What experts say about t

The questions are in the SAT style and well explained and they cover most question types on the Digital SAT.

– Praveen Sharma, Director, Wizius Careers

I appreciate the order of the questions with the divisions (Information and Ideas/ Craft and Structure/Expression of Ideas/Standard English Conventions) and their subdivisions. I believe that for a student or a teacher helping students, these divisions are of great benefit.

I also appreciate the different kinds of genres depicted in the questions. The "key explanations" for the correct answers were on point and I appreciate the inclusion of the distractor explanations as well. The inclusion of the "difficulty level" and "Skill/Knowledge" is great.

Overall, because of the breadth, depth, and organization, I would recommend this book to students and teachers

– Motz Maria, Purchasing Dept, School Board Sarasota County

This page is intentionally left blank

VIBRANT
PUBLISHERS

Digital SAT®
READING AND WRITING
PRACTICE QUESTIONS

2023

Latest information about the
Digital SAT®

**300 Reading and Writing
practice questions** as per
the Digital SAT® format

Detailed answer explanations
including distractor explanations

Questions classified into
easy, medium, and hard

Digital SAT® Reading and Writing Practice Questions

Paperback ISBN–10: 1–63651–158–9
Paperback ISBN–13: 978–1–63651–158–0

Library of Congress Control Number: 2022951785

This publication is designed to provide accurate and authoritative information in regard to the subject matter covered. The Author has made every effort in the preparation of this book to ensure the accuracy of the information. However, information in this book is sold without warranty either expressed or implied. The Author or the Publisher will not be liable for any damages caused or alleged to be caused either directly or indirectly by this book.

Vibrant Publishers books are available at special quantity discount for sales promotions, or for use in corporate training programs. For more information please write to **bulkorders@vibrantpublishers.com**

Please email feedback / corrections (technical, grammatical or spelling) to **spellerrors@vibrantpublishers.com**

For general inquires please write to **reachus@vibrantpublishers.com**

To access the complete catalogue of Vibrant Publishers, visit **www.vibrantpublishers.com**

Table of Contents

This page is intentionally left blank

Dear Student,

Thank you for purchasing **Digital SAT® Reading and Writing Practice Questions.** We are committed to publishing books that are content–rich, concise and approachable enabling more students to read and make the fullest use of them. We hope this book provides the most enriching learning experience as you prepare for your **SAT** exam. Should you have any questions or suggestions, feel free to email us at **reachus@vibrantpublishers.com**. Thanks again for your purchase. Good luck for your Digital SAT!

– Vibrant Publishers Team

ACT/SAT
Books in Test Prep Series

Math Practice Tests for the ACT ISBN: 978-1-63651-085-9	**Winning Strategies For ACT Essay Writing: With 15 Sample Prompts** ISBN: 978-1-63651-125-2
Practice Tests for the Digital SAT ISBN: 978-1-63651-157-3	**Digital SAT Math Practice Questions** ISBN: 978-1-63651-159-7

For the most updated list of books visit

www.vibrantpublishers.com

This page is intentionally left blank

How to use this book

This book is designed to empower you to approach your SAT Reading and Writing section with boldness. The information presented here will only make you fully understand every aspect of the section but also is necessary for you to achieve a high score on your SAT test.

First, read the **About the Digital SAT** chapter to get acquainted with the various features of the digital test. From this chapter, you will learn in detail the differences between the paper-based SAT and the digital one. After reading this chapter, move on to the next chapter on the Reading and Writing section. This chapter contains a plethora of information on the different question types that will be asked in that section.

This book is a compilation of Reading and Writing practice questions from all four domains - Information and Ideas, Craft and Structure, Expression of Ideas, and Standard English Conventions. Start by practicing answering questions of the first domain and after you have mastered them, move on to the next one. While practicing, make a habit of checking your answers from the answer section and reading the detailed answer explanations and distractor explanations.

Recognize a pattern for the same types of questions; this will make it easier for you to classify them on the actual test day and answer them quickly. Learn to analyze the question stems as they will give you a better idea of the question type and what is required to be done.

After thoroughly practicing the different types of questions, you will also find a full-length Reading and Writing test at the end. This test, with a mix of questions like the actual SAT, will give you an authentic testing experience and help you evaluate your test readiness. Appear for this test with the mindset of giving the actual test.

To get complete practice of the Math section, you can also pick up the book *Digital SAT Math Practice Questions* which also has 300 practice questions. After becoming well-versed with the two sections, you can give 5 full-length practice tests from the book *Practice Tests For The Digital SAT*.

To take advantage of the essential information provided in this practice book, read it carefully and attempt the available practice questions with an open mind. Good luck!

This page is intentionally left blank

Chapter 1

About the Digital SAT

Introduction

Now that you have made the important decision to head to college/university, there is one last thing you need to do to achieve your goal—taking the SAT. Most universities or colleges, including the IVY league schools such as Yale, Harvard, and others expect you to have a good SAT score to secure admission in any course of your choice.

But, there is a major change in how students will give the SAT. The College Board has decided to transition the famous pencil–and–paper test into a fully digital one. The College Board's decision to go digital is based on giving a fair testing experience to students. The digital test will be easier to take, easier to administer, will be more secure, and more relevant.

For giving the new test, you need to be aware of the format of the test, the time that will be given to you to answer each question, the possible complexity of the questions, and the scoring method employed to assess your performance in the test. In this chapter, you will discover important information all that including the SAT policy of inclusive accessibility, the newly introduced Multistage Adaptive Testing feature, the modular format of the test, and much more.

The College Board has also streamlined the method of delivery of the digital SAT. With the latest test delivery platform for the digital SAT Suite assessments, students can have access to all their tests and their content, as well as enjoy the chance of practicing with the full–length, adaptive practice test offered for free on the platform so that students can be aware of their knowledge levels before taking the real tests. More so, every question on the digital SAT Suite is in a discrete (standalone) format. This indicates that test takers can answer each question independently. They don't necessarily need to refer to a common stimulus such as an extended passage.

If you are attempting the SAT for the first time, it could be scary not knowing exactly what to expect in the test. This is why this book is specifically designed to expose you to everything you need to know about successfully taking the Digital SAT Suite test.

Customized Test Delivery Platform

The College Board sets up a customized test delivery platform for the Digital SAT Suite assessments. This platform is designed according to the principles of UDA (Universal Design for Assessment) and the main goal of it is to make the testing experience accessible to maximum number of students. The most useful features of this platform are that: (i) all test takers can have complete access to the tests and their content; (ii) students will be able to take full–length, adaptive practice tests for free on the platform so that they can assess their knowledge levels or have an understanding of similar test materials before attempting the real tests.

Multistage Adaptive Testing

The College Board is changing from a linear testing mode, which has been the primary mode of SAT administration to an adaptive mode.

The main difference between the linear and adaptive testing modes is that for the linear testing mode, students are given a test form that contains some questions that have already been set before the test day and do not change during testing, irrespective of the student's performance.

On the other hand, the adaptive testing model makes it possible for the test delivery platform to adjust the questions' difficulty level based on the performance of the individual test takers. Therefore, each student will be given test questions that match their level of understanding.

This adaptive test mode used for the Digital SAT Suite is known as **Multistage Adaptive Testing (MST)**. The MST is administered in 2 stages, and each stage comprises a module or set of questions. The first module consists of test questions with different ranges of difficulty levels (easy, medium, and hard). The performance of the test takers in the first module is appropriately assessed, and the results are used to determine the level of difficulty of questions to be administered to them in the second module.

The set of an administered first–stage module and its second–stage module are referred to as a *panel*.

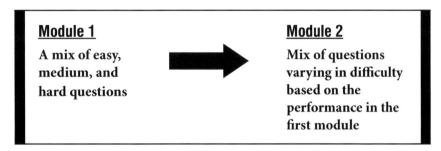

Embedded Pretesting

The digital SAT Suite also includes embedded pretesting in its design. What this means is that a small number of pretest (unscored) questions are incorporated among the operational (scored) questions. Even though they are not administered for a score, students may not be able to distinguish these pretest questions from the operational questions on which their scores are based. It is advisable that students pay maximum attention and effort to these questions, which can be used in estimating their understanding levels to the difficulty of the questions. The number of pretest questions is few so you will not be asked to focus mainly on questions that won't be used to estimate your final SAT score. It is important to note that answers to pretest questions won't contribute to your final score. The pretest questions are mainly used to gather students' performance information so that it can be utilized later to assess if these questions are appropriate for operational use later.

Discrete Questions

One interesting aspect of the Digital SAT is that all their questions are in discreet format; that is they are standalone. You can answer each question on its own, which doesn't necessarily require any reference to a common stimulus such as an extended passage. This is one of the striking differences between the paper–and–pencil SAT and the Digital SAT in the sense that the former uses both discrete and question sets. In practice, the question sets expect you to reference a common stimulus.

Scoring

Students will obtain a section score based on their final performance on the Reading and Writing and Math section. For the SAT, students can get a score between 400–1600. Hence, for each of the tests of the Digital SAT, there will be 3 scores reported: (1) A Reading and Writing section score; (2) A Math section score; (3) A total score, which is the sum of the two section scores. It is important to note that the scales for these scores have the same ranges as for the paper–based SAT Suite. This indicates that the digital SAT total score is on the familiar 400–1600 scale.

Reading and Writing	Math	Total Score
Between 200–800	Between 200–800	Between 400–1600

Overall Test Specifications

The Digital SAT is made up of two sections: A Reading and Writing (RW) section and a Math section. In the linear model, the test has separate sections for Reading and Writing. However, in the Digital SAT, both the Reading and Writing tests are combined in one section. The questions in these two sections concentrate primarily on the skills and knowledge that students need to use in college and/or for getting ready for their careers. The main parts of the digital SAT tests are similar to those of the paper–and–pencil SAT test assessments. More so, all the testing programs within the digital SAT Suite, whether it is the SAT, PSAT 10, PSAT 8/9, or PSAT/NMSQT have similar designs. Although, these tests allow for differences in test takers' ages and levels of understanding.

Digital SAT Suite: Overall Test Specifications

Characteristic	Reading and Writing section	Math section
Administration	Two–stage adaptive design; this section contains two separately timed modules	Two–stage adaptive design; this section contains two separately timed modules
Number of questions	54 questions; 25 questions in each module with 2 pretest question	44 questions; 20 questions in each module with 2 pretest question
Time	64 minutes	70 minutes
Time per question	1.19 minutes	1.59 minutes
Time per module	32 minutes	35 minutes
Content domains	Information and Ideas, Craft and Structure, Expression of Ideas, Standard English Conventions	Algebra, Advanced Math, Problem–Solving and Data Analysis, Geometry and Trigonometry

Test Length

There are a total of 54 questions for the Reading and Writing section. These 54 questions are divided into two equal–length modules; that is, one for each of the section's two stages. Out of the 27 questions for each module, **25 questions are operational**—which means that test takers' performance on them is used to calculate their section score, and **2 questions are pretests**.

For the Math section, the first module has 20 operational questions and 2 pretest questions. Then the second module consists of 20 operational questions and 2 pretest questions. In total, the Math section will comprise 44 questions.

Time Per Module

You will have 32 minutes to complete each module of the Reading and Writing section and 35 minutes to complete each module of the Math section. Once the time for the first module has expired, test takers are automatically advanced to the second module. The second module may contain questions that are of higher or lower difficulty, depending on your performance in the first module. You will not have the opportunity to return to the first–module questions.

Total Number of Questions

The Reading and Writing section consists of 54 questions (4 of which are pretest), while the Math section consists of 44 questions (4 of which are, again, pretest questions)

Total Time Allotted

You will have 64 minutes to complete the Reading and Writing section and 70 minutes to complete the Math section.

Average Time Per Question

You will, on average, have 1.19 minutes to answer each Reading and Writing question and 1.59 minutes to answer each Math question.

Question Format(s) used

The Reading and Writing section mostly utilizes four-option multiple-choice questions, and each question has a single best answer (which is referred to as the keyed response or key). Roughly 75 percent of questions in the Math section also adopt the same four-option multiple-choice format, while the remaining part of the test utilizes the student-produced response (SPR) format. This means that students will be required to answer the latter type of questions by giving their own responses and putting their responses in the field next to the question. These questions measure your ability to be able to solve math problems by yourself. It is possible for the SPR questions to have more than one correct response; however, you are required to provide only one answer.

Text Complexity

It is assumed that the complexity test takers can read is directly related to how ready they are for college and their careers. Therefore, the idea of text complexity is strictly considered when designing and developing the digital SAT Suite. The texts in the Reading and Writing section are given three complexity bands (grades 6–8, grades 9–11, and grades 12–14).

Texts for grades 12–14 have the highest complexity, followed by the texts for grades 9–11, while grades 6–8 have texts with the lowest complexity. While it is possible to use the same texts for grades 12–14 and grades 9–11, those difficult texts cannot be used for grades 6–8 because they don't appropriately assess the literacy knowledge and skills of students in eighth and ninth grades.

On the other hand, text complexity is not an issue in the Math section, because it is not formally measured. It is estimated that about 70 percent of Math questions don't necessarily have a context. You are only required to use the information/data provided to solve some questions that may be related to science, social studies, history, etc.

What is Changing

The College Board continues to maintain fairness and high quality in its administration of SAT Suite, and some aspects of its operations are changing. These changes include:

- Transitioning to digital testing by 2023 or 2024 latest. Once the transition is completed, students can no longer take the paper–and–pencil SAT tests.

- The digital SAT Suite tests are particularly shorter than their paper–and–pencil predecessors—it can be taken in 2 hours 14 minutes instead of 3 hours.

- Test takers now have more time on their hands to answer each question.

- It is now possible for you to receive scores in days instead of weeks, faster than the predecessor paper–and–pencil SAT.

- The SAT Suite now connects students to opportunities based on their scores. They can be connected to information and resources concerning local 2–year colleges, career options, and workforce training programs.

- States, schools, and districts will be given more flexibility concerning when they could give the SAT Suite tests.

- The digital SAT will now have a single Reading and Writing section instead of separate Reading and Writing and Language sections. More importantly, the Reading and Writing section's passages are significantly shorter and more diverse.

- A single (discrete) question is associated with each passage (or passage pair) instead of having several questions associated with a small number of longer passages, as it is for the paper–and–pencil SAT Suite tests.

- You can now use calculators throughout the Math section.

What is Staying the Same

Despite the above–mentioned changes, some aspects of the SAT Suite tests are remaining the same, such as:

- The Digital SAT will still measure skills and knowledge that you are learning in school that can be used in college and/or your future career.

- The test will be scored on the same scales as the paper–and–pencil test.

- The test will be administered in schools and test centers with a proctor.

- You will still be connected to scholarships and the College Board National Recognition Programs.

- Support will be given to all students who need accommodations and/or support to access the tests and their content.

- The Reading/Writing passages will cover a wide range of academic disciplines and text complexities.

- The test will still have both multiple–choice and student–produced response question formats.

1. **When will I be able to register for the digital SAT tests?**

   The first digital SAT administrations at international test centers will start in the fall 2023.

2. **How will students take the digital SAT?**

   You can give the SAT on a laptop or tablet using a custom–built digital exam application that can be downloaded in advance of the test day.

3. **How will the Digital SAT be more secure?**

   At this moment, if one test form is compromised, it can mean that the scores for all the students in that group or at the same test centers will be canceled. However, going digital will make it possible to give every student a unique test form so that it won't be technically possible to share answers.

4. **How will the College Board address test day issues and technical support challenges?**

   The College Board has dedicated customer service resources ready to troubleshoot issues on test day for students and test centers. There is a technology coordinator for each test center to provide additional support and technical help when needed.

5. **What kinds of tools will be available for students taking the digital SAT?**

   You can use the following tools while using the software:

   - Flag questions to come back to them later
   - A countdown clock to know when you are running out of time. You can decide to show or hide it at the top of their testing screen
   - A built–in graphing calculator that you can use on the entire math section (or you can bring their own calculators)
   - A reference sheet, for each math question.

The table below summarizes the specifications of the types of questions and their distribution in the Reading and Writing section.

Content Domain	Skill/Knowledge	Question distribution
Information and Ideas	• Central Ideas and Details • Command of Evidence ▪ Textual and Quantitative • Inferences	12–14 questions (26%)
Craft and Structure	• Words in Context • Text Structure and Purpose • Cross–Text Connections	13–15 questions (28%)
Expression of Ideas	• Rhetorical Synthesis • Transitions	8–12 questions (20%)
Standard English Conventions	• Boundaries • Form, Structure, and Sense	11–15 questions (26%)

Sample Questions

1. The term *"Anthropocene"* introduced by Dutch scientist Paul Crutzen in the mid–1970s, is often used in the context of pollution caused by human activity since the commencement of the Agricultural Revolution, but also pertains largely to all major human bearings on the environment.

    Various start dates for the Anthropocene have been offered by scientists, ranging from the beginning of the first Agricultural Revolution, also known as the *Neolithic Revolution*, to as recently as the 1960s. However, the _____ has not been completed, and hence, a formal, conclusive date remains to be finalized.

    Which choice completes the text with the most logical and precise word or phrase?

    A) Ratification

    B) Investigation

    C) Legality

    D) Approval

    Key: A

    Level: Hard | **Domain:** CRAFT AND STRUCTURE

    Skill/Knowledge: Words in Context

    Key Explanation: Choice A is the correct option because "ratification" refers to the action of signing or giving formal consent to something, making it officially valid. This word is best suited to the context because the second paragraph of the passage talks about how many scientists have offered dates, but a conclusive date has yet to be finalized. The keywords to focus on are "formal, conclusive date" which points to which option (A) might be most suitable in this context.

Distractor Explanations: Choice B is incorrect because there is no evidence provided that an investigation may have been initiated into the subject. Similarly, options **C** and **D** are incorrect because the passage does not talk about any approval process or legalities that need to be completed for a date to be finalized.

2. Brazil's Atlantic Rainforest is among the most biodiverse regions in the world. But despite its spectacular diversity, _____. To counter this, the Society for the Conservation of Birds in Brazil advocates for birds in Brazil, their habitats, and biodiversity in general, and works towards sustainability in the use of natural resources. Their work focuses on educating local people on the importance of birds, biodiversity, and developing environmentally sustainable economic alternatives, along with good governance tools to empower local communities and improve the quality of life of local people.

   What choice most logically completes the underlined space?

   A) there are no more birds in the forest

   B) the Society for the Conservation of Birds in Brazil cannot do much

   C) the rainforest is under extreme threat from human development

   D) there are a number of steps that one can take to preserve the Atlantic Rainforest

   Key: C

   Level: Medium | **Domain:** INFORMATION AND IDEAS

   Skill/Knowledge: Command of Evidence (Textual)

   Key Explanation: Choice C is the best answer because the first sentence talks about the diversity of the Atlantic Rainforest, while the third sentence talks about what the Society for the Conservation of Birds in Brazil is doing to counter said problem in the second sentence. They work by "educating local people" and "developing environmentally sustainable economic alternatives." Therefore, it may be inferred that the problem denoted in the underlined portion of the text involves humans and economics. Hence, using the process of elimination, choice C is the best answer.

   Distractor Explanations: Choice A is incorrect because the text mentions "conservation of birds in Brazil," which means that birds may be endangered but not extinct. **Choice B** is incorrect because there is no information provided that supports this statement. **Choice D** is incorrect because it does not fit in the context of the sentence.

The Math Section at a Glance

The table below summarizes the specifications of the types of questions and their distribution in the Math section.

Content Domain	Skill/Knowledge	Question Distribution
Algebra	• Linear equations in one variable • Linear equations in two variables • Linear functions • Systems of two linear equations in two variables • Linear inequalities in one or two variables	13–15 questions (35%)
Advanced Math	• Equivalent expressions • Nonlinear equations in one variable and systems of equations in two variables • Nonlinear functions	13–15 questions (35%)
Problem–Solving and Data Analysis	• Ratios, rates, proportional relationships, and units • Percentages • One–variable data: distributions and measures of center and spread • Two–variable data: models and scatterplots • Probability and conditional probability • Inference from sample statistics and margin of error • Evaluating statistical claims: observational studies and experiments	5–7 questions (15%)
Geometry and Trigonometry	• Area and volume • Lines, angles, and triangles • Right triangles and trigonometry • Circles	5–7 questions (15%)

Sample Questions

1. The dog park charges $10 for a membership and $3 per hour for the dog to run around in their park. Mindy brings her dog to the park and spends less than $40. Which of the following inequalities represents Mindy's situation, where h is the number of hours at the park and C is the total amount Mindy paid?

   A) $3h + 10 < 40$

   B) $3C - 10 < 40$

   C) $3h + 10 = 40$

   D) $3h + 10 > 40$

   Key: A

   Level: Easy | **Domain:** ALGEBRA

   Skill/Knowledge: Linear inequalities in one or two variables | **Testing Point:** Create a linear inequality

   Key Explanation : Choice A is correct. To determine the inequality that represents the situation, first create the expression that is equal to the total amount that Mindy paid (C).

   The total amount C is the sum of the membership fee ($10) and the fee for having the dog in the park in h hours. This yields $C = 10 + 3h$ or $C = 3h + 10$.

   Since Mindy spent less than $40 in the dog park, then $C < 40$. Substituting the value of C in terms of h in the inequality yields $3h + 10 < 40$.

   Therefore, the inequality $3h + 10 < 40$ is the correct answer.

   Distractor Explanation: Choice B is incorrect. This option is wrong because C is the total amount paid by Mindy and not the rate per hour for the dog to run around the park. **Choices C** and **D** are incorrect. Mindy spent less than $40. Hence, the correct symbol to use is < not > or =.

2. Which expression is equivalent to $2x^2 + 3x + 1$?

   A) $(2x + 1)(2x + 1)$

   B) $(x + 2)(x + 1)$

   C) $(x - 2)(x - 1)$

   D) $(2x + 1)(x + 1)$

   Key: D

   Level: Easy | **Domain:** ADVANCED MATH

   Skill/Knowledge: Equivalent Expressions | **Testing Point:** Factoring a quadratic equation

   Key Explanation : Choice D is correct. To find the equivalent expression, factor the given quadratic equation by splitting the middle term.

   In $2x^2 + 3x + 1$, $a = 2$, $b = 3$ and $c = 1$ using the format $ax^2 + bx + c$.

Getting the product of *a* and *c* yields $ac = (2)(1) = 2$

The factors of 2 whose sum is the value of *b* (where $b = 3$) is 2 and 1.

Hence, the equation can be written as $2x^2 + 2x + x + 1$.

Grouping the binomials in the equation yields $(2x^2 + 2x) + (x + 1)$.

Factoring $2x$ from the first group yields $2x(x + 1) + (x + 1)$.

Factoring $x + 1$ from the two groups yields $(2x + 1)(x + 1)$.

Therefore, **Choice D** is the correct answer.

Distractor Explanation: Choices A, **B**, and **C** are incorrect and may result from a conceptual or calculation error.

Chapter 2

Overview of the Reading and Writing section

Introduction

The Reading and Writing section comprises 54 questions that are divided into two equal-length modules. Each module is for each of the test's two stages, and it has 27 questions, of which 25 are operational and 2 are pretest. But only answers to the operational questions are used in estimating the section's final score. This means that the answers to the pretest questions are not included in calculating the section's final score. The pretest questions are mainly used to collect student performance data to assess if some questions are appropriate for the students when taking the test in the future. So, it is advisable that students focus their attention on the pretest questions as much as they do on the operational questions.

Table 2.1 Digital SAT Reading and Writing section specifications

Characteristic	Total Score
Mode of administering the test	Reading and writing section is designed according to the multi-stage adaptive model and administered through two modules that are timed differently.
Time per module	1st module will take 32 minutes to complete. 2nd module will take 32 minutes to complete. The total time available for the section is 64 minutes.
Average time per question	Each question will take 1.19 minutes to be completed.
Score reported	You will be scored between 200–800. The score for this section represents half of the total score
Question format used	The question format is discreet, with four multiple-choice options.
Passage subject areas	Passages are based on social studies, science, literature, history, and humanities.
Word count by passage	Each passage is between 25 and 150 words, containing at least 6 characters per word.
Informational graphics	Informational graphs can include line graphs, tables, and bar graphs.

Time per section and module

Students are given a total of 64 minutes to complete their Reading and Writing section. Since this time is equally divided between the two modules, test takers can spend 32 minutes answering the questions in each module. After the time for the first module has been used up, test takers have to immediately proceed to the second module and answer questions with lower or higher difficulty levels as per their initial performance in the first module. After moving on to the second module, students will not be able to go back to the questions in the first module.

Average time per question

Every test taker has about 1.19 minutes to answer each Reading and Writing test question.

Question format used

All Reading and Writing test questions are in a multiple-choice format with four answer options that you can choose from. There will be a single best answer referred to as **the keyed response** or **the key**. The questions are discrete in the sense that they all have their own specific passages (or passage pairs).

Passage subject areas

The passages that are used to answer questions in the Reading and Writing section are obtained from the following subject areas: Literature, science, history/social studies, humanities, and science. However, you are not expected to have prior knowledge of each subject.

Word count by passage

The passage (or passage pair) for each Reading and Writing test question is between 25 and 150 words. A word in a passage is made up of six characters (these could be numbers, spaces, letters, symbols, and, of course, punctuation). As a standard, the total number of characters in a passage is divided by six; therefore, when a test question has two short passages as its stimuli, the final word count for the two passages must be between 25 and 150 words.

Informational graphics

You will find some informational graphics in certain passages in the Reading and Writing section. They are basically provided to assess your ability to identify and interpret data. Some examples of informational graphics include bar graphs, tables, and line graphs, being the most common methods of displaying information/data in the subjects the questions are prepared from. However, you are not required to perform any mathematical calculations on the provided data in the informational graphics. In fact, you will not be allowed to bring in calculators while appearing for this section. You need to use your quantitative and literacy skills to discover the relevant information in the graphics, interpret it, and then use that information to make a reasonable conclusion about the appropriate answer for each question.

Domain structure

The questions in the Reading and Writing section depict one of four content domains, which are as follows:

- **Information and Ideas:** This requires you to utilize your knowledge, comprehension, and analytical skills to understand what is stated and implied in texts. You must use the associated informational graphics to identify, interpret, evaluate, and process the information and ideas.

- **Craft and Structure:** In this case, you are expected to use your synthesis, comprehension, vocabulary, analysis, and reasoning skills and knowledge to discover the meaning of high-utility academic words and phrases in context, evaluate texts rhetorically, and make supportable connections between multiple topically related texts.

- **Expression of Ideas:** For this, it is important that you use your revision skills and knowledge to make the written expression effective based on the expected rhetorical goals.

- **Standard English Conventions:** You will be expected to utilize your editing skills and knowledge which should be in accordance with the core conventions of Standard English sentence usage, structure, and punctuation.

To achieve a high score in the SAT Reading and Writing section, pay attention to these tips:

- **What is your "passage" strategy?** If you are weak in answering passage-based questions, you need to come up with a passage strategy. First, lay your hands on some practice tests. Focus on answering those passages in them. While doing this, use a timer to gauge your speed. If a passage seems a bit difficult, move on to the next. After you've completed answering all the passages in the practice test, use the answer key to obtain your score. After you have completed the practice test, analyze those difficult passages and check their answers and explanations. After doing this several times, you will get a better understanding of how the passage-based questions should be answered.

- **Eliminate 3 wrong answers:** Each question in the Reading and Writing section has 4 answer options. You need to train yourself to eliminate 3 wrong answers from the 4 answers provided. Watch out for answers that are: (i) not related to the question; (ii) not specifically addressing the point raised in the question (not supporting the point in the question); (iii) not grammatically correct; and (iv) expressing an opposing view to the point in the question. While it is tricky knowing which answer is correct, these suggestions can guide you to choose the correct answer out of the available four options.

- **Improve your reading skills:** You can improve your level of reading comprehension by practicing with some passages included in this guide. To do this, you should pay attention to these elements of a passage: Its big picture, words and phrases in context, perspective, word choice, textual evidence, inference, and its details. If you analyze each passage, you will discover that they all have the elements mentioned above, and familiarizing yourself with them will help you analyze the passage appropriately.

- **Get interested in the subject matter in the passage:** You should enjoy reading the subject matter in the passages, whether they are derived from science, literature, or history. Once you like the subject matter, you will most likely find answering the questions under it very easy.

- **Finish with extra time and double-checking:** If you can finish with extra time on your hand, use that time to double-check. You may be able to discover some mistakes you have committed in the course of answering the test questions.

- **Thousands of vocabulary:** Many students wrongly assume that by reading thousands of English vocabulary words they will be ready to give the SAT. It is a fact that knowing a lot of vocabulary may aid your understanding of the passages, but it is advisable that you don't waste most of your time on that. The most important thing is knowing the textual and inferred meanings of those vocabulary words when they are eventually used in passages.

In this domain, you will be expected to identify the main idea of the text or a detail or infer and derive a conclusion by reading the passage.

For questions in the Information and Ideas content domain, your skills will be tested in these ways:

Central Ideas and Details

Do you understand the central idea in a text? Are you able to interpret the details used to support the central idea? When reading a passage, it is most likely that the main idea is expressed in the first sentence while the other sentences provide additional information about the main or central idea. Sometimes it is not arranged in that fashion, especially when the passage starts with a dialogue. However, the central idea of a passage is what the entire passage is all about, and you should be able to identify it after reading the entire passage. If the passage is difficult to understand due to its structure and content, you may ask yourself "What is this passage all about?" In this way, you may be able to decode what the passage is trying to tell you.

Sample Question

El Niño is a climate pattern that describes the unusual warming of surface waters in the eastern tropical Pacific Ocean. El Niño is the "warm phase" of a larger phenomenon called the El Niño-Southern Oscillation (ENSO). La Niña, the "cool phase" of ENSO, is a pattern that describes the unusual cooling of the region's surface waters. El Niño and La Niña are considered the ocean part of ENSO, while the Southern Oscillation is its atmospheric changes.

Which choice best states the main theme of the text?

A) It describes the different phases of ENSO

B) It describes the current types of climate patterns

C) It describes the impact of El Niño

D) It describes the patterns of the eastern tropical Pacific Ocean

Key: A

Level: Medium | **Domain:** INFORMATION AND IDEAS

Skill/Knowledge: Central Ideas and Details

Key Explanation: Choice A is correct. The text mainly describes the warm and cold phases of the El Niño-Southern Oscillation (ENSO).

Distractor Explanations: Choice B is incorrect as the text does not mention the current types of climate patterns. **Choice C** is incorrect as the text does not only focus on El Niño. **Choice D** is incorrect because the text describes the El Niño-Southern Oscillation and not the eastern tropical Pacific Ocean.

Command of Evidence

Every passage in the SAT Reading and Writing section has some evidence, details, facts, data, etc. that you, as the test taker, must patiently understand and properly interpret to answer the questions at the end of the passage. Sometimes, you may be given an informational graphic such as a bar graph, pie chart, table, or figure, and the purpose of it is that you will be able to accurately interpret the data and utilize it in answering the questions for that particular passage. You don't necessarily need to be very good at math to interpret pie charts, tables, bar charts, etc. You will discover that the data provided are simple and understandable enough if you understand what the passage is all about.

Sample Question

"Ode to the West Wind" was written by English poet, Percy Bysshe Shelley. The poem addresses the west wind as a formidable force of death and degeneration. However, he also believes that rebirth will happen through the decay brought about by the west wind: _____

Which quotation from "Ode to the West Wind" most effectively illustrates this idea of rejuvenation?

A) A heavy weight of hours has chain'd and bow'd / One too like thee: tameless, and swift, and proud.

B) Thou on whose stream, mid the steep sky's commotion / Loose clouds like earth's decaying leaves are shed / Shook from the tangled boughs of Heaven and Ocean,

C) Be through my lips to unawaken'd earth / The trumpet of a prophecy! O Wind, / If Winter comes, can Spring be far behind?

D) What if my leaves are falling like its own! / The tumult of thy mighty harmonies

Key: C

Level: Hard | **Domain:** INFORMATION AND IDEAS

Skill/Knowledge: Command of Evidence (Textual)

Key Explanation: Choice C is the correct option. The quoted lines point to how the author wants the west wind to speak through him, thereby turning his words into a prophecy of how spring (better times) will follow winter (dark periods of destruction).

Distractor Explanations: Choice A is incorrect as it only describes how time has left the poet tired, even though he used to be fast like the west wind. **Choice B** is incorrect as it talks about the damaging effects of the west wind. **Choice D** is incorrect as it only voices the poet's comparison of how he is declining, just as the leaves of the forest are falling, too.

Inferences

It is not every time that you can find the direct answers to a passage's questions from the information or details provided in the passage. In this case, you will be expected to make an inference about what could be the correct answer according to the information you have at hand. Take for instance, if you read in a passage that all teenagers like to eat ice cream. So, if James is a teenager, you could possibly infer that James likes to eat ice cream. Why? Because James is a teenager! This is how you can make inferences from information or data provided in a certain passage.

Sample Question

Ocean trenches are long, narrow depressions on the sea floor. These chasms are the deepest parts of the ocean—and some of the deepest natural spots on Earth. Ocean trenches are found in every ocean basin on the planet, although the deepest ocean trenches ring the Pacific as part of the so-called "Ring of Fire" which also includes active volcanoes and earthquake zones. Ocean trenches are a result of tectonic activity, which describes the movement of the Earth's lithosphere. In particular, ocean trenches are a feature of _____

Which choice most logically completes the text?

A) Convergent plate boundaries, where two or more tectonic plates meet

B) The deepest layer of the ocean

C) The former sea floor that can rise through volcanoes

D) The most common type of continental crust

Key: A

Level: Hard | **Domain:** INFORMATION AND IDEAS

Skill/Knowledge: Inferences

Key Explanation: Choice A is the best choice. The sentence prior to the one that is to be completed mentions that ocean trenches are due to tectonic activity. Therefore, the text must be completed with a sentence relating to tectonic activity, especially since it begins with "in particular."

Distractor Explanations: All the other choices are incorrect because they do not mention tectonic activity.

Craft and Structure

For questions in the Craft and Structure content domain, you will be expected to use your comprehension, reasoning, vocabulary, analysis, synthesis skills, and knowledge to grasp the meaning of some phrases in context and academic words that are commonly used. You should evaluate texts rhetorically so as to connect multiple texts on the same or similar topic.

These three skills/knowledge testing points are dealt with in this domain:

Words in Context

When reading passages, you have to discover the meaning of some academic words in them, and these are commonly used academic words. You would also need to understand what a phrase means in context and utilize that vocabulary in a correct and contextual manner. Doing this is easy if you understand the passage you are reading; but when dealing with difficult passages, you need to first identify the key phrases and academic words and then try to find out what they mean exactly.

Sample Question

Through various studies and experiments conducted by scientists and social observers, we can safely conclude that human language is far more complex than that of even our nearest and most intelligent relatives, apes. We can comprehend complex beliefs, express subtle emotions, and discuss abstract concepts such as the past and future.

What is astonishing, is that we do this following a set of man-made structural rules that govern how we speak a language. These rules are known as _____. Do only humans use an innate system of rules to govern the order and usage of words?

Which choice completes the text with the most logical and precise word or phrase?

A) Linguistic theory

B) Grammar

C) Language

D) Phonetics

Key: B

Level: Hard | **Domain:** CRAFT AND STRUCTURE

Skill/Knowledge: Words in Context

Key Explanation: Choice B is correct because "grammar" refers to "the rules of a language governing the sounds, words, sentences, and other elements, as well as their combination and interpretation." The second paragraph clearly points to the set of rules that "govern how we speak a language."

Distractor Explanations: Choice A is incorrect because linguistics or linguistic theory refers to the scientific study of language and not the rules that govern the language itself. **Choice C** is incorrect because the question is what word describes the rules that govern the speaking of a language. **Choice D** is incorrect because phonetics is the study of how people produce sounds while speaking a language.

Text Structure and Purpose

You are required to analyze the structure of a text or passage and discover what the main purpose of the text or passage is. Ask yourself these helpful questions to determine the exact purpose of a text or passage: (1) What is this passage talking about? (2) Why is it addressing such a topic? (3) How important is the topic being addressed in the passage? (4) What are the phrases in the passage/text? (5) How do the phrases help in better understanding the text? When dealing with a difficult passage, you need to quickly use the above-mentioned questions to help you identify the central purpose of the test.

Sample Question

Australia is a global leader in tobacco control, having reduced the adult smoking rate from 26.7% in 1998 to 12.9% in 2019. In 2017, 3% of 12–15-year-olds and 9% of 16–17-year-olds reported smoking during the past week, the lowest rates since the first national survey in 1984. These encouraging figures indicate that effective policy (particularly with regard to tobacco pricing), evidence-based media campaigns, and smoke-free indoor environments can significantly reduce smoking among both teenagers and adults. Further reductions will require policy measures and funding for interventions that reach the entire population but also target specific communities.

Which choice best states the main purpose of the text?

A) Australia has attempted to lower its adult smoking rate through various policies

B) Australia's adult smoking rate has been successfully reduced over the years by effectively implementing different campaigns

C) It proves that bringing into effect robust laws and intelligent media drives can have a positive effect on reducing smoking rates in both teens and adults

D) The government must intervene with strict laws to be able to control the use of tobacco among teens and adults

Key: C

Level: Medium | **Domain:** CRAFT AND STRUCTURE

Skill/Knowledge: Text Structure and Purpose

Key Explanation: Choice C is the best choice as the text clearly mentions that "effective policy (particularly with regard to tobacco pricing), evidence-based media campaigns, and smoke-free indoor environments can significantly reduce smoking."

Distractor Explanations: Choice A is incorrect because it is not the main idea of the text. **Choice B** is incorrect because Australia's smoking rate has reduced both in adults and teens, and not specifically in adults as Choice B mentions. **Choice D** is incorrect because there is no information mentioned in the text that supports the idea of strict laws to control the use of tobacco.

Cross-Text Connections

You will be provided with two texts that are somehow related based on their context. For example, Text 1 may be about going to space, while Text 2 expresses NASA's plan to go to Mars. It is important that you learn how to draw a sensible connection between two texts and use the ideas obtained from the two texts to answer the questions for that part of your test.

Sample Question

Text 1

The presence of *Staphylococcus aureus* in the bloodstream (*bacteremia*) can lead to the development of sepsis—a systemic inflammatory response to infection. A typical feature of sepsis is the paradoxical suppression of the immune system, sometimes occurring simultaneously with inflammation. This combination of inflammation and immunosuppression can render the patient defenseless against secondary infections.

Text 2

The *Implementation Guide for the Surveillance of Staphylococcus aureus bloodstream infection* supports prevention, standardized national surveillance, and reporting of this infection in Australian public hospitals. Infection prevention and control within healthcare settings aim to minimize the risk of transmission of infections and the development of antimicrobial resistance.

Based on the texts, how would the author of Text 1 most likely respond to Text 2?

A) Confusion, because the consequences of *Staphylococcus aureus* are dangerous

B) Approval, because preventing the *Staphylococcus aureus bloodstream infection* is key to minimizing its transmission

C) Disappointment, because the *Staphylococcus aureus* infection does not need an implementation guide

D) Disapproval, because this implementation guide wastes precious resources that could be used elsewhere

Key: B

Level: Medium | **Domain:** CRAFT AND STRUCTURE

Skill/Knowledge: Cross-Text Connections

Key Explanation: Choice B is the best answer. The author would approve of the implementation guide since it supports the prevention of the *Staphylococcus aureus* infection which would reduce the transmission of the infection.

Distractor Explanations: Choice A is incorrect because the author is not confused about the infection or the role of the implementation guide in supporting the prevention of the *Staphylococcus aureus* infection. **Choice C** is incorrect because Text 1 mentions the dangerous effects of the infection. Hence, the author of Text 1 would not be disappointed by the idea of an implementation guide to prevent the *Staphylococcus aureus* infection. **Choice D** is incorrect because neither text provides any information regarding wastage of resources.

Expression of Ideas

For questions in the Expression of Ideas content domain, you are required to utilize your knowledge and revision skills to produce effective sentences from all the necessary information you have gathered from the text or passage. You will use these sentences to answer the questions provided for the text/passage.

These are the two skills/knowledge testing in this domain:

Rhetorical Synthesis

As a test taker, you need to understand how to use the information and ideas provided in the text/passage on a topic to form correct or appropriate sentences. You will discover these ideas while reading the text/passage. In order to not forget some core information that you have already read in the text, it is advisable that you jot it down or commit it to your memory. If you don't remember all that you have read, you will find it difficult to create rhetorically correct sentences from the textual ideas or information.

Sample Question

While researching a topic, a student has taken the following notes:

1. Dinosaurs are a diverse group of reptiles of the clade *Dinosauria*, first appearing during the Triassic period, between 243 and 233.23 million years ago.

2. The *fossil record* shows that today's birds are actually feathered dinosaurs, having evolved from earlier theropods during the Late Jurassic epoch.

3. Birds are the only dinosaur lineage known to have survived the Cretaceous–Paleogene extinction event approximately 66 million years ago.

4. Dinosaurs can therefore be divided into avian dinosaurs—birds—and the extinct non-avian dinosaurs, which are all dinosaurs other than birds. Birds and extinct non-avian dinosaurs share many unique skeletal traits, as evidenced by fossils.

The student wants to explain the significance of the *fossil record* to people familiar with dinosaurs. Which choice most effectively uses relevant information from the notes to accomplish this goal?

A) The *fossil record* shows us the importance of dividing dinosaurs into two categories, avian and non-avian

B) The *fossil record* provides solid evidence that today's birds are of dinosaur lineage, with many birds sharing skeletal traits with non-avian dinosaurs

C) Birds are the only creatures of dinosaur lineage that did not perish during the Cretaceous–Paleogene extinction event

D) The *fossil record* proves that the Cretaceous–Paleogene extinction event occurred approximately 66 million years ago

Key: B

Level: Easy | **Domain:** EXPRESSION OF IDEAS

Skill/Knowledge: Rhetorical Synthesis

Key Explanation: Choice B is the best answer. The notes indicate that "today's birds are actually feathered dinosaurs, having evolved from earlier theropods" and that "Birds and extinct non-avian dinosaurs share many unique skeletal traits, as evidenced by fossils."

Distractor Explanations: Choice A is incorrect because the notes provide no information on the importance of dividing dinosaurs into two categories. **Choice C** is incorrect because the given statement does not explain the significance of the *fossil record*. **Choice D** is incorrect because the notes do not state anything about the *fossil record* providing proof of the occurrence of the Cretaceous–Paleogene extinction event 66 million years ago.

Transitions

In English, sentences are formed using some transition words. As a test taker, you need to identify the most important transition words used in the text/passage and understand how they help form the meaning of each sentence. Here is a list of transition words you need to know and familiarize yourself with their purported meanings:

For addition

- As well as
- And
- Too
- Furthermore
- Also
- In addition to
- Not only – but also
- Or

For illustration

- Such as
- In this case
- For one thing
- For instance
- For example
- In the case of
- Illustrated by
- As an example

For cause and effect

- Therefore
- So
- Because
- Thus
- Hence
- Due to
- As a result
- Consequently

For comparison

- As ...as
- As if
- Equally
- Similarly
- Like
- In the same way
- Comparable
- In like manner

For contrast

- But
- However
- On the other hand
- Otherwise
- Unlike
- Conversely

- At the same time
- In spite of

For emphasis
- Especially
- Also
- In particular
- Furthermore
- In addition
- Indeed
- Of course
- Certainly

For time and sequence
- Later
- After
- Before
- Then
- Next
- Soon
- Finally
- First, second…

For direction and place
- Here
- There
- Over there
- Beyond
- Under
- To the left
- In the distance
- Opposite

Sample Question

In 1972, British paleontologist Alick Walker hypothesized that birds arose not from *thecodonts* but from crocodile ancestors like *Sphenosuchus*. Ostrom's work led him to release a series of publications in the mid-1970s in which he laid out the many similarities between birds and theropod dinosaurs. _____ Ostrom's recognition of the dinosaurian ancestry of birds, along with other new ideas about dinosaurs, began what is known as the *dinosaur renaissance*, which continues to this day.

Which choice completes the text with the most logical transition?

A) So

B) While

C) Therefore

D) In fact,

Key: D

Level: Medium | **Domain:** EXPRESSION OF IDEAS

Skill/Knowledge: Transitions

Key Explanation: Choice D is correct because it is used to emphasize a point previously made by adding details about the point being made. Because "Ostrom's work led him to release a series of publications" along with "other new ideas about dinosaurs," he began the *dinosaur renaissance.*

Distractor Explanations: Choice A is incorrect because "so" is a connecting conjunction that does not usually appear at the beginning of a sentence. **Choice B** is incorrect because "while" is usually used to mean "during the time that." This would not make sense in the given context. **Choice C** is incorrect because "therefore" is used when arriving at a valid conclusion of an argument being made in the preceding sentence.

Standard English Conventions

For questions in the Standard English Conventions content domain, you will be required to utilize your knowledge and editing skills to see that the text is according to the conventions of Standard English in punctuation, sentence structure, and usage.

These are the two skills/knowledge testing in this domain:

Boundaries

You should edit the text to make sure that the sentences are completely based on Standard English conventions. For Boundaries questions, you will be asked to focus on how the phrases, clauses, and sentences are linked. It mainly deals with punctuations, such as a full-stop (.), comma (,), colon (:), semi-colon (;), question mark (?), interjection (!), bracket (), and quotation mark (" ").

Sample Question

Riveted: The History of Jeans is a film that reveals the fascinating and surprising story of the iconic American garment. _____ half the people on the planet are wearing them. They have become a staple of clothing the world over, worn by everyone from presidents and supermodels to farmers and artists. More than just an item of apparel, America's tangled past is woven into the indigo-blue fabric.

Which choice completes the text so that it conforms to the conventions of Standard English?

A) At any given moment,

B) At any given moment;

C) At any given moment-

D) At any given moment:

Key: A

Level: Medium | **Domain:** STANDARD ENGLISH CONVENTIONS

Skill/Knowledge: Boundaries

Key Explanation: Choice A is the correct answer. Commas are used after introductory phrases ("At any given moment") to separate them from the main part of the sentence (half the people on the planet are wearing them.)

Distractor Explanations: All the other choices are incorrect because they insert unnecessary punctuation (a semicolon, dash, and colon, respectively) after the sentence's introductory phrase.

Form, Structure, and Sense

You should also edit text so that they are in accordance with the Standard English Conventions. Make sure that the subject-verb agreement is accurate, and that the verbs are in correct tenses.

Sample Question

The following text is from the Farewell Speech given by Dwight D. Eisenhower in 1961.

In the councils of government, we must guard against the acquisition of unwarranted influence, whether sought or unsought, by the military-industrial complex. The potential for the disastrous rise of misplaced power _____ and will persist. We must never let the weight of this combination endanger our liberties or democratic processes. We should take nothing for granted.

Which choice completes the text so that it conforms to the conventions of Standard English?

A) exist

B) exists

C) existing

D) exit's

Key: B

Level: Medium | **Domain:** STANDARD ENGLISH CONVENTIONS

Skill/Knowledge: Form, Structure, and Sense

Key Explanation: Choice B is correct because in most cases, if the subject of a sentence is singular, the verb must be singular, too. A singular verb is that which has an "s" at the end of it.

Distractor Explanations: Choice A is incorrect because "exist" is not a singular verb. **Choice C** is incorrect as the blank space needs a simple/indefinite present tense to make sense of the remainder of the sentence. The word "existing" is the present continuous form of exist. **Choice** D is incorrect as the word does not suit the context of the sentence itself.

Check out the rules for subject-verb agreements in English provided below:

1. If the subject is singular, the verb that follows the subject should be singular too.

2. If the subject is plural, the verb that comes after the subject should also be plural.

3. If the subject of the sentence consists of two or more nouns or pronouns that are connected by and, a plural verb should be used in the sentence.

4. If there is one subject and more than one verb, all the verbs in the sentence should agree with the subject.

5. If a phrase exists between the subject and the verb, you should always remember that the verb must still agree with the subject, not the noun or pronoun that follows the subject in the phrase. .

6. You should use a singular verb whenever two or more singular nouns or pronouns are connected by "or" or "nor". .

7. In case a compound subject has both a singular and a plural noun or pronoun that are connected by "or" or "nor," make sure that the verb must agree with the subject that is nearest to the verb. This is usually referred to as the rule of proximity.

8. Always remember that the words and phrases such as "someone", "each," "neither," "anybody," "everyone," "everybody," "each one"," "either," "nobody," "somebody," "anyone," and "no one" are considered singular and should usually take a singular verb.

9. Uncountable nouns usually have a singular verb.

10. Countable nouns like *proceeds, valuables, odds, surroundings, earnings, contents,* and *goods* are considered a plural form and they usually have a plural verb.

11. For the sentences starting with "there is" or "there are," the noun that follows either of those phrases is the subject, and the verb in the sentence must agree with the subject of the sentence.

12. Collective nouns are used to indicate more than one thing or person; however, they are seen as singular and usually have a singular verb. Some examples are "group," "family," "committee," "team," and "class."

Chapter 3

Information and Ideas

This chapter includes questions on the following topics:

- Central Ideas and Details
- Command of Evidence
    - Textual
    - Quantitative
- Inferences

1

Our observations suggest increasingly that Earth–size planets orbiting within the habitable zone may be common in the galaxy—current estimates suggest that more than 40 percent of stars have at least one. But are any of them inhabited? With no ability to send probes there to sample, we will have to derive the answer from the light and other radiation that come to us from these faraway systems. If we manage to separate out a clean signal from the planet and find some features in the light spectrum that might be indicative of life, we will need to work hard to think of any non biological process that might account for them. We also might not be able to detect biospheres even if they exist.

Which is most likely true according to information suggested in the text?

A) Even if life is present on other planets, we may not be able to recognize it.

B) Life probably exists on about 40 percent of all the planets in the galaxy.

C) It is impossible to find life on other planets using currently available technology.

D) Theories about life on other planets have not considered the practicality of finding it.

2

The following text is adapted from Charles Stearns' 1849 article, "The Way to Abolish Slavery."

The Government of the United States creates no Slaves; it only recognises as lawful the Slavery existing in the several States, or to use the words of the Constitution, "held to service or labor, under the laws thereof." The laws of the several slave-holding States are made the standard for the general government's action upon this subject. No quibble can possibly evade this. From this decision there is no appeal. What then is necessary to be done to remove this prop from under the colossal statue of Slavery? Plainly, to repeal all laws recognising its existence. Do this, and refuse to obey any of the claims of the South in reference to this matter, and Slavery ceases as soon as the earth would cease to turn upon its axis.

Which choice best states the central idea of the text?

A) The U.S. government has no binding authority regarding slavery.

B) The US government rather than states should make laws regarding slavery.

C) Slaveholders should be responsible for proving ownership of slaves.

D) Any legislation that upholds slavery should be rescinded.

3

Scientist James Clark and graduate student Jason McLachlan of Duke University conducted a study to address a central scientific problem in explaining the diversity of tree species in a forest. "In the mathematical models ecologists use to describe how different species compete for resources such as light, moisture and nutrients, it can be difficult to get species to coexist," he said. "In models, slight advantages allow one species to 'out–compete' the other, leading to extinction, that is, loss of biodiversity. And so, ecologists have put a lot of effort into trying to understand the differences among species that allow one species to coexist with another species." Explaining such coexistence that occurs routinely in real life is critical, if ecologists are to truly understand forest biodiversity and the forces that sustain or reduce it.

According to the text, why does Clark feel that mathematical models are insufficient to study biodiversity?

A) They do not account for changes that take place over the course of centuries.

B) Their results do not accurately reflect observations in the natural world.

C) They do not include enough different species of plants from a specific area.

D) Their calculations are based on obsolete data that needs to be updated.

4

Studies have shown that a single, subanesthetic–dose (a lower dose than would cause anesthesia) ketamine infusion can often rapidly relieve depressive symptoms within hours in people who have not responded to conventional antidepressants, which typically take weeks or months to work. However, widespread off–label use of intravenous subanesthetic–dose ketamine for treatment–resistant depression has raised concerns about side effects, especially given its history as a drug of abuse.

According to the text, why is ketamine a preferred drug for treating serious depressive symptoms?

A) Because it acts faster than traditional medications for depression

B) Because it has fewer side effects that most other depression medications do

C) Because there is no apparent risk of addiction when administered long–term

D) Because it can be administered to the patient in multiple different ways

5

In general, deep ocean habitats will be affected by tidal current energy systems due to the change of water flows, materials in the ocean floor, and movement of sediment. Potential other effects include mortality of fish passing through turbines (blade–strike) and the collision risk of marine mammals. A study showed that change in sediment patterns will most likely follow the installation of tidal arrays, impacting the local underwater habitat. This, in turn, could impact animal and plant species. Species of marine mammals and fish could experience distress and discomfort. However, Lewis et al. contend that, "while current technologies have moving parts (rotating rotor blades or flapping hydrofoils) that may harm marine life, there is no evidence to date of harm from tidal current devices to larger marine animals, such as whales, dolphins, seals, and sharks."

Based on the text, why may marine life be harmed by tidal energy systems?

A) The systems have dangerous moving parts.

B) The systems are located where animals are most plentiful.

C) The systems attract animals with their sounds.

D) The systems provide habitats for marine species.

6

A study led by Sarah Mann aimed to provide a fuller picture of the vegan diet in which no animal products are eaten, encompassing both the nutrition and health of the vegan diet as well as related ethical beliefs by studying scientific and popular literature in tandem. Furthermore, the study aimed to provide an insider's perspective of the vegan diet as a means of combating stereotypes and making the diet more relatable/ understandable to those who are not vegan. By combining all three sources, the project aims to educate the public regarding a diet and lifestyle that is often perceived, at least partially, in a negative manner.

According to the text, what is one of the main objectives of Sarah Mann's study?

A) To encourage others to adopt a vegan lifestyle

B) To examine why people are opposed to a vegan diet

C) To teach others about the nature of veganism

D) To determine the anthropological origins of a vegan diet

7

The following text is adapted from Louisa May Alcott's 1868 novel, *Little Women.*

When their father lost his property in trying to help an unfortunate friend, the two oldest girls begged to be allowed to do something toward their own support, at least. Believing that they could not begin too early to cultivate energy, industry, and independence, their parents consented, and both fell to work with the hearty good will which in spite of all obstacles is sure to succeed at last.

According to the text, what is true about the two oldest girls?

A) They were discouraged by all the obstacles.

B) They looked for jobs despite their parents' reservations.

C) They voluntarily accepted their new positions.

D) They lost their money trying to help a friend.

8

The first bottled carbonated mineral water was sold in Geneva in 1783 by Johann Jacob Schweppe, who relocated his business to London in 1792. Not long after, manufacturers started offering flavorings mixed with the mineral water and mostly advertised them as having medicinal purposes; one such drink, ginger beer, is first mentioned in a treatise on beverages written in 1809. However, the drinks were extremely popular, and over time, were consumed for pleasure as well as health purposes.

According to the passage, what is true about ginger beer?

A) It was the most popular flavored drink.

B) It was the first carbonated drink.

C) It was sold as having curative properties.

D) It was first offered for sale by Johann Schweppe.

9

Paleontologists recently found the almost complete skeleton of a new species of dinosaur which they named *Mbiresaurus raathi* after the Mbire region in Zimbabwe where it was found. With parts of the skull, spine, and all four legs, scientists have been able to determine that it was about 5 feet long, fast, and omnivorous, standing on two legs. The little creature may not look very impressive compared to the giant sauropods that are its descendants that roamed the earth on four feet in later eras, but it is notable as the oldest dinosaur fossil found in Africa to date.

According to the text, why is the discovery of the *Mbiresaurus raathi* fossil significant?

A) The dinosaur was much smaller than later sauropods.

B) The dinosaur stood on two legs instead of four.

C) The fossil is the oldest from Africa.

D) The fossil is almost a complete skeleton.

10

The following text is adapted from Mark Twain's 1869 novel, *The Innocents Abroad*.

A little after noon on that distinguished Saturday I reached the ship and went on board. All was bustle and confusion. [I have seen that remark before somewhere.] The pier was crowded with carriages and men; passengers were arriving and hurrying on board; the vessel's decks were encumbered with trunks and valises; groups of excursionists, arrayed in unattractive traveling costumes, were moping about in a drizzling rain and looking as droopy and woebegone as so many molting chickens. The gallant flag was up, but it was under the spell, too, and hung limp and disheartened by the mast. Altogether, it was the bluest, bluest spectacle! It was a pleasure excursion—there was no gainsaying that, because the program said so—it was so nominated in the bond—but it surely hadn't the general aspect of one.

What is the main idea of the text?

A) A voyage has a very inauspicious beginning.

B) The weather is unpleasant where a ship is going.

C) It is busy and exciting as people prepare for a journey.

D) Many people are worried about what will happen.

11

In the 1970s, the California condor, the largest bird in North America with a wingspan of about 9.5 feet (3 meters), was on the brink of extinction and went extinct in the wild in 1987. Conservationists began a captive breeding program, and part of the program was to eliminate all the parasites on the birds. The California condor populations are slowly rebuilding, but the California condor louse, a parasite that had evolved to survive only on that species, has apparently gone extinct. The California condor louse is one of the best–documented cases of the loss of a parasite due to a depletion of the host population.

What is the main idea of the text?

A) California condors have recovered after almost going extinct.

B) California condors have evolved to live with the California condor louse.

C) The California condor louse has gone extinct due to efforts to save the California condor.

D) The California condor louse was one of the causes of the near–extinction of the California condor.

12

The following text is adapted from Kenneth Grahame's 1908 novel, *The Wind in the Willows*.

It all seemed too good to be true. Hither and thither through the meadows Mole rambled busily, along the hedgerows, across the copses, finding everywhere birds building, flowers budding, leaves thrusting—everything happy, and progressive, and occupied. And instead of having an uneasy conscience pricking him and whispering "whitewash!" he somehow could only feel how jolly it was to be the only idle dog among all these busy citizens. After all, the best part of a holiday is perhaps not so much to be resting yourself, as to see all the other fellows busy working.

Based on the text, what is true about Mole?

A) He was traveling through the countryside.

B) He was being encouraged by other animals to work.

C) He never had any type of employment.

D) He usually felt uncomfortable when he was idle.

13

The following text is adapted from Edgar Allen Poe's 1829 poem, *Alone*.

From childhood's hour I have not been

As others were; I have not seen

As others saw; I could not bring

My passions from a common spring.

From the same source I have not taken

My sorrow; I could not awaken

My heart to joy at the same tone;

And all I loved I loved alone.

According to the text, what is true about the narrator?

A) He is an extremely sad person.

B) He has no ambitions and desires.

C) He felt isolated as a child.

D) He is unable to find joy in life.

14

The following text is adapted from Edith Wharton's 1911 novel, *Ethan Frome*.

All the dwellers in Starkfield, as in more notable communities, had had troubles enough of their own to make them comparatively indifferent to those of their neighbours; and though all conceded that Ethan Frome's had been beyond the common measure, no one gave me an explanation of the look in his face which, as I persisted in thinking, neither poverty nor physical suffering could have put there. Nevertheless, I might have contented myself with the story pieced together from these hints had it not been for the provocation of Mrs. Hale's silence, and—a little later—for the accident of personal contact with the man.

According to the text, what is true about the residents of Starkfield?

A) They felt that Ethan Frome overplayed his problems.

B) They tried to hide Ethan Frome's secret from the narrator.

C) They were more concerned about themselves than about Ethan Frome's.

D) They were surprised that the narrator was interested in Ethan Frome.

15

The following text is adapted from a 2011 statement by Jefferson Keel, President of the National Congress of American Indians, in "The Indian Reorganization Act—75 Years Later: Renewing our Commitment to Restore Tribal Homelands and Promote Self–determination."

Today, 75 years later, the Indian Reorganization Act (IRA) is as necessary as it was in 1934. The purposes of the IRA were frustrated first by World War II and then by the termination era. Work did not begin again until the 1970s with the self–determination policy, and since then Indian tribes are building economies from the ground up and they must earn every penny to buy back their own land. Still today, many tribes have no land base and many tribes have insufficient lands to support housing and self–government and culture. We will need the IRA for many more years until the tribal needs for self–support and self–determination are met.

According to the text, what is the only way that present–day Native Americans can acquire their tribal lands?

A) By applying for a grant to reimburse the property owner

B) By proving to the state that the land was historically theirs

C) By paying money to buy the land from the property owner

D) By exercising their right to become a member of the IRA

16

The following text is adapted from Fyodor Dostoevsky's 1866 novel, *Crime and Punishment*.

On an exceptionally hot evening early in July a young man came out of the garret in which he lodged in S. Place and walked slowly, as though in hesitation, towards K. bridge. He had successfully avoided meeting his landlady on the staircase. His garret was under the roof of a high, five–storied house and was more like a cupboard than a room. The landlady who provided him with garret, dinners, and attendance, lived on the floor below, and every time he went out he was obliged to pass her kitchen, the door of which invariably stood open. And each time he passed, the young man had a sick, frightened feeling, which made him scowl and feel ashamed. He was hopelessly in debt to his landlady, and was afraid of meeting her.

According to the passage, what is true about the young man?

A) He felt he had a great obligation.

B) He disliked the landlady's meals.

C) He seldom ran into his landlady.

D) He was extremely ill.

17

The following text is adapted from Sinclair Lewis's 1920 novel, *Main Street*.

On a hill by the Mississippi where Chippewas camped two generations ago, a girl stood in relief against the cornflower blue of Northern sky. She saw no Indians now; she saw flour–mills and the blinking windows of skyscrapers in Minneapolis and St. Paul. Nor was she thinking of squaws and portages, and the Yankee fur–traders whose shadows were all about her. She was meditating upon walnut fudge, the reasons why heels run over, and the fact that the chemistry instructor had stared at the new coiffure which concealed her ears. It is Carol Milford, fleeing for an hour from Blodgett College. The days of pioneering, of lassies in sunbonnets, and bears killed with axes in piney clearings, are deader now than Camelot; and a rebellious girl is the spirit of that bewildered empire called the American Middlewest.

According to the text, what is true about the place where Carol Milford is standing?

A) The hills are covered by cornflowers.

B) Chippewa Indians now reside there.

C) It has become quite industrialized.

D) It is the site of the now–dead Camelot.

18

Snow blindness is a condition in which UV rays from the sun temporarily damage the eyes, causing painfulness and sometimes disrupting vision. Typically, such conditions heal on their own in a few days, but repeated cases can lead to more serious conditions such as vision loss or cancer. Despite the name, snow blindness can occur without the presence of snow. Bright reflected light from sources such as light–colored pavement, white sandy beaches, and water all create the same effect.

Based on the text, what is true about snow blindness?

A) It does not actually harm the eyes at all unless a person repeatedly gets it.

B) It is most severe when caused by snow, but other situations can cause it.

C) It can negatively affect a person's eyesight for several days before recovery.

D) It is impossible to avoid situations that are conducive to causing it.

19

Giant oarfish are the longest bony fish in the world, reaching up to eight meters long, though there have been reports of oarfish as long as seventeen meters. They live in the deep sea around 1,000 meters underwater and seldom come to the surface. Most likely, these unusual fish are the origin of stories of sea serpents from ancient times. In Japan, when a giant oarfish does wash ashore, people say it is an omen of an earthquake.

What is the main idea of the text?

A) Giant oarfish are large fish but not often seen.

B) One of the most famous deep–sea fish is the giant oarfish.

C) Giant oarfish were mistakenly viewed to be different creatures.

D) The longest bony fish in the world is seventeen meters long.

20

Nephi and Golden Griggs worked on their family farm in Ontario, Oregon, raising and selling potatoes and corn. However, their French fry cutting machine was inefficient and resulted in huge amounts of fragments. The brothers experimented with ways to use them until in 1954 they created the iconic food known as the Tater Tot.

Based on the text, what can be inferred about the Griggs's Tater Tot?

A) It was a typical potato product at the time.

B) It was made from material that was considered waste.

C) It was the first product that the family invented.

D) It included both corn and potatoes in the recipe.

21

The ear is a complex organ that is responsible for both hearing and balance. The outer, visible part is called the auricle, and it helps funnel sounds to the tympanic membrane, which is also called the eardrum. The tympanic membrane vibrates and transfers the sound waves to three bones in the middle ear, which in turn conveys the sound to the inner ear, where it is converted into electrical impulses in a fluid–filled part called the cochlea. Those electrical impulses are transferred to the brain, where they are interpreted as sound. The inner ear also contains two structures called the vestibule and semicircular canals, which are both related to maintaining proper balance.

According to the text, what is the function of the cochlea?

A) It funnels sounds into the inner ear.

B) It assists with ensuring good balance.

C) Its fluid slows sound vibrations.

D) It changes sound into electrical impulses.

22

The first restaurant franchise in the United States was an A&W root beer stand. The restaurant was founded in 1919 by Roy Allen and Frank Wright, who used their initials for the name. That first root beer stand was in Lodi, California, and it proved so popular that they leased it for other people to run so that they would be able to expand to other locations, starting with Sacramento, California.

According to the text, why did Allen and Wright create the idea of a restaurant franchise?

A) They hoped to open more restaurants than they could personally operate.

B) They thought that root beer was more marketable in a chain than from only one store.

C) They realized that people did not want to travel far to purchase a root beer.

D) They understood that using their full names might be less marketable.

23

In 2011, treasure hunters Peter Lindberg and Denis Aberg disclosed astounding sonar footage of an unusual object that they had found about 90 meters deep under the Baltic Sea. Further studies revealed a stone structure about 13 meters tall and 60 meters wide, with a similar object about 200 meters away. There also appears to be pavement–like platforms leading to the object. Many people claimed it was a UFO; some geologists theorized it was volcanic material deposited by a melting glacier, and others suspect it is a German military relic from WWII. Since all electronic equipment, even that from reputable scientific institutions, malfunctions when close to the object, the true nature and origin may never be known.

What is the main idea of the text?

A) Treasure hunters have found a stone structure under the Baltic Sea which may be a UFO.

B) A large stone object was found in the Baltic Sea in 2011, but its purpose is a mystery.

C) In 2011, treasure hunters showed sonar images of an undersea object that is likely a hoax.

D) Under the Baltic Sea, there is a stone structure that is 60 meters wide with platforms.

24

Narcissa Whitman (1808–1847) was one of the first female pioneers to travel along the Oregon Trail, and she gave birth to the first white child born in the Oregon Territory. She lived at a mission near Walla Walla, Washington, which became an important stopping point for pioneers heading to the Willamette Valley in Oregon. Unfortunately, she never learned the native language and refused to adopt any of the local culture, which ultimately led to discontent and distrust among the local people.

According to the texts, what was one drawback of Narcissa Whitman's attempts to set up a new life in the Oregon Territory?

A) She gave birth to a child that was not a Native American.

B) She stopped in Washington rather than in Oregon.

C) She did not want to assimilate into the local society.

D) She did not trust any of the Native Americans.

25

The following text is adapted from H.G. Wells's 1925 novel, *Christina Alberta's Father*.

Young Albert Edward Preemby was then a good–looking, slender youth of sixteen, with his father's curliness and his mother's fair hair and eyes of horizon blue, dreamy and indisposed for regular employment. Even as a child he had been given to reverie; at school he would sit with sums or book neglected before him, looking beyond them at unknown things; his early experiences in business were disappointing by reason of this abstraction. After a number of unsuccessful attempts to exploit his gifts at some favourable point in the complex machinery of our civilization, he came to rest for several years in the office of a house–agent and coal–merchant in Norwich to whom his mother was distantly related.

What is the main purpose of the text?

A) It discusses many challenges facing a character.

B) It hints at the personality of a character.

C) It establishes the career of a character.

D) It describes the appearance of a character.

26

It is estimated that more than 91 percent of Australian households own a car and many households own more than one motor vehicle. Cars and private vehicles continue to be the preferred way of getting to work.

The usage of public transport, especially trains, has decreased significantly in the review period (between 2016 to 2021) and only 2.5 percent of the population of Australia walks to work. This may be attributed to the increase in the overall distance people have to commute to work.

Which choice best states the main theme of the text?

A) More Australians are using the train to commute.

B) It is an overview of the work travel statistics of Australia.

C) Many Australians do not like to walk to work.

D) Most Australians like to drive to work.

27

While it may be challenging to find a foolproof tactic for converting a largely state–controlled economy into a free one, the experience of the United Kingdom since 1979 clearly shows one method that works: privatization, where government–owned industries are sold to private companies. By 1979, the total borrowings and losses of public sector industries were operating at approximately £3 billion a year.

By selling many of these industries, the government has reduced these borrowings and losses, adding over £34 billion to the treasury from such sales, and now receives tax revenues from the newly privatized companies.

Which choice best states the dominant theme of the text?

A) There are multiple advantages of privatization.

B) The United Kingdom has been able to overhaul its economy through privatization.

C) It is difficult to find a plan that would help the UK's economy recover.

D) The government is right in selling off public–sector companies

28

Besides vast economic declines, there were also many social consequences of the Great Depression. There was a high demand for most families to have only one full–time paying job. Women were encouraged to stay home and grow their own produce and raise poultry and livestock for their eggs and meat. During the Great Depression, the food eaten was always made with the lowest cost ingredients that could be found. Horse meat was sold because it was cheap, and feeding a horse cost more than selling it to a butcher at a loss.

New clothing was made of cotton sacks used to package goods such as flour, sugar, or grain to feed animals. When these clothes tore or were outgrown, the fabric was recycled into other uses, becoming tablecloths, or quilts for the family.

Which choice best states the main idea of the text?

A) Men were the sole breadwinners of the family.

B) It was difficult for women to find jobs.

C) Horses were sold for their meat at a loss.

D) Most families tried to cut corners to survive the Great Depression.

29

From the First Assessment Report released in 1990, the Intergovernmental Panel on Climate Change (IPCC) has been insisting on its conclusion which attributes modern climate warming to the increase of anthropogenic Greenhouse Gases (GHGs) concentrations in the atmosphere. This conclusion appears to be reinforced continuously by emerging scientific evidence in recent years.

Based on the text, what does the IPCC ascribe modern climate warming to?

A) Emerging scientific evidence

B) Increase in the concentration of GHG

C) Increase in polluting gases

D) Increase in human population

30

The following text is adapted from the book *Emotional Intelligence* by Daniel Goleman.

A view of human nature that ignores the power of human emotion is sadly shortsighted. The very name *homo sapiens*, the thinking species, is misleading in light of the new appreciation and vision of the place of emotions in our lives that science now offers. As we all know from experience, when it comes to shaping our decisions and our actions, feeling counts every bit as much — and often more — than thought. We have gone too far in emphasizing the value and import of the pure rational — of what IQ measures — in human life. Intelligence can come to nothing when the emotions hold sway.

Based on the text, what is the central idea that the author is trying to put forward?

A) Emotions make humans weak.

B) Emotions are stronger than intelligence.

C) Humans should no longer be called homo sapiens.

D) One cannot ignore the power of emotions any longer.

The Pedra D'Anta Reserve, located within the Serra do Urubu forest, protects one of the last large fragments of Atlantic Rainforest left in Brazil's Pernambuco state. Despite the fact that 98 percent of the forest in this area has been destroyed, the reserve sustains a healthy and exceptionally diverse bird population. Scientists have recorded a total of 257 bird species here, including endangered birds like the Orange-bellied Antwren, Scalloped Antbird, and Pinto's Spinetail. The threats to these species increases with each acre of forest that is cleared for charcoal production or illegal timber extraction.

Based on the text, what is true about the Pedra D'Anta Reserve?

A) The Orange-bellied Antwren is found only in the Pedra D'Anta Reserve.

B) The Pedra D'Anta Reserve is located within the Amazon in Brazil.

C) Many habitats are being destroyed due to illegal timber extraction.

D) Only 2 percent of the forest in the area is home to endangered birds.

If you're exploring the planet, Antarctica is the last stop on the train, a continent with no history of a native population, where passports are unnecessary, and where the fringing ocean still boils with life in a way great stretches of the Atlantic and Pacific no longer do. Unexplored valleys and unscaled mountains abound in this white brocade desert, with its ferocious winds and curve–of–the–earth vistas.

Which choice best states the main theme of the text?

A) More people are exploring the planet using trains.

B) Antarctica is the last, unexplored frontier on the planet.

C) Many great stretches of the Atlantic and Pacific are lifeless.

D) Antarctica has a lot to offer tourists.

1. **Level:** Medium | **Skill/Knowledge:** Central Ideas and Details

    Key Explanation: Choice A is the best answer because the passage begins by saying that many planets might potentially host life, but we only can use "light and other radiation" to find out if they do. It is possible that life exists, but "we also might not be able to detect biospheres even if they exist."

    Distractor Explanations: Choice B is incorrect because the passage only says that 40 percent of stars may have planets in the habitable zone. It does not say that all of those planets probably host life. **Choice C** is incorrect because, while the passage points out that identifying life will be hard, it is still possible to do so using light and other radiation detectable by current equipment. **Choice D** is incorrect because the passage does not critique theories about extraterrestrial life; it does not complain that the theories make it appear easy to find.

2. **Level:** Medium | **Skill/Knowledge:** Central Ideas and Details

    Key Explanation: Choice D is the best answer because the author begins by saying that the U.S. government does not create slaves, it only recognizes laws that permit people to own slaves. His conclusion is that if all slavery-related laws were "rescinded" or "removed," then slavery would no longer exist.

    Distractor Explanations: Choice A is incorrect because, while the author feels that laws related to slavery should be revoked, he accepts that the laws are currently "binding" or "can be upheld." **Choice B** is incorrect because the author feels that all laws should be ended; he does not feel that one government is better than another at enforcing slavery. **Choice C** is also incorrect because the

author does not want to continue slavery, so there would be no need to prove ownership of slaves.

3. **Level:** Hard | **Skill/Knowledge:** Central Ideas and Details

    Key Explanation: Choice B is the best answer because Clark says that in mathematical models, "slight advantages allow one species to 'out-compete' the other, leading to extinction, that is, loss of biodiversity," but that in real life, species coexist with each other "routinely" or "very regularly." Therefore, the mathematical models do not accurately "reflect" or "demonstrate" what is observed in natural systems.

    Distractor Explanations: None of the other choices are supported by evidence from the passage. There is no indication that the problem with mathematical models is the time frame, the number of plants included, or the age of the data.

4. **Level:** Medium | **Skill/Knowledge:** Central Ideas and Details

    Key Explanation: Choice A is the best answer because the text says that "ketamine infusion can often rapidly relieve depressive symptoms within hours in people who have not responded to conventional antidepressants, which typically take weeks or months to work," which indicates that ketamine is "preferred" or "often used" because it works quickly in cases where other antidepressants did not work at all.

    Distractor Explanations: Choice B is incorrect because the text does not compare the number of side effects with those of other drugs. **Choice C** is incorrect because the long-term risks are not assessed in the text. There are no apparent short-term risks of addiction when applied once.

Choice D is incorrect because the text addresses only "intravenous subanesthetic–dose ketamine." Other forms of administration are not mentioned in the passage.

5. **Level:** Medium | **Skill/Knowledge:** Central Ideas and Details

    Key Explanation: Choice A is the best answer because the text directly states that there may be "mortality of fish passing through turbines (blade–strike)," meaning that the moving blades kill the fish, and "current technologies have moving parts (rotating rotor blades or flapping hydrofoils) that may harm marine life." This shows that harm may occur, even though there is no documentation of such accidents to larger mammals.

    Distractor Explanations: All of the other choices can be eliminated because there is no evidence in the text to support the claims. For **Choice B**, animals may be present, but there is no indication that they are "most" plentiful. For **Choice C**, sounds are not discussed in the text. **Choice D** is incorrect because it is a benefit rather than a "harmful thing."

6. **Level:** Medium | **Skill/Knowledge:** Central Ideas and Details

    Key Explanation: Choice C is the best answer because the last sentence in the text summarizes the purpose of the study: "By combining all three sources, the project aims to educate the public regarding a diet and lifestyle that is often perceived, at least partially, in a negative manner." In other words, Mann is trying to "educate" or "teach" people about the "nature" or "basic features" of the diet.

Distractor Explanations: Choice A is incorrect because the text does not try to "encourage" or "persuade" anyone to become a vegan. **Choice B** is incorrect because, while the study was trying to fight stereotypes ("Furthermore, the study…are not vegan"), it did not specifically try to analyze why people are "opposed" or "against" it. It just tried to get a better idea of why people choose to become vegan and explain those reasons to others. **Choice D** is incorrect because the study did not delve into "anthropological origins" or "historic al causes" of the diet.

7. **Level:** Medium | **Skill/Knowledge:** Central Ideas and Details

    Key Explanation: Choice C is the best answer because the girls "begged" or "asked strongly" to be able to at least help support themselves, so they "volunteered" or "offered" to get "new positions" or "jobs" to earn money for themselves.

    Distractor Explanations: Choice A is incorrect because the girls were not "discouraged" or "wanted to give up" because of the obstacles; they maintained a "hearty good will" or "good spirit" even though there were obstacles. **Choice B** is incorrect because their parents did not have "reservations" or "concerns" about new jobs; the parents "consented" or "agreed." **Choice D** is incorrect because their father, not the girls, lost his "property" or "money."

8. **Level:** Medium | **Skill/Knowledge:** Central Ideas and Details

    Key Explanation: Choice C is the best answer because "curative properties" refers to "the ability to heal;" it is a synonym for "medicinal." The text says that "one such drink" is ginger beer, with "such drink" referring to those "advertised as having medicinal purposes" in the previous sentence.

Distractor Explanations: Choice A is incorrect because there is no discussion of how popular ginger beer was compared to other bottled drinks. **Choice B** is incorrect because the text states that first Schweppe sold mineral water, and that flavorings like ginger were added later. **Choice D** is incorrect because the text does not say who sold the first ginger beer.

9. **Level:** Easy | **Skill/Knowledge:** Central Ideas and Details

   Key Explanation: Choice C is the best answer because the text directly says that the fossil is "notable" or "significant" because it was "the oldest dinosaur fossil found in Africa."

   Distractor Explanations: All of the other choices are true statements about the fossil according to the text, but they are not listed as the reason that the fossil is "significant" or "important" compared to other fossils.

10. **Level:** Medium | **Skill/Knowledge:** Central Ideas and Details

    Key Explanation: Choice A is the best answer because "inauspicious" refers to something that is "unpromising." It describes the text, in which people are supposed to be going on a "pleasure excursion" or "fun trip," but instead, they are "moping" or "feeling dejected" and "woebegone" or "pathetic." Even the flag was "limp and disheartened." The summary is, "Altogether, it was the bluest, bluest spectacle!" meaning that it was very glum.

Distractor Explanations: Choice B is incorrect because there is no indication that "where the ship is going" is unpleasant; the start of the trip where the people are now is unpleasant. **Choice C** is incorrect because the scene is portrayed as having "bustle" or "busy," there is no indication that it is "exciting" or "fun." Instead, everyone is bleak. **Choice D** is incorrect because there is no discussion of "worry" or "concern," only a lack of energy and spirit.

11. **Level:** Easy | **Skill/Knowledge:** Central Ideas and Details

    Key Explanation: Choice C is the best answer. The concluding sentence summarizes the important part of the text, that the "California condor louse is one of the best–documented cases of the loss of a parasite due to a depletion of the host population." In other words, the parasite was "lost" or "went extinct" because the parasites were removed from the birds in the captive breeding program.

    Distractor Explanations: Choice A is incorrect because it is the reason that the louse went extinct, not the main idea in the text. **Choice B** is incorrect because the fact that the creatures co–evolved is only a minor idea in the description of the louse. **Choice D** is incorrect because there is no indication of why the condor almost went extinct.

12. **Level:** Medium | **Skill/Knowledge:** Central Ideas and Details

    Key Explanation: Choice A is the best answer because Mole is "rambling" or "walking" "hither and thither through the meadows" and along the hedgerows, across the copses." These are fields, bushes, and small clumps of trees, so he must be walking through the countryside.

Distractor Explanations: Choice B is incorrect because he watches others work, but there is no indication that they "encourage" or "urge" him to work, too. **Choice C** is incorrect because the passage refers to him being "on holiday," which implies that he usually has work, but not at the present time. **Choice D** is unsupported by the text, which indicates that Mole likes watching others work when he has nothing to do.

13. **Level:** Medium | **Skill/Knowledge:** Central Ideas and Details

Key Explanation: Choice C is the best answer because the narrator says that the emotions he describes are from "childhood's hour," meaning from when he was very young. The text describes how he was alone and did not enjoy the same things as other people did. "Isolated" can refer to the feeling of being different or apart from others emotionally, not just physically, so fits the context of describing his uniqueness.

Distractor Explanations: The other choices are incorrect because the text does not say that the narrator is without emotions of sadness, desire, or joy. The text only says that his versions of these emotions come from different sources. In other words, he feels happiness and sadness, but for different reasons than most people do.

14. **Level:** Easy | **Skill/Knowledge:** Central Ideas and Details

Key Explanation: Choice C is the best answer because "residents" refers to "dwellers." The first sentence states that "All the dwellers in Starkfield…had had troubles enough of their own

to make them comparatively indifferent to those of their neighbours." In other words, they were more worried about their own "troubles" or "problems" and were "comparatively indifferent" or "relatively unconcerned" about problems of other residents, which would include Ethan Frome.

Distractor Explanations: None of the other choices are supported by evidence from the text. For **Choice A**, the residents "all conceded that Ethan Frome's [troubles] had been beyond the common measure," so they "conceded" or "agreed" that he had more than the usual number of problems rather than feeling that he was "overplaying" or "being too histrionic" about them. For **Choice B**, there is no indication of "hiding" or "trying to conceal" the information from the narrator; the people were just more interested in what was happening to themselves. For **Choice D**, there is no clue how the people felt about the narrator's interest in Frome.

15. **Level:** Medium | **Skill/Knowledge:** Central Ideas and Details

Key Explanation: Choice C is the best answer because the text directly says, "they must earn every penny to buy back their own land." In other words, the tribes must earn the money to buy back land from the people who currently own it.

Distractor Explanations: None of the other choices are supported by evidence from the passage. For **Choice A**, there is no discussion of "grants" or "money given by an organization to use for a specific purpose." For **Choice B**, the text does not refer to who must provide proof of land ownership. For **Choice D**, no one is a "member" of the IRA. Rather, the IRA is legislation that applies to some tribes and not others.

16. **Level:** Medium | **Skill/Knowledge:** Central Ideas and Details

    Key Explanation: Choice A is the best answer because the final sentence says that, "He was hopelessly in debt to his landlady." Therefore, he had an "obligation" or "owed something to" his landlady. This obligation was probably "great" or "large" because he was "hopelessly" in debt, meaning he could not even dream of getting out of the debt.

    Distractor Explanations: Choice B is incorrect because the text only says the young man avoided the kitchen door, presumably because he "avoided meeting his landlady," not that he disliked the food. **Choice C** is incorrect because there is no indication how often the man actually meets the lady. He avoided her this time, but might have been seen often as her kitchen door was "invariably" or "always" open. **Choice D** is incorrect because the man has a "sick feeling," but the text does not say that he is actually sick.

17. **Level:** Medium | **Skill/Knowledge:** Central Ideas and Details

    Key Explanation: Choice C is the best answer because it says that the "girl," who is Milford, saw "flour–mills and the blinking windows of skyscrapers in Minneapolis and St. Paul." In other words, she is looking at "industrialized" or "built–up" areas rather than at fields.

    Distractor Explanations: Choice A is incorrect because the sky is cornflower blue; the plants are not described. **Choice B** is incorrect because the Chippewas "camped two generations ago" or "lived there in the past" rather than the present, as "she saw no Indians now." **Choice D** is incorrect because there is no indication that Camelot was

in that place; the reference is to show that the "pioneering days" are gone, just as Camelot is gone.

18. **Level:** Easy | **Skill/Knowledge:** Central Ideas and Details

    Key Explanation: Choice C is the best answer because the text says that snow blindness "sometimes disrupt[s] vision," so the eyesight is "negatively affected" or "impacted in a bad way." The text also says that "such conditions heal on their own in a few days" or "get better in several days."

    Distractor Explanations: Choice A is incorrect because the text says that snow blindness is when "UV rays from the sun temporarily damage the eyes," so there is "harm" or "damage" even in mild cases, though it gets better. **Choice B** is incorrect because the text does not say that cases are "more severe" or "worse" when there is snow; the text only says that different situations cause it. **Choice D** is incorrect because the text does not say it is "impossible" or "no one can" stay away from situations that are "conducive" or "likely" to cause snow blindness. The text only says that many situations cause it.

19. **Level:** Easy | **Skill/Knowledge:** Central Ideas and Details

    Key Explanation: Choice A is the best answer because the passage describes the size as being the longest bony fish, and it also says they "seldom come to the surface." Since they are "unusual" and the source of legends, they are most likely not seen often.

    Distractor Explanations: Choice B is incorrect because the passage does not say how "famous" or "well–known" giant oarfish are compared to other types of fish. **Choice C** is incorrect because there is no discussion of a "mistake" in recognizing the animal; people just made up stories about sea serpents based on them. **Choice D** is incorrect because it is a minor detail in the text, which only refers to the fish as being up to eight meters long. The comment about seventeen meters is a "report," which means it may or may not be true.

20. **Level:** Easy | **Skill/Knowledge:** Central Ideas and Details

    Key Explanation: Choice B is the best answer because the text says that the brothers "experimented with ways to use" the fragments from the cutting machine, which implies that they did not have a way that was usually used. In other words, the fragments were probably typically thrown away, or wasted, rather than used.

    Distractor Explanations: Choice A is incorrect because the Tater Tot was "iconic," which indicates that it was special or unusual rather than typical or normal. **Choice C** is impossible to determine from the text; it is possible the family invented many foods. **Choice D** is also not explained, as no ingredients other than potatoes are mentioned.

21. **Level:** Easy | **Skill/Knowledge:** Central Ideas and Details

    Key Explanation: Choice D is the best answer because the text directly says that the three bones in the middle ear "convey" or "carry" the sound "to the inner ear, where it is converted into electrical impulses in a fluid–filled part called the cochlea."

    Distractor Explanations: Choice A is incorrect because the auricle funnels sound to the middle

ear, and the tympanic membrane and bones of the middle ear carry the sound to the inner ear. **Choice B** is incorrect because the vestibule and semicircular canals are related to balance. **Choice C** is incorrect because there is no discussion of "slowing" the sound, only that the cochlea contains fluid.

22. **Level:** Medium | **Skill/Knowledge:** Central Ideas and Details

    Key Explanation: Choice A is the best answer because the passage says that they "leased it for other people to run so that they would be able to expand to other locations." In other words, they created the "franchise" or "lease system" in order to expand to other places because they could not "operate" or "run" the restaurants "personally" or "by themselves."

    Distractor Explanations: Choice B is incorrect because the first restaurant was "so popular." In other words, a single store had no problems selling the product. **Choice C** is not supported by the text, as the first stand was popular enough that people probably were willing to travel to buy root beer there. **Choice D** is incorrect because it refers to the reasons for using the name A&W rather than the start of the franchise.

23. **Level:** Medium | **Skill/Knowledge:** Central Ideas and Details

    Key Explanation: Choice B is the best answer because it contains the key ideas of the text. The first three sentences describe the stone object that is very large and was found in the ocean. The final portion delves into possible purposes or origins, but ends by saying that "the true nature and origin may never be known," meaning it is a "mystery."

Distractor Explanations: Choice A is incorrect because the idea of a UFO is a minor detail of the text; the main conclusion is that there are different possibilities about what the structure is, but it is not known. **Choice C** is incorrect because there is no discussion about the object being a "hoax" or "not real." In fact, the text refers to electronic equipment "from reputable scientific institutions," so likely respected places also have verified that the object exists. **Choice D** is incorrect because it does not discuss the speculation about what the object might be caused by or came from, which are essential parts of the text.

24. **Level:** Easy | **Skill/Knowledge:** Central Ideas and Details

    Key Explanation: Choice C is the best answer because the text says that Whitman "never learned the native language and refused to adopt any of the local culture." In other words, she did not make efforts to "assimilate" or "become part of" the Native American society.

    Distractor Explanations: Choice A is incorrect because there is no indication that having a child was a "drawback" or "problem" with starting a new life. **Choice B** is incorrect because the mission where she lived was "an important stopping point," so she was able to settle in enough to help others who were traveling. **Choice D** is not discussed in the text; the "local people" showed distrust, but there is no sign that she did not believe them.

25. **Level:** Medium | **Skill/Knowledge:** Central Ideas and Details

    Key Explanation: Choice B is the best answer. The text says that Preemby was "good-looking" and gives a few general details about his appearance, but then focuses on his "personality"

or "nature," which was "given to reverie" and led to "abstraction" or "absent-mindedness" that made it hard for him to be employed. The reader learns that Preemby finally "comes to rest" or "is employed" by a distant relative, implying that connections helped him get the job rather than that he had the drive and initiative to find a position for himself.

Distractor Explanations: Choice A is incorrect because the text does not discuss "many" challenges, just the fact that his personality makes it hard for him to gain employment. **Choice C** is incorrect because the paragraph says that Preemby "came to rest for several years," but that phrase implies that he moved on to other jobs. The employment was not a "career" or a "lifetime path," only a "rest" or "short stop" along his path. **Choice D** is incorrect because the text does describe the character's "appearance" or "physical looks" in general, but spends more time focusing on the personality. Therefore, the appearance is only a minor part of the overall purpose.

26. **Level:** Medium | **Skill/Knowledge:** Central Ideas and Details

    Key Explanation: Choice B is the correct option. The passage talks about the various methods of transportation Australians use to get to work.

    Distractor Explanations: Choice A is incorrect as the passage mentions that the usage of trains has decreased. **Choices C and D** are also incorrect as they do not represent the main theme but only point to certain characteristics of Australians.

27. **Level:** Easy | **Skill/Knowledge:** Central Ideas and Details

Key Explanation: Choice B is the correct option because the majority of the passage points to how the economy of the United Kingdom has been improved by the process of privatization, and how the government has been able to reduce its losses while receiving taxes from the sold companies.

Distractor Explanations: Choice A is incorrect because while the advantages of privatization are mentioned, the dominant theme is how the UK used privatization to its advantage. Similarly, **choice C** is incorrect because the difficulty of finding a plan to help the UK is not a dominant theme. **Choice D** is incorrect because this option is only an inference from the passage and is not the overarching theme.

28. **Level:** Medium | **Skill/Knowledge:** Central Ideas and Details

Key Explanation: Choice D is the best answer as most of the passage talks about the various ways people tried to save money in order to survive the economic impact of the Great Depression. For example, they grew their own produce, ate cheap meat, used cotton sacks to make clothing, etc.

Distractor Explanations: Choice A is incorrect because it is not the main idea of the passage. In fact, it is an inferred idea as the passage says only one full–time job per family was permitted and women were encouraged to stay home. **Choice B** is incorrect because no evidence has been presented in the passage to support the idea that it was difficult for women to find jobs. **Choice C** is incorrect because similar to **choice A**, it is not the overall theme or main idea of the passage.

29. **Level:** Easy | **Skill/Knowledge:** Central Ideas and Details

Key Explanation: Choice B is correct because the text mentions that the IPCC has attributed "modern climate warming to the increase of anthropogenic Greenhouse Gases (GHGs) concentrations in the atmosphere."

Distractor Explanations: Choice A is incorrect because the text mentions that emerging scientific evidence has only reinforced the conclusion that modern climate warming is caused by an increase in GHGs. **Choices C** and **D** are incorrect because the text does not offer any information to support these options.

30. **Level:** Medium | **Skill/Knowledge:** Central Ideas and Details

Key Explanation: Choice D is the best option because the author has repeatedly mentioned the immense power of emotions and how ignoring emotions is shortsighted. For example, the author says, "A view of human nature that ignores the power of human emotion is sadly shortsighted." He also mentions "feeling counts every bit as much — and often more — than thought."

Distractor Explanations: Choice A is incorrect because the text does not mention anywhere that emotions make humans weak. **Choice B** is incorrect because it is not the central or dominant idea of the text. **Choice C** is incorrect because the text offers no information to support the idea that humans should no longer be called *homo sapiens.*

31. **Level:** Medium | **Skill/Knowledge:** Central Ideas and Details

Key Explanation: Choice C is the correct option because the text mentions "threats to these species increases with each acre of forest that is cleared for charcoal production or illegal timber extraction."

Distractor Explanations: Choice A is incorrect because the text does not mention that the Orange–bellied Antwren is found only in the Pedra D'Anta Reserve. **Choice B** is incorrect because the text mentions that the Pedra D'Anta Reserve is located within the Serra do Urubu Forest and protects the Atlantic Rainforest. **Choice D** is incorrect because the text does not offer any information to support the fact that only 2 percent of the forest in the area is home to endangered birds.

32. **Level:** Medium | **Skill/Knowledge:** Central Ideas and Details

    Key Explanation: Choice B is correct because the text continually emphasizes how remote Antarctica is ("no history of a native population") and how much of this continent remains unexplored ("Unexplored valleys and unscaled mountains abound.")

Distractor Explanations: Choices A and **D** are incorrect because the text offers no evidence to support these claims. **Choice C** is incorrect because the text only mentions that the ocean "still boils with life… no longer do" but it doesn't say that the Atlantic and Pacific are lifeless.

33

As for tidal devices, the environmental impacts are considered comparably small. Wave devices will represent a much lower collision risk compared to offshore wind devices but they could be the risk of underwater collisions for diving birds. Potential positive effects such as the creation of roosting sites and habitat enhancement for marine birds might occur as well. According to Lewis et al., "information on the environmental and social impacts is limited mainly due to the lack of experience in deploying and operating ocean technologies, although adverse environmental effects are foreseen to be relatively low."

Based on the text, which choice best describes the claim that tidal energy systems may improve some aspects of the local environment?

A) It is incorrect, because systems change too many aspects of the region.

B) It is overly optimistic, because there are no examples of improvement.

C) It is justifiable, because systems may create new habitats for birds.

D) It is valid, because many systems have demonstrated unexpected side benefits.

34

An antibody-based drug is one candidate for a more effective, longer-lasting overdose treatment than the current method of using a drug called naloxone. To explore this possibility, a team at Scripps Research Institute led by Kim D. Janda developed a potentially effective biological compound based on antibodies from mice. "Combining the new drug and naloxone could offer treatment that is both fast and long-acting," Janda says. Allegheny Health Network Research Institute's Saadyah Averick, who has worked on extending naloxone's lifetime using nanoparticles, says the work offers a "unique and orthogonal approach to sequester the potent synthetic opioids." He says the antibodies' specificity and longer circulation is interesting but wonders about the antibodies' practicality as a treatment: biological therapies are much more expensive to make because they require special manufacturing facilities and storage, he says.

As described in the text, which choice best describes the relationship between Kim D. Janda and Saadyah Averick?

A) Averick is a researcher in the same field who has reservations about Janda's work.

B) Both researchers are working to create antibody treatments for opiate overdoses.

C) Janda is pursuing research based on preliminary tests conducted by Averick.

D) Averick's research generated different results when duplicating Janda's tests.

35

The vegan diet is one that is chosen by individuals for various reasons, including health and/or ethical reasons. In addition, it is evident that the vegan diet is much more than a diet itself, but has developed into a lifestyle, often associated with animal rights and environmental advocacy as well as a greater concern for physical activity and mindfulness. Findings suggest that a well-rounded vegan diet is healthy and such is evidenced by the variety of whole foods and increased vegetable and fruit intake. Health benefits include a decrease in cholesterol, lipid levels, blood pressure, weight, and a reduced risk for a variety of diseases including obesity, diabetes, cardiovascular disease, and cancer. Despite the benefits, health concerns do exist, especially in regard to nutrient deficiencies, without a well-planned and varied diet. Nutrient concerns include possible deficiencies in calcium, vitamin D, iron, and particularly vitamin B-12, for which supplements should be taken.

The conclusion that veganism offers a well-rounded diet is open to which of the following criticisms?

A) It is not clear whether the results are solely due to partaking in a vegan diet.

B) The diet is sometimes adopted for ethical rather than health purposes.

C) The study relied on a literature review opposed to obtaining firsthand data.

D) It is important to include additions which are not directly deprived from plants.

36

Asheville, North Carolina, has a population of about 95,000 people and around 100 bears. The bears are bold enough to walk down streets during the daylight and cavort around playground equipment. A recent study tagged and tracked female bears that were around one year old and found that the average weight of the urban bears was nearly double that of their rural counterparts, probably due to the addition of human-generated food sources. Another benefit of the close contact was that the female bears were able to reproduce as early as 2 years. However, there are drawbacks to urban cohabitation for the bears: _____

Which choice most logically completes the text?

A) over 40 percent of the cubs died during the 4-year study, mostly due to vehicle strikes.

B) sometimes the bears have attacked and injured people or pets such as small dogs.

C) there are laws preventing residents from using food to entice bears close to their homes.

D) since bears often dig through garbage, the city now offers bear-proof garbage cans.

37

In a recent experiment about salt stress on apples, the temperature, light, and soil were consistent. The only variable was how much salt was applied in the water. Ripe fruits were collected and counted for each treatment of salt at 45 days after the first fruit ripening. The first ripe fruits samples from each treatment were photographed and two ripe fruits were selected from each plant and weighed. Then, the fruits were weighed to determine the average fresh mass of each fruit for each treatment and a nutritional analysis was conducted on them.

Based on the information in the text, what criticism is the experiment open to?

A) The fruits selected for measurement may not have been representative of the other fruits in the group.

B) The change in size may have been based on variations in temperature rather than amount of salt.

C) Fluctuation in light as fruits develop can affect the nutritional value of the mature fruit.

D) The results of the experiment may not be applicable to a wide variety of plant species.

38

Enid Marx was an industrial designer who was hired by the London Passenger Transport Board in 1937 to design textiles for use on the seats of buses and trains. The project was challenging because the patterns needed to hide dirt and wear, yet at the same time, reduce the sense of nausea sometimes experienced when looking at patterns in motion. Marx successfully completed this task, but it took experimentation. At first, she worked with subtle earth colors, but eventually realized that almost the opposite was most effective: _____

Which choice most logically completes the text?

A) her "shield" pattern was used for decades in the London Underground.

B) she was also noted for engraving the designs for several postage stamps.

C) she eventually became a guest lecturer in textile history.

D) her finished designs feature bright colors and strong contrast.

39

If you are a fan of jigsaw puzzles, then you are not alone. It turns out that the first modern jigsaw puzzles were invented in 1947, but the idea predates to 1760, when a cartographer named John Spilsbury glued maps to boards and cut out the shapes along the country lines. These "dissections," as Spilsbury called them, were used for education, and they were technically not "jigsaw puzzles" because _____

Which choice most logically completes the text?

A) they were used for educational purposes.

B) only the wealthy could afford them.

C) Spilsbury was also an engraver.

D) the jigsaw was not even invented until 1855.

40

The narwhal is a medium–sized whale that lives in arctic waters. Its most distinctive feature is a tusk—actually, an overgrown and protruding canine tooth—that can reach 3.1 meters (10.2 feet) long. The tusk usually grows only from the left canine, and typically only in males, though sometimes it is found in females. In the past, biologists speculated that the tusks were used for violent male–to–male combat, but that view has been reassessed upon finding out that _____

Which choice most logically completes the text?

A) the tusks are usually surrounded by vestigial teeth that may be extruded from the bone or which may remain in tooth sockets.

B) about one in 500 males actually grow two tusks when the right canine also extends from the body.

C) the tusk is actually a sensory organ with millions of nerve endings that convey external stimuli about the ocean to the brain.

D) a 2016 survey of feeding narwhals showed them using the tusk to stun prey when hunting fish near the surface of the water.

41

As part of an effort to decrease the power of indigenous tribes, in the 1830s, Canada forced Native American children from Vancouver Island to attend residential schools. This policy was not effective in helping the students integrate into mainstream culture because there were still stigmas against them, and in the process, most were unable to speak their traditional languages. Tla–o–qui–aht tribe member Timmy Masso feels that language is essential to regrow a sense of community, so _____

Which choice most logically completes the text?

A) is employing various media to spread the use of the native language.

B) has made efforts to block roads to prevent disrespectful behavior.

C) has created a performance and healing song to honor the land.

D) is protesting the lack of affordable housing for residents in the region.

42

Bergmann's Rule is a biological observation made in 1847 which points out that within a species, body mass increases as the climate gets colder, so animals at higher latitudes have less surface area compared to the mass. For example, Canadian deer in regions with snow in the winter are bulkier than southern deer of the same species in order to conserve heat. By contrast, the southern deer have lighter builds because _____

Which choice most logically completes the text?

A) the extra surface area allows them to disperse heat in the warmer climate.

B) they do not need to store as much fat to carry them through the winter months.

C) food is more readily available and they do not need to migrate as far.

D) they have not yet replaced the weight for their return to the north.

43

Born in 1914, Hedy Lamarr was an actress who was often considered the most beautiful woman in the world, and she starred in many popular movies such as *Samson and Delilah*. However, she had an insatiable curiosity and spent considerable amounts of time tinkering on inventions during movie takes. In the 1940s, she wanted to contribute to the war effort and helped devise a method of "frequency hopping" that could guide torpedoes while avoiding radio interception. Her techniques were not used by the military at the time, but she changed the world of communication because _____

Which choice most logically completes the text?

A) she died in 2000 without receiving a penny for her incredible invention.

B) her invention became the basis of systems such as WiFi, Bluetooth, and GPS.

C) in 2014, she was inducted into the National Inventors Hall of Fame.

D) she received a patent for the invention in 1942, and in 1943 became a U.S. citizen.

44

Radiocarbon dating offers archaeologists and other scientists a range of dates rather than a precise year in which an object was made. By contrast, dendrochronology, or the science of tree–ring dating, can offer more specific information. Trees add growth every year in predictable patterns called rings, but the exact width of the ring varies depending on certain climatic conditions such as abundance of rain. Comparing rings of different trees allows scientists to determine when the tree lived, and by extension, _____

Which choice most logically completes the text?

A) it is also possible to determine the ages more generally using other techniques.

B) European oak trees from Germany have extremely long lives if not cut

C) when the wood for an object like a panel painting or a historical building was harvested.

D) the species of the tree can also be determined by scientific analysis.

45

Lava tube caves form because molten lava has little silica to give it structure, so it flows like a river. As the lava moves away from the source, the surface cools into a crust that insulates the lava below. The lava inside the crust continues to flow, so when the eruption ends, there is a hollow cavity like a straw. At first the caves are sterile because of the intense heat. However, the caves offer scientists an exciting glimpse into what life might be like on other planets because _____

Which choice most logically completes the text?

A) sometimes the caves are not found for thousands of years until part of the wall collapses.

B) the caves rapidly fill with microbes that thrive in the extreme environment.

C) volcanoes can produce other stone structures depending on the eruption patterns.

D) the largest tube cave in the world is Kazumura Cave in Hawaii, at 40 miles long.

46

Starting around 1200 B.C., the Phoenicians created a fabric dye that was reddish purple in color from snails from the Muricidae family. Making the dye was extremely time–consuming because it required thousands of snails to produce sizeable amounts of pigment, and the process had many complicated steps. The color was so highly coveted that it was mainly used in the early Roman Empire for ceremonial purposes such as senatorial robes, and by the fourth century, there were laws stating that only the emperor could use it. As a result, the dye _____

Which choice most logically completes the text?

A) is frequently referred to as imperial or royal purple.

B) changes color as it ages because it is not completely permanent.

C) can be made from irritating the snails, but that process takes longer.

D) formula was lost and it was not recreated until 1998.

47

Pangaea was the most recent supercontinent to form on Earth. During Paleolithic and Mesozoic times—about 335 to 200 million years ago—the continents were joined together. The theory of the existence of such a supercontinent was first proposed by observing the outlines of the continents along the Atlantic Ocean; when charted to a depth of 910 meters, the match between Africa and South America is almost a perfect fit. Further confirmation of Pangaea came from _____

Which choice most logically completes the text?

A) the fact that scientists theorized that there were earlier supercontinents that formed billions of years prior to Pangaea.

B) Alfred Wegener's theory of continental drift powered by centrifugal force from the Earth's rotation, which was later proved to be unsound.

C) fossil evidence which reveals ancient life forms that are similar or identical in places that are completely isolated from each other today.

D) the hypothesis that the very active volcanism caused by the breaking up of the continent led to global warming and the highest ocean levels to date.

48

Despite the name, an electric eel is not actually an eel, but is part of a group of fish living in South America that are more closely related to catfish. Their preferred prey is smaller fish, and they have the ability to generate an electric charge up to 860 volts, which is enough to stun or even kill prey or predators as large as a cow. They do not just use their electric ability for hunting and defense,

_____

Which choice most logically completes the text?

A) as they have three electricity–producing organs which generate different charges.

B) and the electric battery was invented in 1800 based on studying electric eels.

C) and they get larger by adding additional vertebrae to the spine as they age.

D) because they also have electroreceptors that allow them to use it for navigation.

49

This study about salt stress on chili peppers indicated that increasing NaCl concentrations significantly delayed flowering and fruit ripening and fruits' number, size, and fresh mass. While plants with no NaCl in the soil averaged 23.66 days to produce their first flower and 48 days to the first fruit, the latter in plants with 60 nM of NaCl _____. It also decreased vitamins B6, B12, and C concentrations, but increased capsaicinoid concentration and consequently, the fruit's tangy flavor. Thus, salt stress reduced the fruit yields and deteriorated fruit nutritional quality by reducing vitamins concentrations.

Figure 1: Chili Peppers Exposed to Salt Stress

NaCl concentration (mM)	Average days to first flower	Average days to first fruit	Average number of fruits
0	23.66	48	6
30	23.66	52	3
60	31.66	66	2
90	39.66	0	0
120	40.33	0	0

Which choice most effectively uses data from the table to complete the claim?

A) had only 2 fruit

B) was about 66 days longer on average

C) took an average of 31.66 days

D) took an average of 66 days

50

Average Start-Up Costs for Selected Legitimate Franchises

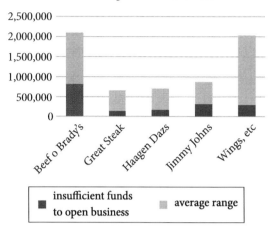

Data adapted from Franchise Direct, 2019 An inconsistency between what a seller tells you about a business opportunity and what you find in online research could be a tell–tale sign of a business opportunity rip–off. However, it is important to remember that many business investments have a wide range of returns, so not all differences in profit are a deliberate attempt to scam a potential buyer. For example, factors such as real estate price may create a large difference in the startup costs of some legitimate franchise opportunities. For example, a Beef o Brady franchise _____

Which choice most effectively completes the text using data from the graph?

A) can cost from about $500,000 to about $2,000,000 to open.

B) ranges from about $750,000 to over $2,000,000 to open.

C) can be opened for any sum up to about $2,000,000.

D) requires about $2,000,000 or it cannot be opened.

51

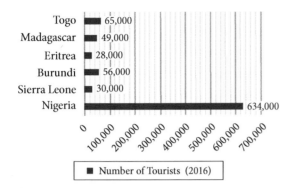

This passage is adapted from *World Regional Geography: People, Places, and Globalization,* copyrighted by the University of Minnesota, 2016.

Even now, Africa excels in attracting tourists to its wildlife and game reserves. Safari tourism highlights exotic creatures, including elephants, lions, rhinos, hippos, and big game. The region is also replete with natural features or attractions that tourists gravitate toward, particularly those in search of outstanding scenic sites or who desire an environmental adventure. There are dozens of awe–inspiring national parks throughout Africa like Zuma Rock in Nigeria, which demonstrates the point: _____

Which choice most effectively completes the text using data from the graph?

A) it had 634,000 more tourists per year than other African countries.

B) Burundi and Sierra Leone had fewer visitors.

C) it has the greatest number of tourists of African countries, 634,000.

D) other countries do not have as many beautiful natural features or safari animals.

Nutrients Found Primarily in Animal Tissues

Nutrient	Function	Natural source	Alternate Source
B12	Used by nervous and circulatory systems	Fish, meat, dairy, eggs	Enriched grain products; some nutritional yeast
Creatine	Increases muscle performance	Animal tissue	Supplements; the body naturally makes small amounts
DHA	Mental health and brain development, especially in children	Fatty fish, fish oil	Microalgae
Taurine	Muscle function, bile production	Fish, meat, poultry, dairy products	Synthetic supplements

Findings suggest that a well–rounded vegan diet is healthy and such is evidenced by the variety of whole foods and increased vegetable and fruit intake. Health benefits include a decrease in cholesterol, lipid levels, blood pressure, weight, and a reduced risk for a variety of diseases including obesity, diabetes, cardiovascular disease, and cancer. Despite the benefits, health concerns do exist, especially in regard to nutrient deficiencies that may arise without a well–planned and varied diet. Nutrient concerns include calcium, vitamin D, iron, and particularly vitamin B–12, for which supplements should be taken. Therefore, _____

Which choice most effectively completes the text using data from the table?

A) vegans should take advantage of the many natural sources for the nutrients, such as fish and poultry.

B) results of interview studies demonstrate that about half of the vegans are potentially at risk for vitamin D deficiency because most do not take vitamin D supplements.

C) it is essential for those who are vegan to consider man–made as well as natural additions to their diet.

D) the popularity of the vegan diet and the question of whether it is nutritionally sound raise issues of anthropological significance.

53

Tiger Population by Year

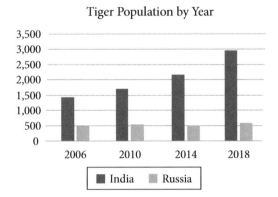

Tigers are listed among the world's endangered species. The large, mostly solitary carnivores require a wide range, and the worldwide population is in jeopardy due to poaching and habitat loss. However, countries are making an effort to preserve these iconic animals. For example, India is home to the largest wild tiger population. In 2014 there were 692 protected areas in the country, but that number has been increased to 860. Those conservation efforts are paying off: _____

Which choice most effectively completes the text with data from the graph?

A) the world population has increased by almost 30% since 2006.

B) India has seen an increase in tigers from about 1,450 in 2006 to almost 3,000 in 2018.

C) in 2018, there were almost 3,000 tigers in India, but only about 550 in Russia.

D) Russia's tiger population has barely increased, but India's has grown to almost 3,000.

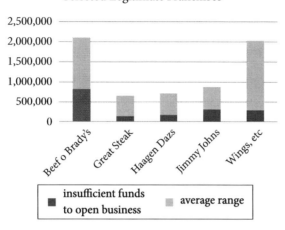

Average Start-Up Costs for
Selected Legitimate Franchises

Data adapted from Franchise Direct, 2019

The Business Disclosure Rule says that a seller has to give you the disclosure document at least seven days before you sign a contract or pay them anything. Use that time to check out the information in the disclosure document, including contacting references. An inconsistency could be a tell–tale sign of a business opportunity rip–off. However, it is important to remember that many business investments have a wide range of returns, so not all differences in profit are a deliberate attempt to scam a potential buyer. For example, factors such as real estate price may create a large difference in the startup costs of some legitimate franchise opportunities.

Which data from the table best supports the author's point that there may be variations in reported costs in legitimate franchises?

A) The cost of opening a Beef o Brady's franchise is significantly higher than opening a Great Steak franchise.

B) The cost of land for building a Wings, etc. franchise is more expensive than for many other franchises.

C) The start–up costs for one franchise, Wings, etc., range from well under $500,000 to about $2,000,000.

D) Investors with less than $500,000 can still have enough money to start a legitimate franchise.

55

Percentage of US Residents who Speak a Language Other than English in the Home (by year)

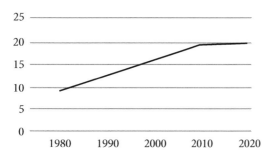

The U.S. Census Bureau asks questions about language use and proficiency as part of its comprehensive demographic profiling of the residents of the country. The information is not just satisfying curiosity, though. It is gathered to ensure that information related to such things as public health, education, and other community services is presented in ways that the community members understand. Such demographics are more important now than ever, since _____

Which choice most effectively completes the text with information from the graph?

A) just over 20% of the population is not comfortable with speaking English.

B) the percentage of bilingual speakers grew greatly after 1980, but tapered off recently.

C) over 20% of the population now speaks a language other than English in the home.

D) the percentage of people who do not speak English in the home has steadily increased since 1980 from about 11% to about 22%.

56

Panda Population in China (by year)

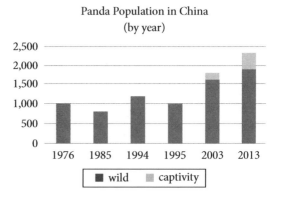

Great pandas have received some of the largest amounts of funding for conservation efforts, as the black–and–white animals are cute and appealing to donors. Some conservationists feel that the money has been wasted because the habitat is too small and fragmented for the long–term continuation of the species. However, the efforts have indeed produced good results as the population has continued to grow since the conservation efforts began around 1976.

Which data from the graph most weakens the claim made by the text?

A) After conservation efforts began, a large number of pandas started living in captivity as well as in the wild.

B) Due to conservation efforts, pandas raised in captivity have been successfully released in the wild.

C) Between 2003 and 2013, the number of pandas both in captivity and in the wild made perceptible increases.

D) Between 1994 and 1995, there was a sharp decrease of about 200 pandas living in the wild.

57

Comparison of Average Heights by Year for Adults

Country	Men–1896	Men–1996	Women–1896	Women–1996
Belgium	167.2	181.7	155.42	165.49
Cuba	159.88	172.0	149.25	157.98
Egypt	158.64	166.68	148.72	157.33
India	161.96	164.95	147.97	152.58
New Zealand	167.48	177.79	155.96	164.94
South Korea	159.75	174.92	142.17	162.34

Scientists agree that genetic makeup is the factor most closely linked to the adult height of an individual, but other components such as activity levels, medical conditions, and hormones, are related. In particular, nutrition during development can significantly alter an individual's end height, with protein, calcium, vitamin A, and vitamin D the most important dietary components for growth.

Which choice best explains the data in the graph using information from the text?

A) The average height of women never exceeds that of men because they consume less protein.

B) In general, people around the world are taller than in the past because they are getting better nutrition.

C) People in Egypt have not changed their diet much over time, and thus have a lower average height than other countries.

D) If everyone in the world ate the same foods, then the average heights would be closer than they actually were.

58

2021 Global Lithium Market (US$6.62 billion)

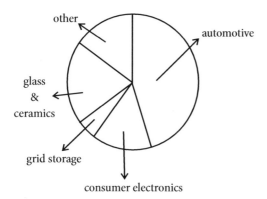

The global lithium market has been expanding greatly in recent years. It was valued at 6.62 billion dollars in 2021, but forecasts predict an annual growth rate of about 12%. Though lithium is used in the production of many useful items in daily life, one of the primary uses is to make rechargeable batteries. As a consequence of the rising push towards electric vehicles, _____

Which choice most effectively completes the text with information from the graph?

A) about 45 percent of all vehicles use lithium in their production.

B) glass and ceramics and consumer electronics use about 15 percent of the lithium.

C) more lithium is used in the automotive industry than in grid storage.

D) the automotive industry comprises about 45 percent of the lithium market.

59

Leading Countries for
International Tourists Arrivals
(in 2019 in millions)

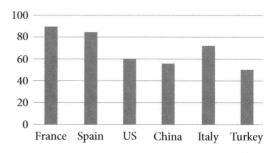

International tourism can greatly affect a country's revenue. If the country has a solid infrastructure, it can safely and comfortably provide the necessary services for visitors to enjoy their journey. As more visitors arrive, they spend money on travel, lodging, food, souvenirs, and entertainment. The tourists also post their impressions—be it positive or negative—on social media for all their friends and family to see. In fact, the development of social media has greatly influenced the number of visitors to different tourist sites around the world.

Which choice most effectively uses information from the text to describe data from the graph?

A) People do not enjoy visits to Turkey and post poor comments on social media.

B) France has the highest number of tourists because it has many famous sites to visit.

C) Spain has a good infrastructure for visitors and is often positively reviewed on social media.

D) China has a less developed infrastructure but better social media reviews than Turkey.

60

Estimated African Elephant Population
(in wild by year)

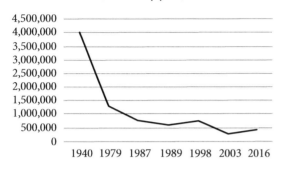

— Estimated African Elephant Population
(in wild by year)

In Africa, there are two types of elephants. One is a savannah elephant, which lives in the wide grasslands. There are also much rarer forest elephants, which are smaller and have straighter, down–pointing tusks. There were over four million at the start of the twentieth century, but hunters prized the giant tusks. Bans on the sale of ivory in 1989 have helped prevent the dramatic decline in numbers that was occurring before that time. Unfortunately, habitat loss and poaching also take a toll on the populations of both. Despite conservation efforts, _____

Which choice most effectively completes the text with data from the graph?

A) savannah elephant populations have declined more than forest elephants.

B) there was a slight increase in total numbers between 2003 and 2016.

C) the combined population of elephants is now less than 500,000.

D) populations have started to rebuild since the ban on the sale of ivory.

61

Most Expensive Prices for Paintings in the World (as of 2021)

Painting	Artist	Year Sold	Price (in millions)	Price adjusted for inflation (in millions)
Salvator Mundi	Leonardo da Vinci (Attributed)	2017	US$400	US$475.4
Interchange	Willem de Kooning	2015	US$300	US$328
The Card Players	Paul Cezanne	2011	US$250	US$288
Nafea Faa Ipoipo	Paul Gaugin	2015	US$210	US$229

The value of art is subjective: some people like one painting, whereas others do not. The fame of the artist or the appeal of the subject may affect the end price, but ultimately, a painting is worth as much as anyone is willing to pay for it. The most expensive painting sold in the world to date is the *Salvator Mundi*, which exists in several copies made by Leonardo da Vinci's students; the one sold in 2017 for US$400 million may have been painted by the great master himself. By contrast, the next most expensive painting _____

Which choice most logically completes the text using data from the table?

A) is *Interchange*, painted by William de Kooning and sold for US$328 million in 2017.

B) cost US$300 million less at the time it was sold: *Interchange*, by William de Kooning.

C) sold in 2017 for US$100 less than *Salvator Mundi*; it is William de Kooning's *Interchange*.

D) is William de Kooning's painting *Interchange*, sold in 2017 for US$300 million.

62

Amount of Chocolate Consumed per Person
(in 2021, in kilograms)

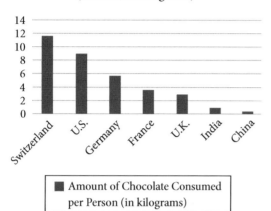

Chocolate is a popular flavor in the United States, and sales skyrocket around Halloween. However, it turns out that the leading country for chocolate consumption in the world is Switzerland, where people average about 11.6 kilograms per year. That figure may not be surprising, as some of the world's premier chocolatiers, and large firms such as Toblerone and Lindt, are based in Switzerland. Though Europeans consume a large amount of chocolate, the same is not as true in Asian countries, where different traditional sweets are still preferred.

Which data from the graph best supports the claims made in the text?

A) The U.S. average chocolate consumption is about 9 kilograms, whereas it is closer to 3.5 kilograms in France.

B) The average chocolate consumption in the U.K. is about 3 kilograms, but consumption in Switzerland is about 11.5 kilograms.

C) The average chocolate consumption in China is about .5 kilograms, but the consumption in Germany is about 5.5 kilograms.

D) People in Germany consume more chocolate on average than people in France or the U.K. do.

63

Client group[a]	Number of clients	Female (%)	Homeless at the beginning of support (%)	Median length of support (days)	Receiving accommodation (%)
Family and domestic violence	116,200	77	37	60	36
Current mental health issue	88,200	62	50	85	37
Indigenous Australians	73,300	61	47	55	41
Young people presenting alone (15–24 years)	41,700	64	51	60	32
Older people (55 years or older)	23,900	56	35	41	20
Children (0–17 years) on care and protection orders[b]	8,300	53	50	102	49

Homelessness is a growing problem in Australia. Australians known to be at particular risk of homelessness include those who have experienced family and domestic violence, young people, children in care and under protection orders, Indigenous Australians, people leaving health or social care arrangements, and Australians aged 55 or older. Older people are especially disadvantaged, as only 20 percent receive housing support. However, Indigenous Australians _____.

Which choice most effectively completes the text using information from the table?

A) receive considerably higher housing support as compared to older Australians

B) receive even lesser housing support than older Australians

C) make up less of the overall clientele as compared to older Australians

D) are the most disadvantaged of all Australians

33. **Level:** Medium | **Skill/Knowledge:** Command of Evidence (Textual)

Key Explanation: Choice C is the best answer because "justifiable" means that a claim is reasonable because it is possibly true. The passage says, "Potential positive effects such as the creation of roosting sites and habitat enhancement for marine birds might occur as well." Therefore, according to the passage, the claim that despite some risks, the idea that there be potential positive effects is reasonable.

Distractor Explanations: Choice A is incorrect because "incorrect" means that the claim is not true at all. Although tidal energy systems may change many aspects of the region, there may also be some positive changes. **Choice B** is incorrect because "overly" means "too." Although the claim is optimistic, there is a potential that it is true, so it is not "too optimistic." **Choice D** is incorrect because, while the claim is valid, side benefits have not been "demonstrated" or "proven." The passage only offers "potential" or "theoretical" advantages.

34. **Level:** Hard | **Skill/Knowledge:** Command of Evidence (Textual)

Key Explanation: Choice A is the best answer because Averick says that Janda's approach is "unique and orthogonal," meaning that it is interesting and unusual. However, he has "reservations" or "doubts" that it will be a usable option for most patients: he "wonders about the antibodies' practicality as a treatment." Since Averick "has worked on extending naloxone's lifetime using nanoparticles," he is also in the field of drug research.

Distractor Explanations: Choice B is incorrect because both researchers are working to treat opiate overdoses, but only Janda is using antibodies. Averick is using nanoparticles to improve the drug naloxone. **Choice C** is incorrect

because both researchers are pursuing different lines of treatment; one is not building on the work of the other. **Choice D** is incorrect because Averick's research was unrelated to Janda's. He did not "duplicate" or "repeat" Janda's tests.

35. **Level:** Medium | **Skill/Knowledge:** Command of Evidence (Textual)

Key Explanation: Choice D is the best answer because the text concludes that "a well-rounded vegan diet is healthy and such is evidenced by the variety of whole foods and increased vegetable and fruit intake." However, she also admits that certain nutrients, such as "calcium, vitamin D, iron, and particularly vitamin B-12" are insufficient from a plant-based diet, so that "supplements" or "additions" need to be taken. Since plants do not provide all the nutrients humans need, then the conclusion that veganism is sufficient to be healthy may be brought into doubt.

Distractor Explanations: Choice A is incorrect because there is no reason to question that stated findings may be in error. **Choice B** is incorrect because even if the diet is "adopted" or "started" for ethical reasons, it still can have health benefits. **Choice C** is incorrect because it is unclear where the research findings were derived from.

36. **Level:** Medium | **Skill/Knowledge:** Command of Evidence (Textual)

Key Explanation: Choice A is the best answer because the sentence says that there are "drawbacks" or "bad points" to "urban cohabitation" or "living in the city" for the bears. **Choice A** shows a problem: "vehicle strikes" or "being hit by cars" accounts for a huge percentage of deaths in the "cubs" or "offspring" of the bears, reducing the chances of survival.

Distractor Explanations: Choice B is incorrect because it is a drawback for people, not for the bears. **Choices C** and **D** show ways that the city has tried to eliminate contact between bears and people, but it is not necessarily something bad for the bears. These options are only inconveniences.

37. **Level:** Medium | **Skill/Knowledge:** Command of Evidence (Textual)

Key Explanation: Choice A is the best answer because the passage only says that some fruits from each plant were selected to determine the nutritional value. It does not give any information about how the fruits were chosen. For example, if only the largest ones were taken from one plant and the smallest from another, the results might be skewed based on that decision.

Distractor Explanations: Choices B and **C** are incorrect because the passage directly states that the temperature and light were kept consistent throughout the experiment. Therefore, the variations resulted from another cause. **Choice D** is incorrect because while it is true that the results may not apply to other plants than apples, the study never claims that they do.

38. **Level:** Medium | **Skill/Knowledge:** Command of Evidence (Textual)

Key Explanation: Choice D is the best answer because the blank portion needs to complete the idea that effective designs were opposite of subtle earth colors. **Choice D** says the designs that were finally used were indeed the opposite; they had bright colors rather than earth colors and were "strong" instead of "subtle."

Distractor Explanations: None of the other choices shows how the effective designs were opposite strong earth colors. **Choice A** refers to

the shape of one finished design, not the color. **Choices B** and **C** refer to different aspects of Marx's career other than textiles for the London buses and trains.

39. **Level:** Medium | **Skill/Knowledge:** Command of Evidence (Textual)

Key Explanation: Choice D is the best answer because the blank is preceded by "because," which shows that the blank needs to contain a reason. The reason needs to state why Spilsbury's "dissections" were not jigsaw puzzles. **Choice D** gives a clear reason: there were no jigsaws when Spilsbury invented them.

Distractor Explanations: None of the other choices offers a logical reason why Spilsbury's "dissections" were not "jigsaw puzzles." For **Choice A**, jigsaw puzzles can be educational, so there must be a different reason. For **Choice B**, cost is not a defining reason to logically explain the name. For **Choice C**, Spilsbury could have had any profession and still his creations could be jigsaw puzzles.

40. **Level:** Easy | **Skill/Knowledge:** Command of Evidence (Textual)

Key Explanation: Choice C is the best answer because the blank is preceded by the claim that the view of using the tusks for "violent male-to-male combat" has been revised. The blank portion needs to provide a reason for a change in the view. **Choice C** gives a logical reason: the tusk is actually extremely sensitive and may have another purpose, so is probably not used for hitting and striking another male.

Distractor Explanations: Choice A is incorrect because it is just an interesting fact about other teeth; there is no reason that the tusk could not be used for violent combat if **Choice A** is true. **Choice B** is also compatible with the idea of violent combat, so can be eliminated. **Choice D** shows a second potential use for the tusk, but if narwhals use the tusk to stun prey, they could also use it to stun an opponent in combat.

41. **Level:** Medium | **Skill/Knowledge:** Command of Evidence (Textual)

Key Explanation: Choice A is the best answer because "so" shows that the blank is finishing the idea of what Masso is doing because language is essential for regrowing a sense of community. **Choice A** gives a logical result of his conviction: he is spreading the use of the language in many ways.

Distractor Explanations: None of the other choices address the result of Masso's belief that language is important for a sense of community. They show different aspects of his activism to protect the land and honor it, but do not show how language is integrated into the efforts.

42. **Level:** Medium | **Skill/Knowledge:** Command of Evidence (Textual)

Key Explanation: Choice A is the best answer because "by contrast" shows that the blank portion needs an answer that acts as the opposite of the previous claim, which is that deer in Canada are bulkier than southern deer "in order to conserve heat." **Choice A** offers a logical contrast: the southern deer do not need to conserve heat; they need to disperse heat because the climate is warmer.

Distractor Explanations: Choice B is incorrect because there is no discussion of storing fat or

"carrying through" or "surviving" certain seasons. The extra mass might be something other than fat. **Choice C** is incorrect because the contrast is not related to food or migration, only retaining heat or not. **Choice D** is incorrect because there is no indication that the deer change their range between north and south.

43. **Level:** Easy | **Skill/Knowledge:** Command of Evidence (Textual)

Key Explanation: Choice B is the best answer because the blank portion must complete the idea of how Lamarr "changed the world of communication." **Choice B** offers a very important change: her invention was the "basis" or "foundation" for systems that are widely used today.

Distractor Explanations: None of the other choices offers any way that Lamarr "changed the world of communication." **Choice A** says she did not get money for her work, but does not say how the work was used. **Choice C** indicates that she was recognized as being important, but does not say why. **Choice D** says that she got a patent, but not that the patent was ever put to use; becoming a citizen is an unrelated detail.

44. **Level:** Easy | **Skill/Knowledge:** Command of Evidence (Textual)

Key Explanation: Choice C is the best answer because "by extension" shows that the idea in the first half of the sentence can be expanded to another situation. **Choice C** offers a similar situation where the process of dating something by tree rings can be applied: dating an object such as a painting on wood or a building.

Distractor Explanations: All of the other choices can be eliminated because they are not another situation that is an "extension" or "supplement" to the discussion of dating trees using the rings. **Choice A** refers to a totally different technique than dendrochronology. **Choice B** only gives an example of a tree with a long life. **Choice D** changes the topic away from dendrochronology and to another aspect of studying trees.

45. **Level:** Medium | **Skill/Knowledge:** Command of Evidence (Textual)

Key Explanation: Choice B is the best answer because the blank portion is preceded by "because," so it needs a reason that explains the previous claim that scientists might be able to understand life on other planets. **Choice B** says that the caves fill with microbes, a form of life, after being sterile, so studying how they appear and thrive in the "extreme environment" or "harsh habitat" may explain how similar microbes appear and survive elsewhere.

Distractor Explanations: Choice A is incorrect because it does not clearly relate to learning about life on other planets. It is possible that the isolated environment can protect a species, but the reader is not given an explanation since the caves are apparently sterile. **Choice C** is incorrect because it discusses another thing that volcanoes do rather than offers a reason that scientists are excited about the possibility of learning about life on other planets. **Choice D** just gives an unrelated fact about a tube cave.

46. **Level:** Medium | **Skill/Knowledge:** Command of Evidence (Textual)

Key Explanation: Choice A is the best answer because the text is talking about how difficult it was to make the dye and how it was so prized that only the emperor could use it. The blank is in a sentence starting with "as a result," which should include a logical conclusion of the previous discussion. The fact that it is called "imperial" or "royal" purple reflects the price and restrictions on who could use the color.

Distractor Explanations: None of the other choices provide a logical result of the text's discussion of an expensive, valued dye. **Choice B** could weaken the argument by making the dye sound less appealing. **Choice C** is a random comment about the production rather than a result of the laws about using the color. **Choice D** is an almost unrelated fact; there is no reason that the process should have been forgotten; if it were valuable, people might want to earn money making it.

47. **Level:** Medium | **Skill/Knowledge:** Command of Evidence (Textual)

Key Explanation: Choice C is the best answer because the unfinished sentence is stating what offers "further confirmation" or "more proof" that Pangaea existed. **Choice C** gives a reason to believe that the supercontinent existed: fossils from places that are "isolated" or "apart" show the same type of creatures from areas that remained connected. That discrepancy would be easy to explain if the places were once together; the animals lived together in the past, but their fossils were carried apart when the continent broke apart.

Distractor Explanations: Choice A is incorrect because it only refers to another theory, so there is no proof that Pangaea existed. **Choice B** also does not show that Pangaea existed because it offers a suggestion that was wrong. **Choice D** is incorrect because it refers to a "hypothesis" or "educated guess" about oceans rather than giving any facts to show that Pangaea existed.

48. **Level:** Medium | **Skill/Knowledge:** Command of Evidence (Textual)

    Key Explanation: Choice D is the best answer because the incomplete sentence should be a continuation of the idea that the eels do "not just use their electricity for hunting and defense." In other words, the sentence should give another reason for using electricity. **Choice D** shows that the electricity can be used for "navigation" or "finding the way."

    Distractor Explanations: All of the other choices are true, but they are not additional uses of the eel's ability. **Choice A** is a fact about how the electricity is produced. **Choice B** is a fact about what observing the electricity led to. **Choice C** is an unrelated fact about the animal.

49. **Level:** Medium | **Skill/Knowledge:** Command of Evidence (Quantitative)

    Key Explanation: Choice D is the best answer because the third row shows the statistics for the chili peppers with a NaCl concentration of 60 mM. The third column shows "average days to first fruit." **Choice D** is the number where the row and column intersect.

    Distractor Explanations: Choice A is the average number of fruit for chili peppers with a NaCl concentration of 60 mM, not the days to first fruit. **Choice B** incorrectly states that the time was 66 days longer, not 66 days total. **Choice C** is the average number of days to the first flower for chili

peppers with a NaCl concentration of 60 mM, not to the first fruit.

50. **Level:** Medium | **Skill/Knowledge:** Command of Evidence (Quantitative)

    Key Explanation: Choice B is the best answer because the graph shows two ranges. The bottom section is "insufficient" or "not enough" funds to open, and the top section shows the "average range" or "usual amount" needed for opening the restaurant. Beef o Brady's is the first column on the left. In that column, the top section starts approximately halfway between $500,000 and $1,000,000 and goes up to just over $2,000,000. Since $750,000 is halfway between $500,000 and $1,000,000, **Choice B** is the closest choice.

    Distractor Explanations: The range in **Choice A** starts lower than the amount of money needed to start a Beef o Brady's restaurant, so is incorrect. **Choice C** shows the maximum, not minimum, investment. Since there is a minimum limit that is needed to open a restaurant, this answer is not complete. **Choice D** is the highest amount needed to open and does not correspond with the idea that there is a large range of start–up prices.

51. **Level:** Medium | **Skill/Knowledge:** Command of Evidence (Quantitative)

    Key Explanation: Choice C is the best answer because it correctly shows that the number of visitors to Nigeria was 634,000, greater than any of the other countries. The nearest country was Togo, with only 65,000 people.

    Distractor Explanations: Choice A is incorrect because the chart shows the total number of visitors to the countries, not the difference between one country and another. **Choice B** is a true statement, but it is not a good choice because it does not illustrate the point that Nigeria has sites that attract visitors. **Choice D** is impossible to determine because the figure does not offer the reasons why visitors do not go to other countries; it is possible that they have beautiful features but have not advertised them.

52. **Level:** Medium | **Skill/Knowledge:** Command of Evidence (Quantitative)

Key Explanation: Choice C is the best answer because it says that vegans should "consider" or "think about" "man–made as well as natural additions to their diet." Since the chart shows that at least taurine comes only from "synthetic" or "man–made" sources, vegans need to take supplements to avoid outcomes such as problems with muscle and bile function.

Distractor Explanations: Choice A is incorrect because it refers to sources that vegans choose not to eat, poultry and fish; it does not show that at least some natural and synthetic options exist to supplement the vegan diet. **Choice B** is incorrect because it refers to a nutrient that is not in the figure, so data from the figure does not support it. **Choice D** is incorrect because it indicates that there is a question about whether veganism is nutritionally "sound" or "complete," but does not actually say that there are possible deficiencies. The topic of "anthropological significance" or "historical importance" is not mentioned in the figure.

53. **Level:** Easy | **Skill/Knowledge:** Command of Evidence (Quantitative)

Key Explanation: Choice B is the best explanation. The blank portion needs to be an example that supports the claim in the first half of the sentence that "Those conservation efforts are paying off." "Those conservation efforts" refers to the previous sentence that says that India raised the number of protected areas. **Choice B** offers support for the claim by showing that the numbers of tigers have greatly increased over time, presumably due to the conservation efforts.

Distractor Explanations: None of the other choices effectively establish that India's increase in preserves has led to success in conservation of tigers. **Choice A** is not supported by evidence because it refers to the world population, but the graph only shows the population in two countries. **Choice C** shows that India has a large number of tigers compared to Russia, but there is no base number to show that the number has grown. For example, the number in India could have been 5,000 and dropped to 3,000. **Choice D** can also be eliminated because it is vague. It does say that the population increased, but it could be by only one tiger.

54. **Level:** Medium | **Skill/Knowledge:** Command of Evidence (Quantitative)

Key Explanation: Choice C is the best answer because the point is that there are "variations" or "differences" in reported costs. **Choice C** emphasizes that point because it highlights the extreme differences found in one specific franchise that is legitimate. An investor might be told that one branch cost $500,000 and another cost $2,000,000, but both are true figures.

Distractor Explanations: Choice A is incorrect because it does not show the variations in cost for one franchise. Therefore, it does not explain why the actual data from branches of one franchise may have a range of different start up investments.

Choice B is incorrect because the graph does not provide data about the cost of land at all. **Choice D** is incorrect because a possible start–up cost of a franchise is not relevant to proving the point that one franchise might have a wide range of start–up investments depending on the conditions related to any given branch.

55. **Level:** Medium | **Skill/Knowledge:** Command of Evidence (Quantitative)

Key Explanation: Choice C is the best answer because the text is asking about a reason that "demographics [about language] are more important than ever." **Choice C** gives a logical reason: there is a large percentage of people who have different language experiences, so it is important to ensure that they get fair access to community services.

Distractor Explanations: Choice A is incorrect because the graph does not say whether people are "comfortable" speaking English; they could speak it well outside the home, but prefer a different language at home. **Choice B** can be eliminated because it does not show why finding out about people's language skills is "more important than ever." If the number of speakers of other languages has "tapered off" or "gotten less," then it may not be as important now. **Choice D** is incorrect because "steadily" refers to something that happens at a constant rate, but the percentage grew extensively between 1980 and 2010, but then remained stable the following ten years.

56. **Level:** Easy | **Skill/Knowledge:** Command of Evidence (Quantitative)

Key Explanation: Choice D is the best answer because the claim in the final sentence is that

"the population has continued to grow since the conservation efforts began around 1976," so the conservation efforts have "good results." The data in **Choice D** shows that the claim is not quite true, as the population also shrank during the conservation period.

Distractor Explanations: Choices A and **C** are incorrect because they support the claim in the text that the conservation efforts have good results, but the question prompt asks for a choice that "weakens" or "goes against" the claim. **Choice B** is incorrect because it is impossible to determine from the graph; there is no information about releasing pandas.

57. **Level:** Medium | **Skill/Knowledge:** Command of Evidence (Quantitative)

Key Explanation: Choice B is the best answer because, based on the text, the factor second after genetics that explains height is nutrition. In all the cases by country and gender, the figures for the past were lower than for the present. Since genetics probably did not change that significantly, one other solution is that nutrition changed and people are eating more things like protein that increase growth.

Distractor Explanations: Choice A is incorrect because "never exceeds" means "never gets higher," but the average height for women in Belgium in 1996 is 165.49 and for men in India is 164.95. **Choice C** is incorrect because both men and women in Egypt had a greater change in the average height between 1896 and 1996 than in India. Their average height is also higher than in India, so this statement has no support in the data. **Choice D** is incorrect because the passage points out that nutrition is important, but genetics is more so. Therefore, there would still be differences in average height, even if the diets were the same.

58. **Level:** Medium | **Skill/Knowledge:** Command of Evidence (Quantitative)

Key Explanation: The passage is discussing the lithium market, and the blank portion needs to complete the idea of something that is "a consequence of" or "a result of" the "rising push" or "trend" towards electric vehicles. The graph shows that just under half of the use of lithium in the world market is used in the automotive industry. Therefore, **Choice D** shows that the increase in electric cars has led to a large percentage of lithium being used in cars.

Distractor Explanations: Choice A is incorrect because the graph does not show how many cars use lithium; it shows what percentage of the total lithium is used in cars. **Choice B** is incorrect because it is unrelated to the result of an increase in electric vehicles. **Choice C** is too vague to be useful because there is no reference for the use of either industry.

59. **Level:** Hard | **Skill/Knowledge:** Command of Evidence (Quantitative)

Key Explanation: Choice C is the best answer because the text refers to two different factors that attract tourists: a good infrastructure and good reviews on social media. Since Spain had the second largest number of tourists per year in 2019 according to the chart, it is most likely strong in both aspects.

Distractor Explanations: Choice A is incorrect because Turkey is the lowest of the six countries given on the chart, but these are the leading countries for tourists in the world. Therefore,

Turkey attracts more tourists than most other countries, so probably gets good enough reviews to do so. **Choice B** is incorrect because there is no discussion in the text about "famous sites." Instead, the text refers to safe and comfortable services. **Choice D** is incorrect because the text says that both infrastructure and reviews are important; since China attracts more tourists, it presumably is good at both. There is no evidence that it has a worse infrastructure than a country that attracts fewer tourists.

60. **Level:** Medium | **Skill/Knowledge:** Command of Evidence (Quantitative)

Key Explanation: Choice C is the best answer because the blank is completing the idea of something that happens "despite" conservation efforts. In other words, the sentence needs to show that even though there are conservation efforts, they are not successful or there is another negative result. **Choice C** offers such a result: despite efforts, the elephant population is very low compared to the past.

Distractor Explanations: Choice A is incorrect because the information is not shown on the graph; the graph only shows the total elephant count. **Choice B** is incorrect because it shows a positive effect of conservation, not a negative effect as indicated by the transition "despite." **Choice D** is incorrect because in 1987, when the ivory ban was implemented, there were about 600,000 elephants. After that, there was a slight increase, but then, the numbers dropped again and are closer to 400,000. There is no overall "rebuilding" or "increase."

61. **Level:** Easy | **Skill/Knowledge:** Command of Evidence (Quantitative)

Key Explanation: Choice D is the best answer because it accurately reports the name of the second–most–expensive painting, who painted it, when it was sold, and the price at the time it was sold.

Distractor Explanations: Choice A is incorrect because it inaccurately says that the painting sold for S$328 million, but that is the price adjusted for inflation. **Choice B** is incorrect because "cost US$300 million less" has no comparison to show what it was less than; US$300 million was the total price. **Choice C** is incorrect because the painting sold for US$100 million less, not US$100 less.

62. **Level:** Medium | **Skill/Knowledge:** Command of Evidence (Quantitative)

Key Explanation: Choice C is the best answer because the passage points out that "Though Europeans consume a large amount, the same is not as true in Asian countries." **Choice C** gives statistics that show people in a European country, Germany, consume significantly more chocolate than people in an Asian country, China.

Distractor Explanations: All of the other choices contain true data, but they do not support claims made by the passage. **Choice A** is incorrect because the passage says that Europeans consume a lot of chocolate, but that does not appear to be true since people in the U.S. consume so much more. **Choice B** is incorrect because the figures make it appear that people in Europe might not eat much chocolate compared to the Swiss. **Choice** is incorrect because the passage does not discuss the relative amounts consumed in most European countries, only that the people consume a lot of chocolate.

63. **Level:** Easy | **Skill/Knowledge:** Command of Evidence (Quantitative)

Key Explanation: Choice A is the correct option as 41 percent of Indigenous Australians receive housing support as compared to only 20 percent of older people.

Distractor Explanation: Choice B is incorrect as Indigenous Australians receive more support as compared to older people. **Choice C** is incorrect as Indigenous Australians make up 73,300 clients as compared to 23,900 clients who are aged 55 years or older. **Choice D** is incorrect because the text offers no information to support the statement that Indigenous Australians are the most disadvantaged of all Australians.

64

The following text is adapted from Jane Austin's 1811 novel, *Sense and Sensibility*.

Mr. John Dashwood told his mother again and again how exceedingly sorry he was that she had taken a house at such a distance from Norland as to prevent his being of any service to her in removing her furniture. He really felt conscientiously vexed on the occasion; for the very exertion to which he had limited the performance of his promise to his father was by this arrangement rendered impractical. The furniture was all sent around by water. It chiefly consisted of household linen, plates, china, and books, with a handsome pianoforte.

Based on the text, what is most likely true about Mr. John Dashwood?

A) He had given his father a pledge regarding his mother's care.

B) He is too busy to assist with the details of his mother's move.

C) He feels that his mother is taking too many belongings.

D) He wishes that his mother would remain at Norland.

65

It is estimated that over 5 million slaves were transported from Africa to Brazil before Brazil abolished slavery in 1888; it was the last country in the Western Hemisphere to do so. Escaped slaves formed small, tight-knit communities called *quilombo* in inaccessible regions and typically survived through farming and raiding. Even after slavery officially ended, the residents suffered prejudice and persecution for their race. Today, there are still about 5,900 quilombo scattered in remote areas around the country.

Based on the text, what is most likely true about modern–day quilombo?

A) A large percentage of the residents are descendants of slaves.

B) They do not have basic facilities such as electricity and running water.

C) Residents of each quilombo seldom have contact with other quilombo.

D) The combined population of all the quilombo is about 5 million.

66

Astronomers from the University of California, Berkeley worked out there could be as many as 40 billion Earth–sized exoplanets in the so–called "habitable zone" around their star, where temperatures are mild enough for liquid water to exist on the surface. There's even a potentially Earth–like world orbiting our nearest neighboring star, Proxima Centauri. At just four light years away, that system might be close enough for us to reach using current technology. With the Breakthrough Starshot project launched by Stephen Hawking in 2016, plans for this are already afoot. It seems inevitable other life is out there, especially considering that life appeared on Earth so soon after the planet was formed.

What is implied in the passage about Stephen Hawking's Breakthrough Starshot project?

A) It was designed to search for Earth–sized planets in the "habitable zone."

B) It intends to send spacecraft to the Proxima Centauri system in the future.

C) It wants to prove that life appeared in the Proxima Centauri system soon after it formed.

D) It is trying to show that humans can survive on a planet circling Proxima Centauri.

67

The following text is adapted from Fyodor Dostoevsky's 1848 book, *White Nights and Other Stories*.

I took long walks, succeeding, as I usually did, in quite forgetting where I was, when I suddenly found myself at the city gates. Instantly I felt lighthearted, and I passed the barrier and walked between cultivated fields and meadows, unconscious of fatigue, and feeling only all over as though a burden were falling off my soul. All the passers–by gave me such friendly looks that they seemed almost greeting me, they all seemed so pleased at something. And I felt pleased as I never had before. It was as though I had suddenly found myself in Italy—so strong was the effect of nature upon a half–sick townsman like me, almost stifling between city walls.

Based on the text, what is the most likely reason that the narrator takes a walk?

A) He wants to spend time with new people.

B) He is displeased with his daily life.

C) He hopes to have an exciting adventure.

D) He is trying to forget a sad event.

68

According to Clark, a neutral model would predict that the variation among the sites would increase over time, as random chance caused different species to go extinct in some areas but not others. Some sites, just by chance, should come to be dominated by one species, while others would come to be dominated by another species. However, the researchers found that variance among the sites did not increase over the millennia, leading them to conclude that stabilizing forces were maintaining forest diversity. Clark emphasized, however, that even though the role of stabilizing mechanisms remains unknown, the results from his and McLachlan's studies offer cautionary lessons: "Our findings suggest that forest biodiversity has probably been stabilized in some important ways, so extinction of species should cause us greater concern than if we believed that biodiversity was maintained in the past by continual replenishment of random extinction by generation of new species."

Based on the text, what is one implication of Clark's study?

A) Due to biodiversity stabilization, there is a smaller chance of ecosystems collapsing than previously theorized.

B) Due to biodiversity stabilization, extinction is a random event that is compensated for by evolution of new species.

C) Due to biodiversity stabilization, as time progresses, fewer new species will evolve than did in the past.

D) Due to biodiversity stabilization, an extinction could indicate a larger–scale collapse of the region's equilibrium.

69

Salt stress, too much salt in the soil for plants to thrive, is one of the major environmental constraints limiting agricultural productivity and influencing the concentration of bioactive compounds of vegetables. A recent study assessed the effect of NaCl salt stress on flowering, fructification and fruit nutritional quality of a local cultivar of chili pepper. Chili pepper belongs to the crops grown throughout the world for their nutraceutical (nutritional and medicinal) and economic virtue. In Benin, chili is the second cash gardening crop after the tomato. Its annual production is about 47.162 tons. Pepper plants produce the compound capsaicin, primarily in the fruits, possibly to deter mammalian herbivores. In Benin, chili pepper is grown only for food partially in the cultivable lands of the coastal areas, where soil salinity and water irrigation are a reality.

Based on the text, which is most likely true about chili pepper production in Benin?

A) Farmers do not realize the problem of salt stress.

B) It an important source of income for many farmers.

C) It is one of the largest sectors of the economy.

D) Most plants produce no fruits because of salt.

70

The following text is adapted from Abraham Lincoln's last public address, given April 11, 1965.

The amount of constituency, so to speak, on which the new Louisiana government rests, would be more satisfactory to all, if it contained fifty, thirty, or even twenty thousand, instead of only about twelve thousand, as it does. It is also unsatisfactory to some that the elective franchise is not given to the colored man. I would myself prefer that it were now conferred on the very intelligent, and on those who serve our cause as soldiers. Still the question is not whether the Louisiana government, as it stands, is quite all that desirable. The question is, "Will it be wiser to take it as it is, and help to improve it; or to reject, and disperse it? Can Louisiana be brought into proper practical relation with the Union sooner by sustaining, or by discarding her new State government?"

Based on the text, Lincoln would most likely agree with which statement regarding former slaves?

A) Most of them are not qualified to vote.

B) They have an inalienable right to vote.

C) Some should be granted the privilege of voting.

D) They are not capable of voting effectively.

71

The global oceans are an important sink for human–released CO_2, absorbing nearly a quarter of the total CO_2 emissions every year. Although it comprises only 26 percent of the total ocean area, the Southern Ocean has absorbed nearly 40 percent of all anthropogenic CO_2 taken up by the global oceans up to the present. By analyzing more than one million surface ocean observations taken over 13 years, the researchers could tease out subtle differences between the CO_2 trends in the surface ocean and the atmosphere. This change is most pronounced in the southern half of the Drake Passage during winter. Although the researchers aren't sure of the exact mechanism driving these changes, it's likely that winter mixing with deep waters that have not had contact with the atmosphere for several hundred years plays an important role.

According to the text, why does the Drake Passage study fall short of being definitive?

A) It did not collect sufficient data to come to a solid conclusion.

B) It was unable to collect data during critical time periods.

C) It only focused on one region rather than the world's oceans.

D) It isolated an effect but not the cause of that effect.

72

Daisy Taugelchee is the most famous Navajo weaver of the 20th century and was noted for the extreme fineness of her tapestries. Typical weavers in her area used the fine gauge of 60 stitches to the inch, but after a dare, she exceeded 80, and in her prime could make a record 115. Moreover, she created unique variations on traditional patterns that made her artwork distinct and popular among collectors. For over 40 years, she won first place in the local art show, the Gallup Ceremonial.

Based on the text, which choice is most likely true about Daisy Taugelchee?

A) She was greatly respected in the Navajo community for her originality.

B) She was able to earn a good living from selling her weaving.

C) Her art used colors that were not typically used by Navajo weavers.

D) No other weaver in her area could make as many stitches per inch.

73

The following text is adapted from Emily Dickinson's poem *Book*, published after her death in 1886.

He ate and drank the precious words,

His spirit grew robust;

He knew no more that he was poor,

Nor that his frame was dust.

He danced along the dingy days,

And this bequest of wings

Was but a book. What liberty

A loosened spirit brings!

Based on the text, what is the benefit of a book?

A) It can increase a person's tangible wealth.

B) It can return a person to his youth.

C) It can free a person from true bondage.

D) It can provide sustenance for a person's soul.

74

Tapirs are ancient animals that date back about 50 million years, and they are one of the few large mammals to survive the megafauna extinctions of the last ice age. Tapirs live in Brazilian lowlands and help regrow the degraded forests though seeds that are spread when they defecate. Unfortunately, all tapir species are now categorized as either vulnerable or endangered due to hunting, vehicle strikes, and habitat loss.

Based on the text, what is most likely true about tapirs?

A) They did not go extinct because they are intelligent.

B) They used to have a much wider range than Brazil.

C) They are too slow to get out of the way of vehicles.

D) They are not purely carnivorous animals.

75

Inbal Ben–Ami Bartal of Tel Aviv University conducted a series of experiments to determine whether rats had the emotion of empathy. She placed a rat in a clear, narrow tube in a cage where another rat roamed freely. The free rats had been taught the method to open the door and release the trapped rat. Invariably, if the free rat and the rat in the tube had been raised together, the loose rat would rapidly release the trapped one. Interestingly, the free rat would often ignore the plight of the trapped rat as if it were a complete stranger.

Based on the text, what is most likely true about rats?

A) They do not like other rats that are complete strangers.

B) They feel compelled to assist only if there is an established relationship.

C) They are genetically inclined to help others of their species.

D) They only feel the need to help if there is a proven danger to the other.

76

Afghanistan has one of the highest child mortality rates and levels of malnutrition in the world because large portions of the population live in poverty. That is sadly ironic because geologists estimate that there are trillions of dollars of untapped mineral reserves within the country, but there is a dearth of infrastructure to extract and purify them.

Based on the text, what is most likely true about the mineral reserves in Afghanistan?

A) If the minerals were to be mined, there would be enough money to raise the standard of living.

B) The people in Afghanistan are currently mining the minerals using ineffective or dangerous tools.

C) The country is spending its money on addressing the problem of poverty rather than extracting the minerals.

D) The leaders in Afghanistan do not want any foreign companies to invest in infrastructure.

77

A vicious cycle is occurring in Lope National Park in Gabon. Low rainfall and higher temperatures led to a decline in tree fruits, which are the staple food of African forest elephants. The seeds are usually dispersed in the dung over the wide range of each elephant. The elephant population now faces pressures from starvation, as well as the ongoing problem of poaching. In fact, the population has decreased by over eighty percent in the past thirty years.

Based on the text, what is most likely true about the fruit trees in Lope National Park?

A) Elephants are changing to different food sources because there are fewer trees.

B) The seeds are not being dispersed as effectively because there are fewer elephants.

C) Conservationists are starting to plant more fruit trees to provide food for the elephants.

D) The elephants are no longer dispersing the seeds very far from the original trees.

78

The Rosetta Stone, discovered in 1799, was the key to understanding how to read ancient Egyptian hieroglyphic writing. The stone is a fragment of a larger stele carved in 196 B.C. in Memphis, Egypt, under the reign of King Ptolemy V Epiphanes. The first bilingual text known to contain hieroglyphics, scholars circulated copies in the hopes of translating the language, which was written in ancient Greek, Egyptian hieroglyphics, and also a more casual form of Egyptian writing called Demotic. Jean–Francois Champollion found the key to solving the puzzle in 1822, when _____

Which choice most logically completes the text?

A) he realized that both the Demotic writing and hieroglyphs contained phonetic spellings.

B) he gave a lecture about his findings at the Académie des Inscriptions et Belles–Lettres.

C) others assumed the writing was pictographic but he was curious about the meaning.

D) his announcement led to a new wave of learning about the Egyptian language.

79

The Amish might not be considered the most technologically advanced people in North America, seeing as to how they denounce the usage of modern essentials, including electricity and motor vehicles.

Yet the most extraordinary things to note about the Amish are not their quaint routines and their self–made clothes, but the organic growth of their community, their rapid efficiency in building structures, and their socially cohesive nature. Although they till their lands using archaic horse–drawn machines, and farm without the use of chemical fertilizers, their _____ is, interestingly, among the most productive in North America.

Which word most logically completes the text?

A) Agriculture

B) Lifestyle

C) Methods

D) Culture

80

The following text is adapted from Jane Austen's *Mansfield Park*.

Sir Thomas was indeed the life of the party, who at his suggestion, now seated themselves round the fire. He had the best right to be the talker; and the delight of his sensations in being again in his own house, in the centre of his family, after such a separation, made him communicative and chatty in a very unusual degree; and he was ready to give every information as to his voyage, and answer every question of his two sons almost before it was put. His business in Antigua had latterly been prosperously rapid, and he came directly from Liverpool, having had an opportunity of making his passage thither in a private vessel, instead of waiting for the packet; and all the little particulars of his proceedings and events, his arrivals and departures, were most promptly delivered, as he sat by Lady Bertram and looked with heartfelt satisfaction on the faces around him — interrupting himself more than once, however, to remark on his good fortune in finding them all at home — coming unexpectedly as he did — all collected together exactly as he could have wished, but dared not depend on.

Based on the text, what is most true about Sir Thomas?

A) He was a rich man.

B) He was not usually a talkative man.

C) He was fortunate to see his friends and family together.

D) He had many sad tales about his voyage.

81

As ancient Egyptian rulers, pharaohs were both the heads of state and the religious leaders of their people. The word "pharaoh" means "great house," a reference to the palace where the pharaoh resides. As the religious leader of the Egyptians, the pharaoh was considered the divine intermediary between the gods and Egyptians. Maintaining religious harmony and participating in ceremonies were part of the pharaoh's role as head of the religion. As a statesman, the pharaoh made laws, waged war, collected taxes, and oversaw all the land in Egypt (which was owned by the pharaoh).

Based on the text, what is true about ancient Egyptians?

A) Ancient Egyptians did not own any land.

B) The pharaoh was an ancient Egyptian God.

C) The Egyptians believed in one God.

D) The pharaoh did not participate in social conventions and were religious leaders only.

82

In the fall of 1954, at the age of 18, I discovered the other half of the world. I began that journey through the eyes of an encyclopedic professor who guided me to China and the neighboring Altay Mountains, to Japan and their elaborate methods of making swords. Then India, Tibet and the Potala Palace, Burma and the Burma Road, and, of course, the Khmer Empire and Cambodia. These places had all been hidden from my view by my Philadelphia suburban education.

Based on the text, what is most likely true about the author?

A) The author was transfixed by the world because he had not traveled before

B) The author grew up in a small town of Philadelphia

C) The author was helped by a professor in China

D) The author had already traveled extensively

83

The London and Northwestern Railway War Memorial is a First World War memorial outside Euston Station in London, England. The memorial was designed by Reginald Wynn Owen and _____ employees of the London and Northwestern Railway (LNWR) who were killed in the First World War.

Which word most logically completes the text?

A) Commemorates

B) Idolizes

C) Celebrates

D) Overlooks

84

Onomatopoeia is the process of creating a word that phonetically imitates, resembles, or suggests the sound that it describes. Such a word itself is also called an onomatopoeia.

Based on the above text, which of the following is the best example of an onomatopoeia?

A) Bell

B) Twinkle

C) Miaow

D) Glitter

64. **Level:** Easy | **Skill/Knowledge:** Inferences

Key Explanation: Choice A is the best answer because the text says, "the very exertion to which he had limited the performance of his promise to his father was by this arrangement rendered impracticable." Therefore, it can be determined that Mr. Dashwood had made a "promise" or "pledge" to take care of his mother, but could not because she was moving too far away.

Distractor Explanations: Choice B is incorrect because Mr. Dashwood is "vexed" that he cannot help due to the distance, not due to a lack of time. **Choice C** is incorrect because, while Mrs. Dashwood is taking many things, there is no indication that her son feels that the number is too large. **Choice D** is incorrect because there is no discussion that Mr. John Dashwood wishes that his mother would stay, only that she would not travel so far away.

65. **Level:** Medium | **Skill/Knowledge:** Inferences

Key Explanation: Choice A is the best answer. The passage points out that the quilombo were tight-knit communities of escaped slaves, and after slavery ended, the residents "suffered prejudice and persecution for their race." This sentence implies that most of the residents had a race that was different from local people in Brazil. In other words, the communities are probably still close-knit groups of people whose ancestors were slaves.

Distractor Explanations: Choice B is incorrect because there is no discussion in the passage about the situation of quilombo today. It is possible that most have electricity and running water, though being "remote," they might not have extremely advanced technology. **Choice C** is impossible to

determine from the passage because there is no discussion of how often quilombo residents travel or meet. Even if the quilombo are remote, the residents might interact with each other and not outside groups. **Choice D** is also impossible to tell from the passage. Just because there were about 5 million slaves does not mean that all of them escaped, nor that all of them averaged one child each.

66. **Level:** Medium | **Skill/Knowledge:** Inferences

Key Explanation: Choice B is the best answer because the Breakthrough Starshot project is introduced in a sentence with "with" showing that it is the method of achieving the main part of the sentence. The main clause is "plans for this are already afoot," and "this" refers to the previous sentence, "that system might be close enough for us to reach using current technology." Therefore, the Breakthrough Starshot project is the method that may be possible for reaching the star system of Proxima Centauri, presumably via a spacecraft of some sort.

Distractor Explanations: Choice A is incorrect because there is no indication of how the researchers worked out or searched for Earth-sized planets in the "habitable zone." **Choice C** is incorrect because, while the project is designed to look for life, it is not trying to prove that life appeared at a certain time period. The project would presumably be a success if it proved that life appeared at any time, even very recently. **Choice D** is incorrect because there is no evidence to support the claim that the project wants to send humans to a different planet, only that it wants to look for life.

67. Level: Medium | **Skill/Knowledge:** Inferences

Key Explanation: Choice B is the best answer because the narrator says he felt "lighthearted" when he saw the city gates and felt "as though a burden were falling off my soul" when he left the city. Later, he refers to the walk as making him feel better because he had been "half–sick" and "stifling between city walls." Therefore, it can be presumed that he was "displeased" or "not happy" with being in town all the time, which would have been his "daily" or "regular" life since he was a "townsman." He felt discontent with his conditions, feeling trapped within a city, rather than with a specific event.

Distractor Explanations: Choice A is incorrect because, while the narrator greets people on his walk, there is no indication that meeting them was the purpose of his going for the walk. **Choice C** is incorrect because there is no indication that the narrator was trying to find adventure, only that he was trying to relax. **Choice D** is incorrect because there is no reference to the narrator having a "sad event." He does not refer to a specific occurrence that bothered him, only the stifling nature of living in the city.

68. Level: Hard | **Skill/Knowledge:** Inferences

Key Explanation: Choice D is the best answer because Clark claims, "extinction of species should cause us greater concern than if we believed that biodiversity was maintained in the past by continual replenishment of random extinction by generation of new species." In other words, he feels that if one species goes extinct, it would show that the biodiversity is not being maintained as it should be; the stabilizing forces would not be functioning properly. That could indicate a "collapse" or "failure" of the entire system.

Distractor Explanations: Choice A is incorrect because Clark implies that because of stabilization, ecosystems remain in balance, but if one part of the balance is disrupted, the entire system may collapse. Therefore, a total collapse is more likely than if the system is random. **Choice B** is incorrect because it refers to the situation in the neutral theory, not the biodiversity stabilization theory. **Choice C** is incorrect because the stabilization theory proposes that the number of species remains about the same. It is implied that the rate of addition and extinction would therefore be about the same.

69. Level: Medium | **Skill/Knowledge:** Inferences

Key Explanation: Choice B is the best answer because the passage states that "in Benin, chili is the second cash gardening crop besides tomato." This statement shows that chili is the second largest crop grown to be sold rather than used by the farmer. Without chili, one of the major crops that provides income would be missing, so it is important to many farmers.

Distractor Explanations: Choice A is incorrect because the passage states that "This stress is known to negatively affect plant growth at all developmental stages," which indicates that the farmers also know about the negative effect. **Choice C** is incorrect because there is no discussion of other sources of income in Benin. In reality, textiles and cotton are more important than the cash crops sold for food. **Choice D** is impossible to determine from the text because, while the passage hints that many plants are raised in areas with salt, it does not say that the plants are very unproductive. Since it is an important cash crop, the implication is that the plants grow and make fruit.

70. **Level:** Easy | **Skill/Knowledge:** Inferences

Key Explanation: Choice C is the best answer because Lincoln expresses his personal opinion, "I would myself prefer that it were now conferred on the very intelligent, and on those who serve our cause as soldiers." This quote indicates that he feels that some former slaves, such as intelligent men and soldiers, should be "granted" or "given" the right to vote.

Distractor Explanations: Choice A is incorrect because "most" implies over half. Lincoln expresses his view that some former slaves should be able to vote, suggesting that others are not capable of doing so. However, there is no indication that the "incapable" or "not qualified" group is over half of the former slave population. **Choice B** is incorrect because "inalienable" means "absolute" or "inherent." Lincoln, though, does not say that there is an obligation to give all former slaves the right to vote. He limits his suggestion to giving voting rights to intelligent men and soldiers. **Choice D** is incorrect because Lincoln indicates that some freed slaves would be capable of voting effectively; otherwise, he would not suggest allowing intelligent men and soldiers to vote.

71. **Level:** Medium | **Skill/Knowledge:** Inference

Key Explanation: Choice D is the best answer because "definitive" means "conclusive" or "final." The data was complete enough to determine that "the Southern Ocean has absorbed nearly 40 percent of all anthropogenic CO_2 taken up by the global oceans up to the present." so the "effect" of removing CO_2 was "isolated" or "identified." However, the cause of the removal of CO_2 is still unknown: "the researchers aren't sure of the exact

mechanism driving these changes." Therefore, the study does not conclusively answer all questions.

Distractor Explanation: Choice A is incorrect because the researchers were able to collect "sufficient" or "enough" data to come to the "solid" or "well-supported" conclusion that the Southern Ocean has recently been removing more CO_2 from the atmosphere. **Choice B** is incorrect because the passage says that the research took place over 13 years, and there is no indication that "critical" or "important" time periods were missed during the study. **Choice C** is incorrect because there is no indication that the results are missing important information because they focused on one region—the Southern Ocean—rather than a wider area. The conclusion drawn from that data about CO_2 absorption is valid.

72. **Level:** Easy | **Skill/Knowledge:** Inferences

Key Explanation: Choice D is the best answer because the text says that she could weave "a record 115," which implies that no one else was able to reach her record.

Distractor Explanations: Choice A is incorrect because there is no indication about how other Navajos viewed Taugelchee's work; since she used non-traditional designs and was popular among collectors, it is possible that the local community thought she was too different. **Choice B** is incorrect because there is no indication about how much Taugelchee earned from selling to collectors; they could have purchased her work for very little. **Choice C** is incorrect because the text only refers to designs; it is possible she used traditional colors.

73. **Level:** Hard | **Skill/Knowledge:** Inferences

Key Explanation: Choice D is the best answer because "sustenance" refers to "support" or "food and drink." In the text, the person "ate and drank" the words, showing that he received support as if he were eating. His "soul" or "spirit" grew "robust" or "healthy."

Distractor Explanations: Choice A is incorrect because "tangible" refers to real wealth. Though the person "knew no more" or "forgot" that he was poor, he remained poor financially. **Choice B** is incorrect because there is no indication that the person felt or became young, only less tired. **Choice C** is incorrect because "true bondage" means "real imprisonment." Though the person mentally escaped the imprisonment of his poor situation, he did not actually leave the living conditions.

74. **Level:** Medium | **Skill/Knowledge:** Inferences

Key Explanation: Choice D is the best answer because the text states that tapirs "help regrow the degraded forests though seeds that are spread when they defecate." In other words, they must eat something that has seeds in order to defecate them, so they must be eating some kind of plant. Therefore, they are not purely "carnivorous" or "meat–eating" animals.

Distractor Explanations: Choice A cannot be determined based on the text because there is no discussion about why tapirs survived the Ice Age extinction; they could just be well–adapted to cold. **Choice B** is also not supported by any evidence from the text. **Choice C** is one possible explanation for the vehicle strikes, but there could be other reasons such as having poor

eyesight so they do not see the cars, or being well–camouflaged when cars travel at night.

75. **Level:** Easy | **Skill/Knowledge:** Inferences

Key Explanation: Choice B is the best answer. The passage says that the rats helped if "they had been raised together," meaning that the rats had a connection of some kind to the other when releasing it. However, the fact that they "would often ignore the plight" of strange rats indicates that they did not feel "compelled" or "forced" to help strangers in any way.

Distractor Explanations: Choice A is incorrect because there is no indication of liking or disliking, only assisting or not. The choice could be based on survival benefits and not emotions. **Choice C** is incorrect because, if they were "inclined" or "had a tendency" to help others in the species, they would help the strange rats, as all rats are the same species. **Choice D** is incorrect because there is no discussion of "danger" to the rat in the tube, only the inability to free itself. It is referred to as "trapped" but not as being at risk of injury or death.

76. **Level:** Easy | **Skill/Knowledge:** Inferences

Key Explanation: Choice A is the best answer because the paragraph says it is "sadly ironic" that the people live in poverty with health issues while there is a wealth of mineral resources. That comparison implies that the resources would provide enough money to solve some of the problems, raising the overall standard of living, if the resources were mined and sold.

Distractor Explanations: Choice B is incorrect because the minerals are referred to as "untapped," meaning they are not yet being removed.

Therefore, no equipment has been used to take the minerals out yet. **Choices C** and **D** are not addressed by the passage; there is no indication of where the country's money is being spent, or whether the leaders want other countries to participate. It is possible that Afghanistan could set up the infrastructure without foreign assistance.

77. **Level:** Easy | **Skill/Knowledge:** Inferences

Key Explanation: Choice B is the best answer because the passage refers to the "vicious cycle," which refers to one thing causing something else to happen, and that result causes the first thing to happen again. The text describes a decrease in fruit trees and the "pressure from starvation" on the elephants that eat the fruit. In other words, there are not enough fruits for the elephants, who spread the seeds. As a result, elephants starve and there are fewer elephants to eat and "disperse" or "spread" the seeds. Fewer trees then grow in different places around the forest, creating even less food for the elephants.

Distractor Explanations: Choice A is incorrect because there is no indication that the elephants eat anything other than their "staple" or "main" diet of fruit; otherwise, they might not be facing starvation. **Choice C** is incorrect because there is no discussion of conservation in the text. **Choice D** is incorrect because the text refers to a "wide range" for the elephants. There is no indication that the range has changed, only the number of elephants.

78. **Level:** Medium | **Skill/Knowledge:** Inferences

Key Explanation: Choice A is the best answer because it gives a reason that Champollion was able to "find the key" or "decipher" the writing:

he noticed a similarity between the texts that had "phonetic" or "sound–based" letters.

Distractor Explanations: Choice B is a true event about Champollion's presentation of solving the meaning of the writing, but it does not complete the sentence saying "when" he "found the key" or "solved" the problem of how to read the texts. **Choice C** is weak because it is too vague for the reader to know how Champollion solved the problem; it only suggests that he was "curious" or "interested" in it. **Choice D** is incorrect because it shows what happened after he "found the key" and announced what he had found.

79. **Level:** Medium | **Skill/Knowledge:** Inferences

Key Explanation: Choice A is correct because the sentence is talking about how the Amish are able to be productive without the use of modern farming equipment and fertilizers. Therefore, logically, choice A is the most fitting in this context.

Distractor Explanations: Choice B is incorrect because their lifestyle has already been mentioned in the first sentence of the second paragraph as not being the most extraordinary. **Choice C** is incorrect because the sentence will be grammatically incorrect if one inserts the option in the blank space ("their methods is" isn't grammatically correct). Option D is incorrect because the sentence is talking about their farming methods and not about the culture or lifestyle of the Amish.

80. **Level:** Medium | **Skill/Knowledge:** Inferences

Key Explanation: Choice B is the best answer because the text mentions that Sir Thomas was happy to be back home, and this made him "communicative and chatty to a very unusual degree." This implies that he wasn't usually this talkative.

Distractor Explanations: Choice A is incorrect because the text does not mention that he is rich, and his business has only "latterly been prosperously rapid." **Choice C** is incorrect because the text doesn't say he is fortunate, but that Sir Thomas considers himself fortunate. **Choice D** is incorrect because the text does not mention that his stories are sad.

81. **Level:** Medium | **Skill/Knowledge:** Inferences

Key Explanation: Choice A is the correct answer since the text mentions that all the land in Egypt was owned by the pharaoh.

Distractor Explanations: Choice B is incorrect because the text mentions that the pharaoh was the "divine intermediary between the gods and Egyptians." **Choice C** is incorrect because the text mentions that the pharaoh was the divine intermediary between the gods and the Egyptians, implying that there were several Gods. **Choice D** is incorrect because the text mentions the pharaoh's responsibilities included "participating in ceremonies."

82. **Level:** Easy | **Skill/Knowledge:** Inferences

Key Explanation: Choice C is correct because according to the text, the author "began that journey through the eyes of an encyclopedic professor who guided me to China,"

Distractor Explanations: Choice A is incorrect because there is no evidence to support the claim that the author had not traveled before. He only mentions he "discovered the other half of the world," meaning he was familiar with one

half. **Choice B** is incorrect because the text only mentions a "Philadelphia suburban education." **Choice D** is incorrect because the text offers no evidence that the author had already traveled extensively.

83. **Level:** Medium | **Skill/Knowledge:** Inferences

Key Explanation: Choice A is correct because to commemorate something means to remember the event and by doing so, to honor it. Here, the memorial commemorates the employees of LMWR killed in the First World War.

Distractor Explanations: Choice B is incorrect because to idolize is to respect or admire someone extensively. Here the memorial has been built to remember martyrs and not only show respect. **Choice C** is incorrect because "celebrate" is not a word used to describe the purpose of a memorial. **Choice D** is incorrect because the memorial has been built for the fallen LNWR employees and hence, cannot overlook or ignore them.

84. **Level:** Hard | **Skill/Knowledge:** Inferences

Key Explanation: Choice C is correct. According to the text, an onomatopoeia is a word that sounds exactly like the sound that it describes. The word "miaow" sounds exactly like the sound of a cat, which is what the word is describing.

Distractor Explanation: All the other choices are incorrect because they are not words that sound like what they are describing. For example, "glitter" does not make a sound, and neither does "Twinkle."

Chapter 4

Craft and Structure

This chapter includes questions on the following topics:

- Words in Context
- Text Structure and Purpose
- Cross–Text Connection

85

While life is a special _____ of complex chemistry, the elements involved are nothing special: carbon, hydrogen, oxygen, etc., are among the most abundant elements in the universe. Complex organic chemistry is surprisingly common. Amino acids, just like those that make up every protein in our bodies, have been found in the tails of comets. There are other organic compounds in Martian soil. And 6,500 light years away, a giant cloud of space alcohol floats among the stars.

Which choice completes the text with the most logical and precise word or phrase?

A) model

B) kind

C) unit

D) design

86

The following text is adapted from Herman Melville's 1851 novel, *Moby Dick; or The Whale*.

Call me Ishmael. Some years ago—never mind how long precisely—having little or no money in my purse, and nothing particular to interest me on shore, I thought I would sail about a little and see the watery part of the world. Whenever I find myself growing grim about the mouth; whenever it is a damp, drizzly November in my soul; whenever I find myself involuntarily pausing before coffin warehouses, and bringing up the rear of every funeral I meet—then, I account it high time to get to sea as soon as I can. With a philosophical flourish Cato throws himself upon his sword; I quietly take to the ship. There is nothing surprising in this. If they but knew it, almost all men in some _____ , some time or other, cherish very nearly the same feelings towards the ocean with me.

Which choice completes the text with the most logical and precise word or phrase?

A) rank

B) degree

C) standard

D) diploma

87

Behavioral activation is a type of talk therapy that helps teens get unstuck from negative mood spirals by noticing a _____ between what they do and how they feel, and gradually adding more small and enjoyable actions back into life. Behavioral activation has the goal of decreasing avoidance, bolstering peer connection, and improving engagement in rewarding activities. It also incorporates parent involvement so parents gain tools for supporting their adolescent children.

Which choice completes the text with the most logical and precise word or phrase?

A) relevance

B) bond

C) correspondence

D) attachment

88

The researchers found that variance among the sites did not increase over the millennia, leading them to conclude that stabilizing forces were maintaining forest diversity. "Our findings indicate there are factors that _____ populations at relative abundances that are consistent from one place to another," said scientist James Clark. "Our study doesn't identify what those stabilizing forces are, however."

Which choice completes the text with the most logical and precise word or phrase?

A) supervise

B) manage

C) balance

D) administer

89

Mann's research was conducted in two parts – a literature review and interview study. A literature review of both the scientific and the popular literature was conducted and reviewed from August to November, 2013. The interview study involved semi–structured, one–time, in–person private interviews conducted the same year. Twenty vegans were interviewed, and questions targeted personal history of veganism, related health beliefs, factors influencing the decision to become vegan, and diet _____. Once all data was obtained, it was analyzed in tandem.

Which choice completes the text with the most logical and precise word or phrase?

A) arrangement

B) disposition

C) constitution

D) amalgam

90

The following text is adapted from Abraham Lincoln's last public address, given April 11, 1965.

To the Blacks we say, "This cup of liberty which these, your old masters, hold to your lips, we will dash from you, and leave you to the chances of gathering the spilled and scattered contents in some vague and undefined when, where, and how." If this course, discouraging and paralyzing both white and black, has any tendency to bring Louisiana into proper practical relations with the Union, I have, so far, been unable to perceive it. If, on the contrary, we <u>recognize</u> and sustain the new government of Louisiana, the converse of all this is made true.

As it is used in the text, what does the word "recognize" most nearly mean?

A) identify

B) accept

C) realize

D) appreciate

91

HEPHL1 belongs to a family of proteins known as multicopper oxidases (MCOs). One unique property of MCOs is the presence of three copper–binding sites that can _____ six copper atoms. Mutations that alter the structure of these sites are likely to affect their ability to bind copper.

Which choice completes the text with the most logical and precise word or phrase?

A) house

B) quarter

C) lodge

D) shelter

92

The following text is adapted from Charles Stearns's 1849 treatise, "The Way to Abolish Slavery."

The Government of the United States creates no Slaves; it only recognises as lawful the Slavery existing in the several States, or to use the words of the Constitution, "held to service or labor, under the *laws* thereof." The laws of the several slave–holding States are made the <u>standard</u> for the general government's action upon this subject.

As it is used in the text, what does the word "standard" most nearly mean?

A) guideline

B) quality

C) ideal

D) worth

93

It was an audacious idea: To send an unmanned research vehicle called a *saildrone* on a 13,670–mile journey around Antarctica alone, at the mercy of the most <u>hostile</u> seas on the planet. In winter. "The assumption was the Southern Ocean would eat the saildrone...and that would be that," said NOAA oceanographer Adrienne Sutton. "But we were willing to try, given the large role the ocean plays in the trajectory of climate change."

As used in the text, what does the word "hostile" most nearly mean?

A) aggressive

B) antagonistic

C) unforgiving

D) conflicting

Digital SAT Reading and Writing Practice Questions   **102**

94

Demographic, transportation, and environmental changes will drive employment growth for planners. Within cities, urban planners will be needed to develop revitalization projects and _____ issues associated with population growth, environmental degradation, the movement of people and goods, and resource scarcity.

Which choice completes the text with the most logical and precise word or phrase?

A) remit

B) address

C) communicate

D) approach

95

Behavioral activation is a type of talk therapy that helps teens get unstuck from negative mood spirals by noticing a _____ between what they do and how they feel, and gradually adding more small and enjoyable actions back into their lives. Behavior activation has the goal of decreasing avoidance, bolstering peer connection, and improving engagement in rewarding activities. It also incorporates parental involvement so parents learn tools for supporting their adolescents.

Which choice completes the text with the most logical and precise word or phrase?

A) relevance

B) bond

C) correspondence

D) attachment

96

We need to look for robust biospheres (atmospheres, surfaces, and/or oceans) capable of creating planet–scale change in order to find life on other planets. Presently, Earth is the only body in our solar system with a biosphere detectable by its light spectrum, despite the possibility that habitable conditions might _____ in the subsurface of Mars or inside the icy moons of the outer solar system. Even if life exists on these worlds, it is very unlikely that it could yield planet–scale changes that are both telescopically observable and clearly biological in origin.

Which choice completes the text with the most logical and precise word or phrase?

A) exist

B) triumph

C) overcome

D) endure

97

The researchers found that variance among the test sites did not increase over the millennia, leading them to conclude that stabilizing forces were maintaining forest diversity.

"Our findings indicate there are factors that _____ populations at relative abundances that are consistent from one place to another," said Clark. "The variation from place to place is not 'neutral.' Ecologists have long known that, within a region, some species tend to be more abundant and some species less abundant. Our study doesn't identify what those stabilizing forces are, but it clearly shows they do not arise from neutral dynamics."

Which choice completes the text with the most logical and precise word or phrase?

A) supervise

B) oversee

C) regulate

D) administer

98

Although an antibody–based overdose drug would be more expensive than standard treatments, the authors say, it would cost less than cancer immunotherapy, which is now routinely used to treat patients. In the coming weeks, the team will test the antibodies' ability to _____ synthetic opioids' effects in nonhuman primates.

Which choice completes the text with the most logical and precise word or phrase?

A) rebuff

B) dismay

C) contradict

D) counter

99

The nature of the interviews conducted for this paper was such that a comprehensive but diverse collection of information was obtained, precisely because the interviewees have chosen the vegan diet for a multitude of reasons, and approach their diet and lifestyle in varied ways. However, there are some commonalities that were _____ when we analyzed the data carefully.

Which choice completes the text with the most logical and precise word or phrase?

A) uncovered

B) betrayed

C) confessed

D) circulated

100

Black bears in North Carolina have adapted to city life so well that their behavioral and biological habits are changing. They are unafraid to forage during the daytime, and many residents place food outside to entice the bears closer for easy viewing. Resulting conflicts have led the city of Asheville to create laws that _____ feeding bears.

Which choice completes the text with the most logical and precise word or phrase?

A) denigrate

B) embargo

C) prohibit

D) endorse

101

In Timbulsloko, Indonesia, the rice crops failed in the 1990s because the land was sinking and the saline ocean water entered the rice paddies. Residents changed to raising milkfish and tiger prawns in the brackish pond water. However, they can no longer survive on aquaculture because the ocean continues to _____ and the region is now about one mile away from the mainland area.

Which choice completes the text with the most logical and precise word or phrase?

A) encroach

B) conquer

C) vanquish

D) subjugate

102

The following text is adapted from Robert Louis Stevenson's 1882 novel, *Treasure Island*.

Well, mother was upstairs with father and I was laying the breakfast–table against the captain's return when the parlour door opened and a man stepped in on whom I had never set my eyes before. He was a pale, tallowy creature, <u>wanting</u> two fingers of the left hand, and though he wore a cutlass, he did not look much like a fighter. I had always my eye open for seafaring men, with one leg or two, and I remember this one puzzled me. He was not sailorly, and yet he had a smack of the sea about him too.

As used in the text, what does the word "wanting" most nearly mean?

A) craving

B) lacking

C) requiring

D) hoping for

103

Honing knives on a stone wheel is becoming a lost art, but craftsmen who still use that method can tell the percentage of carbon in a blade based on the color and number of sparks _____ that fly the instant the metal touches the wheel.

Which choice completes the text with the most logical and precise word or phrase?

A) evolved

B) manufactured

C) generated

D) assembled

104

Known as the Abominable Snowman in Western Culture, the Yeti is a giant, mythological, ape–like creature that has its basis in sherpa tales from the Himalayan Mountains. Many people have reported seeing the creature, and some even offer blurry videos, damaged photographs, and other _____ evidence to support their vague claims.

Which choice completes the text with the most logical and precise word or phrase?

A) coherent

B) hesitant

C) dubious

D) unrestricted

105

Recent research has determined that rattlesnakes can alter the rate of vibrations in their tail to produce sounds that make them appear closer than they really are to a creature that is approaching. This cunning manipulation of sound, similar to the way an ambulance siren seems to increase in pitch as it comes closer, is one attempt to scare off _____ predators.

Which choice completes the text with the most logical and precise word or phrase?

A) preventative

B) pretentious

C) prosperous

D) potential

106

Over the past three decades, scientists have revealed emotional responses such as grief and play in a surprising array of animal and even insect species. However, researchers who study emotions in animals are often accused of anthropomorphizing their _____.

Which choice completes the text with the most logical and precise word or phrase?

A) questions

B) volunteers

C) subjects

D) specialties

107

NASA's Artemis I mission will feature a mannequin _____ Campos to record such information as seat vibrations, gravity, and radiation as part of the preparations for another manned mission to the Moon.

Which choice completes the text with the most logical and precise word or phrase?

A) entitled

B) granted

C) dubbed

D) termed

108

The Leaning Tower of Pisa is known for its precarious–looking 4–degree tilt, which started to _____ during construction in the twelfth century because the soft ground was unable to support the massive weight of the structure.

Which choice completes the text with the most logical and precise word or phrase?

A) initiate

B) confirm

C) evince

D) manifest

109

Alexander Calder (1898–1976) was a sculptor and inventor who is best known for his mobiles, which are kinetic sculptures that employ either motors or wind currents to add a level of _____ to the arrangement of the parts at any given time.

Which choice completes the text with the most logical and precise word or phrase?

A) prosperity

B) serendipity

C) accountability

D) feasibility

110

Though Cuba is known for censorship, it is ironically also known for having one of the highest literacy rates in the world because in 1961, the government sent out "literary brigades" to the countryside to build schools and educate the locals. The result was that 700,000 people _____ basic reading skills in less than one year.

Which choice completes the text with the most logical and precise word or phrase?

A) obtained

B) collected

C) sustained

D) derived

111

The Russian–American actor known on stage as Yul Brynner is best remembered for his portrayal of King Monkut in the musical *The King and I*. He performed the part 4,625 times on stage and is one of the few actors who has been _____ with both a Tony and an Oscar for the same role.

Which choice completes the text with the most logical and precise word or phrase?

A) granted

B) accepted

C) dedicated

D) conceded

112

The following text is adapted from Abraham Lincoln's last public address, given April 11, 1965.

Some twelve thousand voters in the heretofore slave–state of Louisiana have sworn allegiance to the Union, assumed to be the rightful political power of the State, held elections, organized a State government, adopted a free–state constitution, giving the benefit of public schools equally to black and white, and empowering the Legislature to confer the elective franchise upon the colored man. Their Legislature has already voted to ratify the constitutional amendment recently passed by Congress, abolishing slavery throughout the nation. These twelve thousand persons are thus fully <u>committed</u> to the Union, and to perpetual freedom in the state––committed to the very things, and nearly all the things the nation wants––and they ask the nation's recognition and its assistance to make good their committal.

As used in the text, what does the word "committed" most nearly mean?

A) engaged

B) performed

C) dedicated

D) consigned

113

We know a lot about the Nabataean culture, which flourished in what is now modern Jordan between the fourth and first century B.C. However, they had no literary texts or records, so it is difficult to _____ a full picture of daily life at that time.

Which choice completes the text with the most logical and precise word or phrase?

A) reconstruct

B) fabricate

C) refurbish

D) imbue

114

Juvenile bald eagles are dark brown and have irregular white streak patterns, dark bills, and dark eyes. They do not gain the distinctive markings of an adult until they reach _____ at about five years of age.

Which choice completes the text with the most logical and precise word or phrase?

A) precedence

B) maturity

C) primacy

D) security

115

Knitting is actually based on two basic stitches, a knit stitch through the back of a loop and the purl stitch through the front, though these two basic stitches can be combined in _____ ways to create an infinite number of complex patterns.

Which choice completes the text with the most logical and precise word or phrase?

A) sizeable

B) immense

C) impervious

D) myriad

116

Manatees are herbivorous aquatic mammals that require water temperatures over 68 degrees Fahrenheit, so many flock to water heated by coal-fired power plants _____ hot springs that are no longer in their habitat range.

Which choice completes the text with the most logical and precise word or phrase?

A) as well as

B) along with

C) in lieu of

D) let alone

117

After a long search, in March, 2022, autonomous underwater vehicles _____ the three-masted, oak-hulled *Endurance*, which sank off the coast of Antarctica in 1915. Fortunately, explorer Ernest Henry Shackleton and his entire crew survived.

Which choice completes the text with the most logical and precise word or phrase?

A) perceived

B) located

C) noticed

D) obtained

118

Snakes and other reptiles do not create their own body heat, so when _____ temperatures decrease, their metabolism slows down and they enter a special form of hibernation that is called *brumation*.

Which choice completes the text with the most logical and precise word or phrase?

A) adjacent

B) surrounding

C) contiguous

D) accessible

119

Succotash is a mixture of sweet corn and lima beans, though any other shell beans can be _____ in the recipe. The word means "broken corn kernels" in the Narragansett language, though the food was eaten by a wide range of indigenous peoples in North America.

Which choice completes the text with the most logical and precise word or phrase?

A) reciprocated

B) exchanged

C) nurtured

D) substituted

120

Amphora are jars that were used in ancient Greece and Rome that had two vertical handles and typically a pointed bottom. These jars were used to store and transport food, olive oil, and wine. It may seem impractical to have a pointed base, but that shape was ideally _____ for placement in sand.

Which choice completes the text with the most logical and precise word or phrase?

A) suited

B) acclimatized

C) converted

D) adjusted

85. **Level:** Easy | **Skill/Knowledge:** Words in Context

    Key Explanation: Choice B is the best answer because the blank portion shows what part of "complex chemistry" "life" is. **Choice B** refers to a class or category, so fits the context of saying that life is a category of chemistry that uses simple elements.

    Distractor Explanations: Choice A is incorrect because it refers to a replica, an original that replicas are made from, or an ideal. None of these fit the context because there are no copies of the general concept of life. **Choice C** is incorrect because it refers to one part of a larger set of identical things. However, "life" is different from the other parts of complex chemistry. **Choice D** refers to a pattern for something. However, life is a changing process that does not follow a specific set of guidelines or blueprint.

86. **Level:** Medium | **Skill/Knowledge:** Words in Context

    Key Explanation: Choice B is the best answer because the blank should infer that most men cherish feelings towards the ocean. **Choice B** means "quantity," so it accurately shows that all men have some quantity of desire to go to the sea.

    Distractor Explanations: All of the other choices can be eliminated because they do not describe what most men feel about the ocean. **Choice A** refers to status. **Choice C** refers to a measurement or level of attainment. **Choice D** refers to an official document showing that a course of study was completed.

87. **Level:** Medium | **Skill/Knowledge:** Words in Context

    Key Explanation: Choice C is the best answer because the blank portion is something that is noticed which helps "teens get unstuck from

negative mood spirals." It is something "between what they do and how they feel." **Choice C** refers to a close similarity or equivalence, so it shows that what the teens do is equivalent to how they feel and vice versa.

    Distractor explanation: None of the other choices adequately explain the relationship "between what they do and how they feel." **Choice A** refers to the state of being closely connected or important to the subject of the sentence or topic at hand; it is not typically used with "between" and two objects. **Choices B** and **D** refer to joining or uniting two things together rather than showing a parallel between two ideas.

88. **Level:** Hard | **Skill/Knowledge:** Words in Context

    Key Explanation: Choice C is the best answer because the blank portion is what the factors do to the populations so that the populations are "at relative abundances that are consistent from one place to another." **Choice C** refers to making something stable, so it fits the context of saying that the populations are relatively the same.

    Distractor Explanations: None of the other choices fits the context of describing what the factors do to the populations. The other choices all refer to a deliberate action of overseeing the actions of someone or something else, but "factors" are inanimate and cannot decide to direct anything else.

89. **Level:** Hard | **Skill/Knowledge:** Words in Context

    Key Explanation: Choice C is the best answer because the blank portion refers to an aspect of the diet that Mann questioned twenty vegans about. **Choice C** refers to the makeup or structure of something, so fits the context of explaining that Mann asked about the makeup or balance of parts in the diet.

Distractor Explanations: None of the other choices adequately show what part of the diet Mann discussed with the twenty vegans. **Choice A** refers to how things are spaced and organized rather than the balance of things. **Choice B** refers to the inherent personality of someone. **Choice D** refers to a mixture.

90. **Level:** Medium | **Skill/Knowledge:** Words in Context

    Key Explanation: Choice B is the best answer because "recognize" is what "we," the Union, could do to the new government of Louisiana that would make the "converse" or "opposite" of the previous discussion true. The previous discussion is about what happens if the Union does not support Louisiana. **Choice B** refers to welcoming or integrating something, in this case, Louisiana, so it fits the context of showing the opposite of rejecting Louisiana.

    Distractor Explanations: None of the other choices show the opposite of rejection. **Choice A** refers to indicating what something is or naming it. **Choice C** refers to either fully understanding something or achieving a goal. **Choice D** refers to knowing the value of something.

91. **Level:** Medium | **Skill/Knowledge:** Words in Context

    Key Explanation: Choice A is the best answer because it means "hold" or "provide sufficient space for." It fits the context of saying that MCOs have three copper–binding sites that can provide space for or hold six copper atoms.

    Distractor Explanation: None of the other choices sufficiently fits the context of explaining what the three copper–binding sites do to the six

copper atoms. **Choice B** refers to providing space for a person or people to stay; it does not apply to inanimate objects such as atoms. **Choice C** refers to providing a person a room to stay in for a rental fee. **Choice D** refers to protecting something from something harmful, but there is no evidence that the copper–binding sites are trying to help the copper atoms remain safe.

92. **Level:** Medium | **Skill/Knowledge:** Words in Context

    Key Explanation: Choice A is the best answer because, in the context, "standard" refers to what the laws of the several slave–holding states are in relation to the government's action. **Choice A** refers to a general rule or requirement. Therefore, it accurately shows that the laws of the states are the rules that the government follows.

    Distractor Explanations: None of the other choices adequately establishes the relationship between the laws and the government's action. **Choice B** refers to the general excellence of something, so does not act as a measure. **Choice C** refers to the most perfect example, but the laws are not necessarily perfect. **Choice D** refers to how valuable something is rather than how it is used.

93. **Level:** Hard | **Skill/Knowledge:** Words in Context

    Key Explanation: Choice C is the best answer because it is used to describe a place that is harsh and severe. It fits the context of saying that the Southern Ocean contains some of the most harsh and severe water conditions on the planet.

    Distractor Explanation: None of the other choices fits the context of describing a harsh environment. **Choice A** refers to something that is ready to attack or confront something else.

It is not used to describe something that is not deliberately trying to inflict harm. **Choice B** refers to an emotional state in which someone feels hostility towards something; it is not used to describe an inanimate object. **Choice D** refers to things which are at variance with each other. However, "hostile" is only referring to the "seas," not to more than one thing that could be incompatible with each other.

94. **Level:** Medium | **Skill/Knowledge:** Words in Context

Key Explanation: Choice B is the best answer because the blank is used to show what urban planners will be needed to do with different types of issues. **Choice B** refers to "dealing with" or "solving" a problem or difficulty. Therefore, it fits the context of saying that in cities, urban planners will have to deal with problems such as population growth.

Distractor Explanations: None of the other choices effectively explains what the planners do with issues. **Choice A** refers to canceling or sending something rather than solving something. **Choice C** refers to sharing information. However, the planners do not just need to talk about issues; they need to solve issues. **Choice D** is incorrect because it refers to starting or beginning something, but it does not include the idea of following through until the problem is solved.

95. **Level:** Medium | **Skill/Knowledge:** Words in Context

Key Explanation: Choice C is the best answer because the word in the blank describes the correlation between what teens do and what teens feel. – something that has been noticed to help break negative mood spirals. **Choice C** refers to

a similarity or relationship, so it shows that by seeing the relationship between what the teens do and feel, the mood spiral can be fixed.

Distractor Explanations: None of the other choices adequately explain the relationship "between what they do and how they feel." **Choice A** refers to the state of being closely connected or important to the subject of the sentence or topic at hand; it is not typically used with "between" and two objects. **Choices B** and **D** refer to joining or uniting two things together rather than showing a parallel between two ideas.

96. **Level:** Easy | **Skill/Knowledge:** Words in Context

Key Explanation: Choice A is the best answer because the blank portion is used to describe what the "habitable conditions" do in the "subsurface of Mars or inside the icy moons of the outer solar system." **Choice A** means "occur" or "be found," so shows that the habitable conditions may occur in places like under the surface of Mars or inside icy moons.

Distractor Explanations: Choices B and **C** are incorrect because they refer to having a victory or success over something else. However, the habitable conditions do not win in a contest against places like inside Mars or icy moons. **Choice D** refers to lasting or continuing, often despite hardship. However, the habitable conditions do not continue on despite problems; the habitable conditions just occur.

97. **Level:** Medium | **Skill/Knowledge:** Words in Context

Key Explanation: Choice C is the best answer because **Choice C** refers to making something stable. The word in the blank is what the factors do to the populations so that the populations are "at relative abundances that are consistent from one place to another," in other words, they remain stable or the same. **Choice C**, therefore, fits the context of saying that the populations are relatively the same.

Distractor Explanations: None of the other choices fits the context of describing what impact the factors have on the populations. The other choices all refer to a deliberate action of directing the actions of someone or something else, but "factors" are inanimate and cannot decide to direct anything else.

98. **Level:** Hard | **Skill/Knowledge:** Words in Context

Key Explanation: Choice D is the best answer because the underline should describe what the antibodies' ability does to the synthetic opioids' effects. **Choice D** refers to opposing or making something ineffective, so accurately shows that the researchers are trying to determine how effective the antibodies are at making the opioids ineffective.

Distractor Explanation: Choice A refers to refusing something in a way that is not gracious. It describes a deliberate action in response to an offer or request. **Choice B** refers to being upset, so does not apply to an inanimate object. **Choice C** refers to claiming that something is incorrect. However, the antibodies do not disagree or say that the opioids are wrong.

99. **Level:** Easy | **Skill/Knowledge:** Words in Context

Key Explanation: Choice A is the best answer because the blank portion is what happened to the "commonalities" or "similarities." **Choice A** refers

to detecting or discovering something, which fits the context of explaining that the study discovered some similar points.

Distractor Explanations: Choices B and **C** are incorrect because they refer to telling a secret, but the study did not decide to share information that it was supposed to keep hidden. **Choice D** refers to flowing continuously through a closed system, which would imply that the commonalities moved around between members of a certain group of people.

100. **Level:** Easy | **Skill/Knowledge:** Words in Context

Key Explanation: Choice C is the best answer because the blank portion is a verb that shows what the laws have done regarding feeding bears. The text says that the residents place food outside, but the "resulting conflicts" or "problems that have occurred as a consequence" have caused the laws. Therefore, the laws probably stop the people from feeding the animals. **Choice C** means "stop," so fits the context well.

Distractor Explanations: None of the other choices accurately describe what the laws do about feeding bears. **Choice A** refers to criticizing something severely, but a law does not criticize, it prevents an action. **Choice B** refers to a law banning trade or another official action between countries; the word is not applicable to stopping a private citizen from doing something. **Choice D** means "encourages." Though it grammatically fits the context, it does not logically describe what the law does to prevent conflicts between people and bears due to the people feeding bears.

101. **Level:** Medium | **Skill/Knowledge:** Words in Context

Key Explanation: Choice A is the best answer because it refers to invading or moving gradually beyond accepted limits. It is acceptable to use with inanimate objects, so fits the context of explaining that the ocean moves forward into areas that the residents of Timbulsloko do not want it to enter.

Distractor Explanations: None of the other choices fits the context of explaining what the ocean does. All of the choices refer to dominating or taking over something, but they include the idea of an active desire to have the area. The ocean is inanimate, so it does not actively want to take over the land.

102. **Level:** Medium | **Skill/Knowledge:** Words in Context

Key Explanation: Choice B is the best answer because it means "missing." In the text, "wanting" refers to two fingers on the hand of a person who appears to be a sailor. **Choice B** clearly shows that two fingers are not there.

Distractor Explanations: Choices A and **D** can be eliminated because they refer to the desire for something, but there is no indication in the text that the sailor desires new fingers, at least in the described scene. The narrator is just describing the appearance of the man. **Choice C** refers to needing something, but the sailor is not fumbling or having difficulties without the fingers, so he can get by without them.

103. **Level:** Easy | **Skill/Knowledge:** Words in Context

Key Explanation: Choice C is the best answer because it means "created" or "produced," so fits the context of saying that sparks are produced when the knife touches the wheel.

Distractor Explanations: Choice A is incorrect because it refers to slow changes over time rather than an instantaneous action. **Choices B** and **D** are incorrect because they refer to producing something on purpose, such as a product to sell. They are not used to describe the by–product of a process. Sparks are not made on purpose; they are a by–product of "honing" or "sharpening" a knife.

104. **Level:** Medium | **Skill/Knowledge:** Words in Context

Key Explanation: Choice C is the best answer because it refers to something which is not to be relied on. It fits the context of saying that people have questionable evidence like blurry videos to try to prove that they have seen the Yeti.

Distractor Explanations: None of the other choices aptly describes the evidence that people use to support their claims about the Yeti. The word "other" shows that the word needs to be similar to blurry photographs and damaged photographs. **Choice A** means "very logical," so is not consistent with things that are not very convincing. **Choice B** refers to being slow to make a decision, but the evidence is not an animate, thinking thing. **Choice D** refers to having no limits.

105. **Level:** Easy | **Skill/Knowledge:** Words in Context

Key Explanation: Choice D is the best answer because the blank portion needs to describe the "predators" or "things which might eat the snake." The snake "attempts" or "tries" to scare it off, so the predator is not yet successful. **Choice D** refers to something that is possible, so indicates that it is possible for the creature to eat the snake.

Distractor Explanations: None of the other choices aptly describe the "predators" in this context. **Choice A** refers to something that stops another thing from happening. Though the action of manipulating sound is preventative for the snake, it does not describe the predators. **Choice B** refers to something that is trying to impress. **Choice C** refers to something that is wealthy.

106. **Level:** Medium | **Skill/Knowledge:** Words in Context

Key Explanation: Choice C is the best answer because it refers to the object of a study or experiment. In the context, in the blank portion, researchers are accused of "anthropomorphizing" or "giving human qualities to" their subjects. The passage says that they are studying emotions in animals and insects, **Choice C** correctly shows that some people say the researchers give human emotional qualities to the things they study.

Distractor Explanations: None of the other choices adequately show that the researchers are accused of "anthropomorphizing" or "giving human qualities to" their subjects. **Choice A** refers to doubts or inquiries, but those do not have human qualities . **Choice B** refers to someone who offers to be in an experiment, but animals do not offer to join, they are selected to participate. **Choice D** refers to the field of study, not to the things being studied.

107. **Level:** Medium | **Skill/Knowledge:** Words in Context

Key Explanation: Choice C is the best answer because the blank portion shows how "mannequin" and "Campos" are related. **Choice C** means "named" or "called," so it fits the context of saying the name of the mannequin is Campos.

Distractor Explanations: Choices A and **B** are incorrect because they refer to giving an honor or rights to something, but "Campos" is a name. **Choice D** is incorrect because it is used to show that the following word is an established definition or expression for something.

108. **Level:** Medium | **Skill/Knowledge:** Words in Context

Key Explanation: Choice D is the best answer because the blank portion needs to show what the 4–degree tilt started to do during construction. **Choice D** means "display" or "demonstrate," so shows that the tower started to show its tilt.

Distractor Explanations: None of the other choices adequately explains what the 4–degree tilt started to do during construction. **Choice A** refers to causing something to begin, but the soft ground caused the tilt rather than the other way around. **Choice B** is incorrect because it refers to establishing that something is true rather than appearing. **Choice C** is incorrect because it refers to revealing an emotion.

109. **Level:** Hard | **Skill/Knowledge:** Words in Context

Key Explanation: Choice B is the best answer because it refers to "chance" or "accident," so it shows that the moving parts add a certain amount of unpredictability to the arrangement of the parts of the sculptures.

Distractor Explanations: None of the other choices show what the motors and wind currents do to the arrangement of parts. **Choice A** refers to wealth and good fortune. **Choice C** refers to responsibility. **Choice D** refers to the degree of something being able to be done.

110. **Level:** Medium | **Skill/Knowledge:** Words in Context

Key Explanation: Choice A is the best answer because the blank portion needs to refer to what the "people" did to the "reading skills" because of the educational campaign. **Choice A** refers to receiving or getting something, so it accurately states that the people got reading skills, and that is why the country has a high literacy rate.

Distractor Explanations: None of the other choices accurately shows what the people did to the reading skills. **Choice B** refers to actively gathering or bringing something together rather than learning something. **Choice C** refers to undergoing something, typically negative. **Choice D** refers to getting something from a specific source, but the source is not given.

111. **Level:** Medium | **Skill/Knowledge:** Words in Context

Key Explanation: Choice A is the best answer because it is used to show that something such as a title or award is given to someone. **Choice A** fits the context of saying that the Tony and Oscar awards were given to Brynner.

Distractor Explanations: None of the other choices aptly explains the relationship between Brynner and the awards. **Choice B** refers to agreeing to take something, but is an active verb. As a result, the passive "has been accepted" is illogical in the context, as Brynner accepted the awards. **Choice C** refers to devoting time or formally unveiling something like a monument. **Choice D** refers to admitting that something is true after first denying it.

112. **Level:** Medium | **Skill/Knowledge:** Words in Context

Key Explanation: Choice C is the best answer because "are committed" is the action that "these twelve thousand persons" do to "the Union." The sentence goes on to say that the people intend to do "nearly all the things the nation wants." **Choice C** means "faithful to," so fits the context that the people are faithful to the Union.

Distractor Explanations: Choice A refers to being busy with something else rather than a promise to follow the orders of a governing body. **Choice B** refers to doing an action, but does not specify what kind. **Choice D** refers to something that is sent to a place, but the people choose to enter the Union rather than being sent there by a different authority.

113. **Level:** Easy | **Skill/Knowledge:** Words in Context

Key Explanation: Choice A is the best answer because the blank portion is a verb that shows what it is difficult to do to the whole picture of daily life. **Choice A** refers to forming a model based on available evidence, so fits the context of saying that there are no literary texts to help round out the idea of what daily life might be like.

Distractor Explanations: Choice B refers to making something up in the effort to deceive, but the passage is referring to understanding the truth about a culture. **Choice B** can also refer to assembling something from pre-made component parts, but that definition also does not fit the idea of determining what a culture was like from archaeological clues. **Choice C** refers to renovating and remodeling something that exists to make it better. **Choice D** is incorrect because it refers to inspiring something or permeating it with a characteristic or quality.

114. **Level:** Easy | **Skill/Knowledge:** Words in Context

Key Explanation: Choice B is the best answer because it refers to the time when something is completely grown into an adult stage. It fits the context of saying that bald eagles are different colors until they become adults at about five years old.

Distractor Explanations: Choices A and **C** are incorrect because they refer to being first or higher in a ranking, but there is no indication that the eagles must be more important than other eagles in some way to get the coloration of an adult. **Choice D** is incorrect because it refers to the state of being protected from harm, not to a growth phase.

115. **Level:** Medium | **Skill/Knowledge:** Words in Context

Key Explanation: Choice D is the best answer because it refers to a great, possibly uncountable number. It fits the context of describing the "ways" that the stitches can be combined: there are so many ways to combine the stitches that there are infinite patterns.

Distractor Explanations: Choices A and **B** are incorrect because they refer to something great as far as physical size, not number. The ways are not large, they are multiple. **Choice C** does not fit the context of describing the ways because it refers to something that is strong and durable.

116. **Level:** Medium | **Skill/Knowledge:** Words in Context

Key Explanation: Choice C is the best answer because it means "instead of," so fits the context of saying that the manatees go to water heated by man instead of using hot springs, as hot springs are "no longer" or "not now but were in the past" part of the habitat.

Distractor Explanations: Choices A and **B** are incorrect because they mean "and," but the hot springs are no longer in the range where the manatees live, so they do not use both heat sources. **Choice D** is incorrect because it is used to show that something is less suitable than something else, but it reverses the order and makes it appear like the hot springs are less suitable than the manmade hot water.

117. **Level:** Easy | **Skill/Knowledge:** Words in Context

Key Explanation: Choice B is the best answer because it refers to finding the place where something is, so fits the context of saying that the vehicles found the place that the ship sank.

Distractor Explanations: Choices A and **C** are incorrect because they refer to finding something by chance rather than deliberately searching for something, but the underwater vehicles were sent on "a long search." **Choice D** is incorrect because it refers to getting or taking possession of something, not just finding it.

118. **Level:** Medium | **Skill/Knowledge:** Words in Context

Key Explanation: Choice B is the best answer because it refers to everything that is all around something. It fits the context of showing that when the temperatures all around the reptile "decrease" or "get lower," the reptile's metabolism drops and it enters a form of hibernation.

Distractor Explanations: Choices A and **C** are incorrect because they refer to two things which are next to each other or share a border, such as two countries that have the same border. They do not show that the temperature is everywhere around the reptile. **Choice D** means "in easy reach," but temperatures do not have a physical location that is near or far away.

119. **Level:** Medium | **Skill/Knowledge:** Words in Context

Key Explanation: Choice D is the best answer because the blank must explain how the "other shell beans" can be used in the recipe. **Choice D** refers to something that replaces something else, so accurately shows that other shell beans can be used in place of lima beans.

Distractor Explanations: Choices A and **B** are incorrect because they refer to something that is given in return for something else, so they do not fit the context because the chef does not receive lima beans when using shell beans. **Choice C** is incorrect because it refers to growing or caring for something, but beans are not grown in a recipe, they are made into a food.

120. **Level:** Medium | **Skill/Knowledge:** Words in Context

Key Explanation: Choice A is the best answer because it refers to being convenient or acceptable for something. It fits the context of showing that the amphora's odd shape allowed it to be placed in sand.

Distractor Explanations: None of the other choices explains how the amphora were "ideally" or "perfectly" related to sand. **Choice B** refers to getting used to something by degrees, but the amphora did not change over time. **Choices C** and **D** refer to changing from one thing to another, but there is no indication that amphora were a different shape before being designed with pointed bases.

121

The following text is adapted from Mother Jones's 1912 speech to coal miners picketing in Charlestown, West Virginia.

I want to show you here that the average wages you fellows get in this country is $500 a year. Before you get a thing to eat there is $20 taken out a month, which leaves about $24 a month. Then you go to the "pluck–me" stores and want to get something to eat for your wife, and the child comes back and says, "Papa, I can't get anything." "Why," he says, "there is $24 coming to me?" The child says, "They said there was nothing coming to you." And the child goes back crying without a mouthful of anything to eat. The father goes to the "pluck–me" store and says to the manager, "There is $24 coming to me," and the manager says, "Oh, no, we have kept $26 for rent."

What is the main purpose of including a quote from the miner's child?

A) To explain the amount of money that is needed to pay bills

B) To indicate that the miners are too busy to do their own shopping

C) To highlight the cruelty of the practice being described

D) To emphasize that children are also forced to work in the mines

122

Spix's macaw is a gorgeous bird that was declared extinct in its wild habitat of Brazil in 2000. Its range was historically limited to dry forests, and due to its dependence on trees for nesting and feeding, the little bird was not able to adapt to the combined challenges of habitat loss and poaching. Collectors who owned captive birds were concerned about this turn of events and collaborated with conservators to initiate a captive breeding program. In June 2022, eight banded Spix's macaws were reintroduced into the wild, and more are scheduled to be released at a later date.

What is the main purpose of the text?

A) It issues a warning.

B) It describes a situation.

C) It details steps for a solution.

D) It is a request for assistance.

123

The following text is adapted from Mother Jones's speech to coal miners picketing in Charlestown, West Virginia, on August 15, 1912.

They wouldn't keep their dog where they keep you fellows. You know that. They have a good place for their dogs and a slave to take care of them. The mine owners' wives will take the dogs up, and say, "I love you, dea–h." My friends, the day for petting dogs is gone; the day for raising children to a nobler manhood and better womanhood is here! You have suffered; I know you have suffered. I was with you nearly three years in this State. I went to jail. I went to the Federal courts, but I never took any back water!

In the text, what is the main purpose of the discussion of the mine owners' pet dogs?

A) To offer one point of consolation for the mine workers

B) To point out one of the adversaries faced by the miners

C) To illustrate that some mine owners can be compassionate

D) To emphasize the sordid conditions of the mine workers

124

By analyzing data on tree pollen extracted from ancient lake sediments, ecologists have sharpened the understanding of how forests can maintain a diversity of species. Their findings indicate that stabilizing processes have been more important than previously thought, and that the human–caused loss of species could upset that stability in ways that remain poorly understood. "Quantifying the link between stability and diversity, and identifying the factors that promote species diversity, have challenged ecologists for decades," said Saran Twombly, program director in the National Science Foundation (NSF)'s division of environmental biology, which funded the research. "The contribution of this study is unique, as the scientists used a clever blend of long–term data and statistical modeling to test the opposing hypotheses of neutrality and stability as key factors promoting community assembly and diversity."

What is the main function of the quote by Saran Twombly in the overall structure of the text as a whole?

A) It clarifies a key term used throughout the passage.

B) It presents a counterargument that is refuted by the passage.

C) It offers an expert opinion about the study described in the passage.

D) It highlights one limitation of the methodology described in the passage.

Salt stress, too much salt in the soil for plants to thrive, is one of the major environmental constraints limiting agricultural productivity and influencing the concentration of bioactive compounds of vegetables. In this study, we assessed the effect of NaCl salt stress on flowering, fructification, and fruit nutritional quality of a local cultivar of chili pepper. In Benin, chili is the second cash gardening crop after the tomato. Pepper plants produce the compound capsaicin, primarily in the fruits, possibly to deter mammalian herbivores. In Benin, chili pepper is grown in the cultivable lands of the coastal areas, where soil salinity and water irrigation are a reality. Salt stress is known to negatively affect plant growth at all developmental stages, but sensitivity varies greatly at different stages. Crop production in saline areas largely depends on successful germination, seedling emergence, and establishment of an efficient reproductive phase.

What is the function of the underlined portion in the overall structure of the text?

A) It emphasizes the need for a different crop.

B) It shows that the environment is suitable for crops.

C) It highlights the importance of the study.

D) It describes methods to combat salt stress.

A new range of technologies, devices, and sub-systems regarding wave and tidal current energy production need in-depth analysis. Competing pressures and uses such as climate change, fishing, and marine transport should be considered when looking at environmental impacts of such systems. The literature research shows that only a small number of LCA on wave and tidal energy converters have been performed. The main focus was on devices that are in advanced stages of development, so there is little data for prototype models. So far, most of the studies focused only on the impact of energy and carbon. Existing data are very much dispersed among countries, researchers, and developers. Since most wave energy and tidal energy technologies are at an early development stage, no data exists on environmental effects from large integrated systems.

What is the main function of the underlined sentence in the overall structure of the text?

A) It shows the data set is very incomplete.

B) It shows the groups are sharing data.

C) It shows the data is comprehensive.

D) It shows the sources are incompatible.

The following text is adapted from Mother Jones's 1912 speech to coal miners picketing in Charlestown, West Virginia.

To me, the proper thing to do is to read the purpose of our meeting here today. The guards of the mining companies beat, abuse, maim, and hold up citizens without process of law; deny freedom of speech, a provision guaranteed by the Constitution. We hold that the companies in maintaining such guards are detrimental to the best interests of society and an outrage against the honor and dignity of the State. I hope, my friends, that you and the mine owners will put aside the breach and get together before I leave the State. But I want to say, make no settlement until they sign up that every bloody murderer of a guard has got to go. This is done, my friends, beneath the flag our fathers fought and bled for, and we don't intend to surrender our liberty.

What is the main purpose of the text?

A) To describe the working conditions suffered by miners

B) To encourage miners to avoid making compromises

C) To convince the government to change conditions of miners

D) To initiate negotiations with the guards at the mines

How the gene HEPHL1 mechanistically regulates hair growth and development will require further in–depth analysis, and the curly whiskers from *HEPHL1* knockout mice could help these investigations. Our preliminary results showed that HEPHL1 regulates the activity of an enzyme, lysyl oxidase, which needs copper for its enzymatic activity. In conclusion, our study identified HEPHL1 as a <u>novel</u> gene responsible for hair abnormalities and highlights the importance of exploring the role of HEPHL1—and its interconnections with other key regulators—in developing new therapeutic strategies to treat hair disorders and even more insidious genetic diseases.

In the text, what is the primary function of using the word "novel"?

A) To show HEPHL1 has never before been classified by researchers

B) To emphasize the relationship between HEPHL1 and hair anomalies has only just been identified

C) To illustrate HEPHL1 is the newest solution in the fight against genetic diseases

D) To point out no one had realized that HEPHL1 existed in mice as well as humans

Under the Business Opportunity Rule, as well as the other documents, sellers have to give you a one–page disclosure document that offers five key pieces of information. Use the information in the disclosure document to fact–check what the seller tells you about the opportunity and what you find out from your own research. The document has to identify the seller and tell you about certain lawsuits or other legal actions involving the seller or its key personnel. It must tell you if the seller has a cancellation or refund policy and what the terms are. The seller must also give you a list of references.

What is the main purpose of the text?

A) It outlines the key documents required by the Business Opportunity Rule.

B) It describes one of the essential documents that sellers must provide in a sale.

C) It explains how the Business Opportunity Rule protects buyers.

D) It establishes that sellers must give references to potential buyers.

The following text is adapted from F. Scott Fitzgerald's 1922 novel, *The Beautiful and the Damned*.

Anthony's recollections of the gallant Ulysses were much more vivid. After Henrietta Lebrune Patch had "joined another choir," as her widower huskily remarked from time to time, father and son lived up at grampa's in Tarrytown, and Ulysses came daily to Anthony's nursery and expelled pleasant, thick–smelling words for sometimes as much as an hour. He was continually promising Anthony hunting trips and fishing trips and excursions to Atlantic City, "oh, some time soon now"; but none of them ever materialized. One trip they did take; when Anthony was eleven they went abroad, to England and Switzerland, and there in the best hotel in Lucerne his father died with much sweating and grunting and crying aloud for air. In a panic of despair and terror Anthony was brought back to America, wedded to a vague melancholy that was to stay beside him through the rest of his life.

What is the main purpose of including details about the episode in the hotel in Lucerne?

A) To show that Ulysses ultimately kept his promises

B) To highlight the pain during Ulysses' last moments

C) To explain why Anthony decided to live in America

D) To provide background for a feature in Anthony's personality

The following text is from Frances Hodgson Burnett's 1905 novel, *A Little Princess*.

If Sara had been older or less punctilious about being quite polite to people, she could have explained herself in a very few words. <u>But, as it was, she felt a flush rising on her cheeks.</u> Miss Minchin was a very severe and imposing person, and she seemed so absolutely sure that Sara knew nothing whatever of French that she felt as if it would be almost rude to correct her. The truth was that Sara could not remember the time when she had not seemed to know French.

Which choice best states the function of the underlined sentence in the text as a whole?

A) It gives a description of the physical appearance of one of the characters.

B) It establishes why one of the characters was not comfortable in the situation.

C) It reinforces an emotional state alluded to in the previous sentence.

D) It introduces the interaction between two characters in the following sentences.

The following text is adapted from Mother Jones's 1912 speech in Charlestown, West Virginia, on August 15, 1912.

The proper thing to do is to read the purpose of our meeting here today - why these men have laid down their tools and come to the statehouse. The guards of the mining companies beat, abuse, maim, and hold up citizens without process of law; deny freedom of speech; deny the citizens the right to assemble in a peaceable manner for the purpose of discussing questions in which they are concerned. I hope, my friends, that you and the mine owners will put aside the breach and get together before I leave the State. But I want to say, make no settlement until they sign up that every <u>bloody murderer</u> of a guard has got to go.

What is the main function of the phrase "bloody murderer"?

A) It describes the tactics used by certain guards.

B) It offers the reason that guards must be removed.

C) It suggests that guards overreached the orders of the mine owners.

D) It emphasizes the inhumanity exhibited by the guards.

The following text is adapted from F. Scott Fitzgerald's 1922 novel, *The Beautiful and the Damned*.

Early in his career Adam Patch had married an anemic lady of thirty, Alicia Withers, who brought him one hundred thousand dollars and an impeccable entré into the banking circles of New York. Immediately and rather spunkily she had borne him a son and, as if completely devitalized by the magnificence of this performance, she had thenceforth effaced herself within the shadowy dimensions of the nursery. The boy, Adam Ulysses Patch, became an inveterate joiner of clubs, connoisseur of good form, and driver of tandems—at the <u>astonishing</u> age of twenty–six he began his memoirs under the title "New York Society as I Have Seen It." On the rumor of its conception this work was eagerly bid for among publishers, but as it proved after his death to be immoderately verbose and overpoweringly dull, it never obtained even a private printing.

What is the main function of the word "astonishing" in the overall structure of the text?

A) It indicates irony.

B) It expresses admiration.

C) It highlights respect.

D) It emphasizes talent.

The following text is adapted from Chapter 1 of *Moby Dick; or The Whale*, copyright 1851 by Herman Melville.

I always go to sea as a sailor, because of the wholesome exercise and pure air of the fore–castle deck. For as in this world, head winds are far more prevalent than winds from astern, so for the most part the Commodore on the quarter–deck gets his atmosphere at second hand from the sailors on the forecastle. He thinks he breathes it first; but not so. But wherefore it was that after having repeatedly smelt the sea as a merchant sailor, I should now take it into my head to go on a whaling voyage; this the invisible police officer of the Fates, who has the constant surveillance of me, and secretly dogs me, and influences me in some unaccountable way—he can better answer than any one else. <u>It came in as a sort of brief interlude and solo between more extensive performances.</u>

What is the main function of the final sentence in the context of the text?

A) It indicates that whaling was not the narrator's usual occupation.

B) It foreshadows a tragedy that the narrator does not want to repeat.

C) It offers the narrator's rationale for embarking on a whaling voyage.

D) It explains that the narrator could not find longer employment at the time.

135

The vegan diet has gained momentum in recent years, with more people transitioning to the diet, whether for health or more ethically–based reasons. The vegan diet, often characterized as very restrictive, is associated with health benefits but raises concerns. Controversy regarding the diet exists within the public sphere, with those actively supporting and advocating for it, and others questioning its purpose and proposed benefits, even disparaging its existence, perhaps because of a lack of knowledge about the diet. Therefore, a study led by Sarah Mann aimed to provide a fuller picture of the vegan diet in which no animal products are eaten, encompassing both the nutrition and health of the vegan diet as well as related ethical beliefs by studying scientific and popular literature in tandem.

What is the main function of the text?

A) To define key terms about veganism

B) To provide background for a study

C) To establish the author's side of a debate

D) To explain the rationale for a decision

136

The following text is adapted from Emily Bronte's 1847 novel, *Wuthering Heights*.

Wuthering Heights is the name of Mr. Heathcliff's dwelling. "Wuthering" being a significant provincial adjective, descriptive of the atmospheric tumult to which its station is exposed in stormy weather. Pure, bracing ventilation they must have up there at all times, indeed: one may guess the power of the north wind, blowing over the edge, by the excessive slant of a few stunted firs at the end of the house; and by a range of gaunt thorns all stretching their limbs one way, as if craving alms of the sun. Happily, the architect had foresight to build it strong: the narrow windows are deeply set in the wall, and the corners defended with large jutting stones.

What is the main purpose of the text?

A) To describe the local weather

B) To hint at the personality of a character

C) To give an impression of a building

D) To clarify a definition

137

The vegan diet is one that is chosen by individuals for various reasons, including health and/or ethical reasons. While many health benefits exist, it is essential for those who are vegan or are planning to become vegan to be educated about potential nutrient deficiencies to prevent adverse outcomes. In addition, it is evident that the <u>vegan diet is much more than a diet itself,</u> but has developed into a lifestyle, often associated with animal rights and environmental advocacy as well as a greater concern for physical activity and mindfulness. Further research begs the question of whether the health benefits associated with the diet are solely attributable to the diet or in conjunction with a greater physical activity level and mindful living.

Which choice best describes the function of the underlined portion in the overall structure of the text?

A) It shows that people who are concerned about protecting animals should consider veganism.

B) It points out that adopting veganism is a good way for people to help the environment.

C) It indicates that many vegans consider factors other than food to be part of being a vegan.

D) It establishes that people who are vegans have healthier lifestyles than non–vegans do.

138

This poem is adapted from Emily Dickenson's poem *The Outlet,* published after her death in 1886.

> My river runs to thee:
>
> Blue sea, wilt welcome me?
>
> My river waits reply.
>
> Oh sea, look graciously!
>
> I'll fetch thee brooks
>
> From spotted nooks, —
>
> Say, sea,
>
> Take me!

What is the function of the image of a sea in the overall structure of the text?

A) It shows the difficulties of expressing love.

B) It refers to the person that the author loves.

C) It represents the depth of the author's love.

D) It indicates that the course of love is complicated.

139

On November 16, 2022, NASA launched an unmanned spacecraft that is the first step of the Artemis program, an ambitious plan to send manned missions to Mars. The spacecraft was recording valuable information about flight characteristics such as gravity and vibrations that will be vital in keeping astronauts safe on a voyage to the Moon. A successful Moon landing and return is essential in the preparations for the much longer trip to the Red Planet.

What is the main purpose of the text?

A) To introduce a project that will culminate with a trip to Mars.

B) To discuss the importance of gravity and vibrations to space travel.

C) To argue that unmanned missions are safer than manned ones.

D) To explain the steps NASA is taking to land a person on the Moon.

140

The following text is adapted from Horatio Alger, Jr.'s 1865 novel, *Paul Prescott's Charge*.

Squire Benjamin Newcome, as he was called, in the right of his position as Justice of the Peace, Chairman of the Selectmen, and wealthiest resident of Wrenville, was a man of rule and measure. He was measured in his walk, measured in his utterance, and measured in all his transactions. He might be called a dignified machine. He had a very exalted conception of his own position, and the respect which he felt to be his due, not only from his own household, but from all who approached him. If the President of the United States had called upon him, Squire Newcome would very probably have felt that he himself was the party who conferred distinction, and not received it.

What is the function of the last sentence in the overall structure of the text?

A) It emphasizes how important a person Squire Newcome was.

B) It highlights the self–esteem with which Squire Newcome held himself.

C) It remarks on an event that Squire Newcome was involved in.

D) It shows that most people did not care for Squire Newcome.

141

The vegan diet has gained momentum in recent years, with more people transitioning to the diet, whether for health or more ethically–based reasons. The vegan diet, often characterized as very restrictive, is associated with health benefits but raises concerns. Controversy regarding the diet exists within the public sphere, with some actively supporting and advocating for it, and others questioning its purpose and proposed benefits, even disparaging its existence. A study led by Sarah Mann aimed to provide a fuller picture of the vegan diet in which no animal products are eaten, encompassing both the nutrition and health of the vegan diet. The study also delved into related ethical beliefs by studying scientific and popular literature in tandem. Furthermore, the study aimed to provide an insider's perspective of the vegan diet as a means of combating stereotypes and making the diet more relatable to those who are not vegan.

What is the main purpose of the text?

A) It presents rationale for adopting an increasingly popular diet.

B) It challenges a popular stereotype regarding a certain diet.

C) It discredits the supposed benefits of a popular diet.

D) It introduces a study that analyzes different facets of a diet.

142

Hibiscandelphis wilderianus was a relative of the hibiscus, a popular flower found in tropical regions. *H. wilderianus* had a limited range, as it was only known to grow on the lava fields on Mount Haleakala on Maui Island in Hawaii. It probably went extinct between 1910 and 1913, <u>when ranchers slashed the forest to make room to raise cattle.</u> In 2019, the scent was recreated using DNA from a preserved specimen.

What is the function of the underlined portion in the overall structure of the text?

A) It clarifies a potential misunderstanding.

B) It gives the logic for the following claim.

C) It provides a reason for a hypothesis.

D) It offers justification for an action.

143

The following text is adapted from Charles Dickens's 1853 novel *Bleak House*.

Fog everywhere. Fog up the river, where it flows among green meadows; fog down the river, where it rolls defiled among the tiers of shipping and the waterside pollutions of a great (and dirty) city. Fog on the Essex marshes, fog on the Kentish heights. Fog creeping into the cabooses of collier-brigs; fog lying out on the yards and hovering in the rigging of great ships; fog drooping on the gunwales of barges and small boats. Fog in the eyes and throats of ancient Greenwich pensioners, wheezing by the firesides of their wards; fog in the stem and bowl of the afternoon pipe of the wrathful skipper, down in his close cabin; fog cruelly pinching the toes and fingers of his shivering little 'prentice boy on deck.

What is the main purpose of the text?

A) It establishes the typical weather pattern of an area.

B) It introduces the range of industry in an area.

C) It shows the activities of a variety of characters.

D) It uses a metaphor to instill a sense of oppression.

144

The following text is adapted from Lewis Carroll's 1869 poem, *Poeta Fit, Non Nascitur*.

"In verse, when you are describing

  A shape, or sound, or tint;

Don't state the matter plainly,

  But put it in a hint;

And learn to look at all things

  With a sort of mental squint."

"For instance, if I wished, Sir,

  Of mutton-pies to tell,

Should I say 'dreams of fleecy flocks

  Pent in a wheaten cell'?"

"Why, yes," the old man said: "that phrase

  Would answer very well."

What is the purpose of the reference to mutton pies in the overall structure of the text?

A) It is given as a method for producing verse.

B) It offers an example to confirm some advice.

C) It is a sarcastic allusion to a shared reference.

D) It indicates that the speaker wants to change the subject.

145

Earth has over 200,000 glaciers, but global warming has been greatly accelerating the melting process so that they are now shrinking at unprecedented rates. One study hypothesizes that manmade contributions to global warming are accountable for the loss of one hundred percent of the glacial ice since 1850. Actually, <u>the number may be over one hundred percent</u>, as without those pressures placed on them, many glaciers might have added ice and increased in size during that time period.

What is the function of the underlined portion in the overall structure of the text?

A) It points out a discrepancy in calculations.

B) It emphasizes the extent of a problem.

C) It gives an alternative explanation.

D) It offers the reason for an observation.

146

The following text is adapted from Charlotte Bronte's 1853 novel, *Villette*.

My godmother lived in a handsome house in the clean and ancient town of Bretton. Her husband's family had been residents there for generations, and bore, indeed, the name of their birthplace—Bretton of Bretton: whether by coincidence, or because some remote ancestor had been a personage of sufficient importance to leave his name to his neighbourhood, I know not. When I was a girl I went to Bretton about twice a year, and well I liked the visit. The house and its inmates specially suited me. The large peaceful rooms, the well–arranged furniture, the clear wide windows, the balcony outside, looking down on a fine antique street, where Sundays and holidays seemed always to abide—so quiet was its atmosphere, so clean its pavement—these things pleased me well.

What is the main purpose of the text?

A) It describes a character's appearance.

B) It establishes an agreeable setting.

C) It hints at a change in circumstances.

D) It shows where the narrator resides.

147

The following text is adapted from Emily Dickenson's poem, *With a Flower*, published after her death in 1886.

> I hide myself within my flower,
>
> That wearing on your breast,
>
> You, unsuspecting, wear me too —
>
> And angels know the rest.
>
> I hide myself within my flower,
>
> That, fading from your vase,
>
> You, unsuspecting, feel for me
>
> Almost a loneliness.

Which choice best describes the overall structure of the text?

A) One paragraph shows the writer's love and the other shows the recipient's rejection of that love.

B) One paragraph shows how love grows and the second explains that love always dies.

C) The writer describes her desire to share her love and then what happens when she does express it.

D) The writer describes situations where she wants to show love but the recipient does not know.

148

The brightly-colored board game known as Parcheesi was introduced into the United States in the late 1860s, but the game actually predates that debut. In 1860, the British brought it from India, where it was known as *pachisi*. But that game, too, has older origins: it was derived from a game called *chaupar* that is referred to in texts as early as 540 to 300 B.C.

What is the overall purpose of the text?

A) To offer a counterargument to a claim

B) To give a brief historical outline

C) To explain the rules of a game

D) To point out a factual error

149

The following text is adapted from a speech given in 326 BC by Alexander the Great to his exhausted and dispirited soldiers on the banks of the Hydaspes River.

I could not have blamed you for being the first to lose heart if I, your commander, had not shared in your exhausting marches and your perilous campaigns; it would have been natural enough if you had done all the work merely for others to reap the reward. But it is not so. You and I, gentlemen, have shared the labour and shared the danger, and the rewards are for us all. The conquered territory belongs to you; already the greater part of its treasure passes into your hands, and when all Asia is overrun, the utmost hopes of riches or power which each one of you cherishes will be far surpassed, and whoever wishes to return home will be allowed to go, either with me or without me.

What is the main purpose of the underlined sentence in the text?

A) To explain that he would share the rewards with his soldiers

B) To motivate his soldiers to fight harder because the rewards would be shared

C) To emphasize that the wars being fought were a shared effort

D) To tempt his soldiers with the spoils of war

150

William Wordsworth was one of the founders of English Romanticism and one its most central figures and important intellects. He is remembered as a poet of spiritual and epistemological speculation, a poet concerned with the human relationship to nature and a fierce advocate of using the vocabulary and speech patterns of common people in poetry.

What is the main purpose of the text?

A) It describes the work of William Wordsworth.

B) It details the legacy of William Wordsworth.

C) It talks about the life of William Wordsworth.

D) It shows how important William Wordsworth was to English poetry.

151

Wordsworth's deep love for the "beauteous forms" of the natural world was established early. The Wordsworth children seem to have lived in a sort of rural paradise along the Derwent River, which ran past the terraced garden below their ample house. He began writing poetry as a young boy in grammar school, and before graduating from college, he went on a walking tour of Europe, which deepened his love for nature and his sympathy for the common man: both major themes in his poetry.

What is the main purpose of the text?

A) It explains the early life of Wordsworth.

B) Wordsworth's poetry was solely based on nature.

C) It explains why and how Wordsworth was influenced by nature.

D) It shows how important nature was to Wordsworth.

152

Dzoodzo Baniwa, a member of an Indigenous community in Brazil's Amazonas state, has been collecting data on the region's biodiversity for around 15 years. He lives in a remote village called Canadá on the Ayari River, a tributary of the Içana, which in turn, feeds the Rio Negro, one of the main branches of the Amazon. The nearest city, São Gabriel da Cachoeira, is a three–day trip by motorboat.

What is the purpose of the underlined portion in the overall structure of the text?

A) It emphasizes how remote the village of Canadá is.

B) It shows the vastness of the Amazonas state.

C) It highlights Dzoodzo Baniwa's life.

D) It describes the river network of the Amazon.

121. **Level:** Medium | **Skill/Knowledge:** Text Structure and Purpose

Key Explanation: Choice C is the best answer because the child says that there is not enough money for food and is hungry. The quote emphasizes that not only the miners are affected by the problem at hand; the families, including little children, are also suffering. Mother Jones could have introduced the fact that pluck–me stores take more than the monthly wage using statistics. However, using the voice of a child makes the issue seem more personal and pitiful, highlighting cruel or inhumane aspects of the practice rather than just the financial aspect.

Distractor Explanations: Choice A is incorrect because Mother Jones could show the difference needed using many different methods, such as quoting statistics. Therefore, she deliberately uses the voice of a child to emphasize a point other than just the specific amount of money. **Choice B** is incorrect because the description says that the miner goes shopping; it appears that the family goes together because the miner talks to the manager after the child reports that there is not enough money. **Choice D** is incorrect because the speaker is a child of a miner, but there is no reference that the child also works.

122. **Level:** Easy | **Skill/Knowledge:** Text Structure and Purpose

Key Explanation: Choice B is the best answer. The text adopts a neutral tone in describing or discussing the "situation" or "conditions" surrounding the Spix's macaw; the bird was extinct in the wild, but efforts have led to people breeding the bird to release in the wild again.

Distractor Explanations: Choice A is incorrect because the text does not identify something which should be changed, done, or avoided. A "warning" includes a message that needs to be followed, but the reader is not asked to do anything. **Choice C** is incorrect because "details" refers to specific information, but the passage only gives a broad overview of the general plan to breed and release birds into the wild. "Detailed steps" need more facts, such as where the breeding program occurs, how many birds are in it, when the program started, and how the new population will be monitored in the wild. **Choice D** is incorrect because a "request for assistance" is "asking for help." However, there is nothing mentioned which the average reader can do: for example, it does not ask for birds or money to be donated.

123. **Level:** Medium | **Skill/Knowledge:** Text Structure and Purpose

Key Explanation: Choice D is the best answer because pet dogs are brought up to show that there is a contrast between the way that the dogs are treated and the way that the miners are treated. The dogs have "a good place" and "a slave to take care of them," as well as attention from the wives of the mine owners. These conditions are contrasted with the conditions of the miners: "They wouldn't keep their dog where they keep you fellows." In other words, the conditions that the miners live in are more "sordid" or "foul" than the conditions that dogs live in.

Distractor Explanation: Choice A is incorrect because "consolation" is "comfort for a loss." However, the idea of dogs having better living conditions is not comforting to the miners. **Choice B** is incorrect because an "adversary" is an "opponent." There is no evidence that the dogs are competing with the miners. **Choice C** is incorrect because the description of the dogs does not show any "compassion" or "caring" on the part of the mine owners. The owners keep the miners in conditions worse than they keep their dogs. The wives may be compassionate towards the dogs, but **Choice C** refers to the mine owners.

124. **Level:** Hard | **Skill/Knowledge:** Text Structure and Purpose

Key Explanation: Choice C is the best answer because Saran Twombly is described as being the program director in the National Science Foundation's division of environmental biology, which implies that she is an "expert" or "authority" on the subject. Twombly's opinion is that the contributions are "unique" or "one–of–a–kind" because they use a creative method of matching different types of data. Twombly indicates that the study's methods have helped solve a problem that has "challenged ecologists for decades."

Distractor Explanations: Choice A is incorrect because Twombly's quote does not "clarify" or "define" any vocabulary. **Choice B** is incorrect because Twombly praises the study rather than giving a "counterargument" or "point that goes against" the premise of the study. **Choice D** is incorrect because, while Twombly talks about the "methodology" or "techniques" of the study, she does not mention "limitations" or "restrictions" that make the data less applicable.

125. **Level:** Medium | **Skill/Knowledge:** Text Structure and Purpose

Key Explanation: Choice C is the best answer because the study is about salt stress on chili peppers in Benin. Chili peppers are an important cash crop, but if they were raised in environments

that didn't have salt, there would be no need beyond curiosity to see how salt affects the plants. The comment that the soil has salt in it and irrigation is by water (rather than, for example, in controlled hydroponic tanks) shows that the farmers must deal with salt. The study can, therefore, help them understand ways in which the soil could be amended or growing practices altered to increase crop yield and nutrition.

Distractor Explanations: Choice A is incorrect because the author does not say that farmers should try growing different crops. The author is just trying to learn more about how the environment affects the crops. **Choice B** is incorrect because salinity is bad for the crops. Therefore, the comment that the soil salinity "is a reality" or "exists" shows that the environment is less than ideal. **Choice D** is incorrect because there are no suggestions for how to raise plants in salty conditions.

126. **Level:** Hard | **Skill/Knowledge:** Text Structure and Purpose

Key Explanation: Choice A is the best answer because the paragraph is discussing gaps in the current research. The claim that the data is "dispersed" or "spread out" shows that there are bits of data from sources that are far apart. The authors are trying to show that there needs to be a more comprehensive collection that "fills in the blanks" before conclusions can be drawn.

Distractor Explanations: Choice B is incorrect because "dispersed" refers to "spread out" rather than "announced to everyone." **Choice C** is incorrect because "comprehensive" refers to something that is complete, but the authors discuss many areas that are lacking information or "not complete." **Choice D** is incorrect because "incompatible" means "not able to get along with each other." There is no evidence that the groups are hostile to each other, only that there are many different groups that have pieces of data related to the field.

127. **Level:** Medium | **Skill/Knowledge:** Text Structure and Purpose

Key Explanation: Choice B is the best answer because Mother Jones is addressing the miners. She describes the conditions they suffer in order to show why change is needed. She emphasizes that they should not "compromise" or "accept lower terms" when they negotiate with mine owners: "But I want to say, make no settlement until they sign up that every bloody murderer of a guard has got to go."

Distractor Explanations: Choice A is incorrect because Mother Jones is not trying to "describe" or "explain" working conditions because her audience is the miners who undergo the conditions. She gives examples of conditions to support her argument that complete change is needed. **Choice C** is incorrect because she is not addressing members of the government. She is telling the miners not to give up when they request help from the government. **Choice D** is incorrect because she is not talking to the guards; if anything, she might be talking to the mine owners.

128. **Level:** Hard | **Skill/Knowledge:** Text Structure and Purpose

Key Explanation: Choice B is the best answer because "novel" is used to describe the gene HEPHL1 and how it is responsible for hair abnormalities. The gene itself is a natural part of the human chromosome, so has presumably been around for a long time. Therefore, "novel" is referring to the newly–discovered relationship with hair abnormalities rather than to the existence of the gene itself. "Novel" can refer to something that is "groundbreaking" or "innovative," so shows that the gene is an innovative answer for why hair abnormalities occur.

Distractor Explanations: Choice A is incorrect because there is no indication that HEPHL1 has never been classified, only that it hasn't been associated as "responsible for hair abnormalities." If the gene itself were newly found, "novel" would be better placed in the first line, "how the novel gene…." **Choice C** is incorrect because there is no indication that the gene is a "solution," only that "exploring the role" or "understanding how it works" might help find solutions in the future. There is not enough evidence to support **Choice D**; it is possible that the gene was known before the study.

129. **Level:** Medium | **Skill/Knowledge:** Text Structure and Purpose

Key Explanation: Choice B is the best answer because the text describes the one–page disclosure document. It suggests that the document can be used to check data and offers some of the main pieces of information that need to be on the document.

Distractor Explanations: Choice A is incorrect because the text only describes the disclosure agreement, one document, but there are "other documents" mentioned in the first sentence. **Choice C** is weak because the text lists what facts must be included in the document, but it does not "explain" or "clearly describe" how the rule itself protects the buyer. **Choice D** is incorrect because references are only a small portion of the text, not its main topic. The comment about references only rounds out the larger discussion of what is required on the disclosure document.

130. **Level:** Medium | **Skill/Knowledge:** Text Structure and Purpose

Key Explanation: Choice D is the best answer because the description of Ulysses' death in the hotel gives a valid reason for Anthony to have a "panic of despair and terror." The scene implies that Anthony saw his father die in an unpleasant way, and provides a logical reason that he had a "vague melancholy" for the rest of his life. Without knowing about the traumatic event, the reader might wonder why Anthony took his father's death so hard.

Distractor Explanations: Choice A is incorrect because Ulysses promised many trips, but only took one. Therefore, the death scene is a somewhat paradoxical image because it shows that Ulysses did not even keep the promise of completing one whole trip with his son; he died before it was over. **Choice B** is incorrect because, while the scene indicates that Ulysses had a painful death, that is not the reason that the author included the information. If there was no need to establish why Anthony had terror and panic that stayed with him for life, it would be sufficient to know only that his father died. **Choice C** is incorrect because the passage does not say that Anthony chooses to live in America. He was "brought back," which implies that others made the decision for him when he was too panicked to think for himself.

131. **Level:** Medium | **Skill/Knowledge:** Text Structure and Purpose

Key Explanation: Choice C is the best answer. The underlined sentence says that Sara flushed, which typically happens in anger or embarrassment. In this context, she appears embarrassed because she is not old or experienced enough—and was too "punctilious" or "careful"—to explain how she felt in a few words. The fact that she flushes highlights her sense of awkwardness and embarrassment.

Distractor Explanations: Choice A is incorrect because the sentence only says that Sara flushed. It does not explain what she looked like; she could be tall, short, dark–haired or blonde, dressed nicely, etc. **Choice B** is incorrect because the underlined sentence only establishes that Sara blushes. It does not give a reason why; the following sentences show she could speak French but was reluctant to tell Miss Minchin so. **Choice D** is incorrect because there is no interaction between characters in the following sentences. The underlined portion is expanded upon with a reason for blushing, not actions.

132. **Level:** Medium | **Skill/Knowledge:** Text Structure and Purpose

Key Explanation: Choice D is the best answer because "inhumanity" refers to actions that are extremely cruel or brutal. The passage says that the "guards of the mining companies beat, abuse, maim, and hold up citizens without process of law," which are all cruel or bad acts. The phrase "bloody murderer" shows that Mother Jones feels that the guards are not just "bad," but have reached the worst possible level of crime and brutality.

Distractor Explanations: Choice A is incorrect because the passage does not say that the guards actually murder anyone, only that they "beat, abuse, maim, and hold up citizens without process of law." Therefore, "bloody murderer" is not a literal description of the methods they use. **Choice B** is incorrect because, while murder would be a reason to remove the guards, there is no evidence that the guards murdered. The phrase only shows the extent of Mother Jones's contempt for the guards. **Choice C** is incorrect because the passage implies that the mine owners approve of the guards' tactics. There is no evidence to show that the mine owners think that the guards have gone too far in their actions.

133. **Level:** Medium | **Skill/Knowledge:** Text Structure and Purpose

Key Explanation: Choice A is the best answer because "astonishing" is used to describe the age, 26, when Adam Ulysses began his memoirs. Memoirs are typically a person's reflections on life that draw upon extensive experience, often as the person approaches old age. Therefore, the fact that a 26-year-old is writing about New York society is relatively presumptuous. The author is highlighting the "irony" or "incongruity" that the person has not seen much of life by that age, let alone enough to write a detailed analysis on a complex portion of society. The use of "astonishing" is further explained by showing that the book was "dull" or "boring," indicating that it did not capture the excitement or depth that Adam Ulysses was trying to achieve.

Distractor Explanation: Choices B and **C** are incorrect because the author is not trying to say that people have a high opinion—"admire" or "respect"—Adam Ulysses. They may be curious about his views, but do not necessarily think that he is a great person for writing memoirs. **Choice D** is incorrect because the book was not published because it was boring; this shows that Adam Ulysses was not a "talented" or "skilled" writer. Therefore, the author is not highlighting Adam's abilities, only the fact that he chose to write at a young age.

134. **Level:** Medium | **Skill/Knowledge:** Text Structure and Purpose

Key Explanation: Choice A is the best answer because the narrator is using the analogy of the theater to show that the whaling voyage was "brief" or "short" compared to his "extensive performances" or "longer jobs" as a merchant

sailor. The word "solo" hints that he only went on one whaling voyage, so it was not his "usual" or "regular" employment.

Distractor Explanations: Choice B is incorrect because the final sentence does not give any clue that a "tragedy" or "sad story" will follow. It only indicates that the narrator's experiences on the whaling boat, whatever they were, were a short break in his regular work. **Choice C** is incorrect because the final sentence does not give a "rationale" or "reason" for going on the voyage. The narrator indicates in the previous sentence that he does not really know why he chose to go; the final sentence explains that he only went once. **Choice D** is incorrect because, although the final sentence says that the narrator had had longer positions, it does not say that the narrator had no other choices when he decided to go on a whaling voyage.

135. **Level:** Medium | **Skill/Knowledge:** Text Structure and Purpose

Key Explanation: Choice B is the best answer because "background" refers to the context and circumstances related to the study. The text explains that the vegan diet is gaining "momentum" or "popularity" for various reasons. It also explains that there is "controversy" or "argument" about many aspects of the diet, including its "purpose and proposed benefits." Therefore, the paragraph gives the context so the reader understands the situation and offers a reason that Mann decided to conduct a study clarifying points about the diet, including why people choose to become vegan and whether it is nutritionally sound.

Distractor Explanations: Choice A is incorrect because no terms are "defined" or "explained"

in the text. "Vegan diet" is only described as "restrictive." **Choice C** is incorrect because the author's view is not given in the text, which only introduces the fact that there is a lot of controversy. **Choice D** is incorrect because "rationale" refers to the reasons behind something. There are general statements in the text about why someone might become vegan and for opposing veganism, but it does not delve into complete reasons for any specific decision or course of action regarding the matter.

136. **Level:** Medium | **Skill/Knowledge:** Text Structure and Purpose

Key Explanation: Choice C is the best answer because the text starts by explaining that Wuthering Heights is where a character lives, then defines the word to show that the place has extreme weather. The weather has formed the appearance of the exterior of the building with "stunted firs" and "gaunt thorns." The building is described as strong with deep-set windows and large, jutting stones. The result is an "impression" or "feeling" of a building that is imposing and durable.

Distractor Explanations: Choice A is incorrect because the weather is not the main purpose but a detail used to describe the building. **Choice B** is incorrect because the text does not say what Mr. Heathcliff is like at all. **Choice D** is incorrect because, while "wuthering" is defined, that word is used to describe the building. The definition is not the purpose of the text.

137. **Level:** Easy | **Skill/Knowledge:** Text Structure and Purpose

Key Explanation: Choice C is the best answer because the author expands on the quote by saying that veganism "has developed into a lifestyle" that incorporates other beliefs, such as animal or environmental activism and concern for physical

activity. Therefore, the author is trying to say that the vegan diet includes factors or beliefs that are not solely related to a "diet" or "food."

Distractor Explanations: Choices A and **B** are incorrect because while concern for animals and environmental advocacy are often aspects of veganism, on their own, they are not the only reasons to become a vegan. **Choice D** is incorrect because the quote is not comparing vegans and non-vegans. It is broadening the scope of veganism to include aspects that create a lifestyle, not just the food a person eats.

138. **Level:** Medium | **Skill/Knowledge:** Text Structure and Purpose

Key Explanation: Choice B is the best answer because in the poem, the author asks of the sea, "wilt welcome me?" and implores "Take me!" In other words, the author is talking to the sea as if it were the person that she hopes will accept her love.

Distractor Explanations: Choice A is incorrect because the author has no problems talking to the sea, asking questions about whether love will be accepted. **Choice C** is incorrect because no "depth" or "deepness" imagery is given in relation to the sea; more importantly, the sea refers to the other person, not the author's emotions. **Choice D** is incorrect because the complexities of love are better embodied by the brook that runs to the sea and might not get accepted.

139. **Level:** Medium | **Skill/Knowledge:** Text Structure and Purpose

Key Explanation: Choice A is the best answer because the text discusses the "first step" of the program "to send manned missions to Mars." The text says a spaceship was launched to gather information that will be used on a trip to the

Moon, which will then be a step towards the "much longer" trip to Mars.

Distractor Explanations: Choice B is incorrect because while gravity and vibrations are important to space travel, they are not the focus of the text. Gravity and vibrations are examples of "flight characteristics" that are being recorded, so they are a minor detail in the text. **Choice C** is incorrect because the author does not try to "argue" or "prove" that unmanned missions are safer; it appears that the author takes this idea for granted because the unmanned missions are "vital" for keeping astronauts safe on future missions. **Choice D** is incorrect because, while the text does discuss steps towards getting to the Moon, that is one part of the overall topic of getting humans to Mars.

140. **Level:** Medium | **Skill/Knowledge:** Text Structure and Purpose

Key Explanation: Choice B is the best answer. The sentence is a hypothetical situation, as indicated by the "if" at the start. The sentence shows that Squire Newcome thought that he "conferred distinction" or "gave honor" rather than "received it." In other words, Squire Newcome thought himself to be more important than the U.S. President, so he has a high "self–esteem" or "sense of importance."

Distractor Explanations: Choice A is incorrect because the sentence implies that Squire Newcome might not be as important as he thinks he is; the U.S. President is still more important. **Choice C** is incorrect because the situation is not true, as shown by the "if." **Choice D** is incorrect because, while some people might not like a person who has an inflated view of his own importance, the

sentence does not show that it is true in the case of Squire Newcome.

141. **Level:** Medium | **Skill/Knowledge:** Text Structure and Purpose

Key Explanation: Choice D is the best answer because the passage is telling about a study by Sarah Mann that is "aimed to provide a fuller picture of the vegan diet."

Distractor Explanations: Choice A is incorrect because, while the passage indicates that veganism is increasing in popularity ("The vegan diet has gained momentum in recent years"), the main point is not just to discuss "rationale" or "reasons" to become a vegan. **Choice B** is incorrect because the passage says that there are stereotypes regarding the diet, but it does not specifically attempt to show that one is wrong. **Choice C** is incorrect because the passage does not try to "discredit" or "prove something wrong."

142. **Level:** Medium | **Skill/Knowledge:** Text Structure and Purpose

Key Explanation: Choice C is the best answer because the underlined portion states that between 1910 and 1913, ranchers "slashed" or "severely cut" the forest. Since that is the time period that the *H. wilderianus* plant most likely went extinct, the underlined portion gives a reason for the "hypothesis" or "guess" about when the plant died: it was destroyed along with the forest.

Distractor Explanations: Choice A is incorrect because there is no obvious "misunderstanding" or "mistaken idea" that the reader might have that is changed by reading the underlined portion. **Choice B** is incorrect because the fact that ranchers cut the forest is not "logic" or "reason" that the scent was recreated; the fact that the plant went extinct is a reason to recreate it. **Choice D is** incorrect because "justification" refers to a valid reason for something, but destroying the forest to raise cattle is not a good reason for doing anything else mentioned in the text.

143. **Level:** Medium | **Skill/Knowledge:** Text Structure and Purpose

Key Explanation: Choice D is the best answer because "oppression" refers to misery and hardship. In the text, the fog is "defiled," which highlights the pollution of a city. The fog adds misery and hardship to a variety of people: pensioners who wheeze with fog in their lungs, puts out the pipe of a skipper, and pinches the toes of the cold apprentice. The paragraph creates the effect of gloom.

Distractor Explanations: Choice A is incorrect because there is no indication that the fog is "typical" or "usual"; it only appears unpleasant. **Choice B** is incorrect because the "range or industry" or "types of businesses" is not the focus of the paragraph; the different people suffering is most important. **Choice C** is incorrect because the paragraph is not designed to show what the people are doing so much as how their activities are made more difficult or uncomfortable by the fog.

144. **Level:** Hard | **Skill/Knowledge:** Text Structure and Purpose

Key Explanation: Choice B is the best answer because the first person gives instructions about not stating a matter plainly. The mutton pies are part of a question about wording, since they are paraphrased as dreams of fleecy flocks / Pent in a wheaten cell'? The response is that the phrase "would answer well" or "is good." Therefore, the mutton pies are an example that the old man "confirms" or "agrees are acceptable."

Distractor Explanations: Choice A is incorrect because the method is given in the first verse: describe things vaguely with a "mental squint." **Choice C** is incorrect because there is no indication that the question is "sarcastic" or spoken with irony; furthermore, there is no indication that there is a specific reference or backstory that both the speakers know about pies. **Choice D** is incorrect because the speaker is asking a question that is on the topic of writing verse, not changing the topic to something else.

145. **Level:** Hard | **Skill/Knowledge:** Text Structure and Purpose

Key Explanation: Choice B is the best answer because the underlined portion says that the percentage of ice melting due to human causes may be greater than one hundred percent. That number expands on the previous claim that a study shows one hundred percent of the ice has been lost. In other words, the underlined portion stresses the fact that the problem of melting may be even greater than the study suggests.

Distractor Explanations: Choice A is incorrect because the passage does not say that there is a "discrepancy" or "error," only that the true situation might be even greater if another factor, the lack of rebuilding ice, is taken into account. **Choice C** is incorrect because the added information is not an "alternative" or "different" explanation, it is an expansion on the same idea. **Choice D** is incorrect because the underlined portion only offers a statistical fact; the following portion is the reason that the numbers might be true.

146. **Level:** Medium | **Skill/Knowledge:** Text Structure and Purpose

Key Explanation: Choice B is the best answer because "agreeable" refers to "pleasant," and the entire passage is about the "handsome house" where the godmother lived. The description is a comfortable place that the narrator says "pleased me well."

Distractor Explanations: Choice A is incorrect because the passage describes a place, not a "character" or "person." The grandmother is discussed, but not her "appearance" or "how she looks." **Choice C** is incorrect because there is no "hint" or "clue" that the "circumstances" or "situation" will change. The story could be a pleasant memory that took place in Bretton. **Choice D** is incorrect because the passage shows where the godmother, not the narrator, resides. The narrator says she only went "about twice a year."

147. **Level:** Hard | **Skill/Knowledge:** Text Structure and Purpose

Key Explanation: Choice D is the best answer. The writer talks about two situations: when the recipient is wearing the flower and when the flower is in a vase. In both situations, the recipient is "unsuspecting" or "does not know" that the author has "hidden herself within the flower," meaning that she is giving her love but not saying anything.

Distractor Explanations: Choice A is incorrect because both paragraphs include references to the author's love, but the recipient never "rejects" or "turns down" the love. Instead, the recipient does not realize that the author feels that way; he is "unsuspecting." **Choice B** is incorrect because while the first paragraph may show that the author's love flourishes while the man is wearing her flower on his lapel, the second does not

explain that love "always" or "every time" dies. **Choice C** is incorrect because the author never "expresses" or "tells" about her love.

148. **Level:** Medium | **Skill/Knowledge:** Text Structure and Purpose

Key Explanation: Choice B is the best answer because the text offers the various dates that led up to the invention of the game Parcheesi. Therefore, it offers the "history" or "background" of the game.

Distractor Explanations: Choice A is incorrect because there is no claim that is being disproved with a "counterargument" or "opposing view." **Choice C** is incorrect because the reader does not learn how to play the game. Choice D is incorrect because there is no "factual error" or "untrue detail" discussed; the text just says that the game was invented elsewhere before it was introduced to the United States.

149. **Level:** Medium | **Skill/Knowledge:** Text Structure and Purpose

Key Explanation: Choice B is the best answer because it is initially mentioned that the soldiers are dispirited. Hence, Alexander is trying to motivate his soldiers to fight harder so that they may get a larger share.

Distractor Explanations: Choice A is incorrect because as mentioned in the underlined sentence, the reward has already been shared. **Choice C** is incorrect because he is not only emphasizing the shared effort. Rather, he is focused on sharing the rewards with his soldiers. **Choice D** is incorrect because there is no evidence that he is tempting his soldiers.

150. **Level:** Easy | **Skill/Knowledge:** Text Structure and Purpose

Key Explanation: Choice B is the best answer as the passage mainly talks about what William Wordsworth is remembered for, aka, his legacy.

Distractor Explanations: Choice A is incorrect because the text does not describe the work of Wordsworth. **Choice C** is incorrect because no information is given about his life. **Choice D** is incorrect because the majority of text does not give us information about Wordsworth's importance. Rather, the text details his legacy.

151. **Level:** Medium | **Skill/Knowledge:** Text Structure and Purpose

Key Explanation: Choice C is the best answer as the text primarily focuses on the ways Wordsworth was influenced by nature. For example, he lived in a "rural paradise along the Derwent River" and he went on a walking tour of Europe, which deepened his love for nature.

Distractor Explanations: Choice A is incorrect because the text does not focus only on his early life. **Choice B** is incorrect because the text does not mention that his poetry was solely based on nature, instead mentioning that "sympathy for the common man" was also a major theme. **Choice D** is incorrect because the text does not focus on the importance of nature to Wordsworth.

152. **Level:** Medium | **Skill/Knowledge:** Text Structure and Purpose

Key Explanation: Choice A is correct because the underlined portion only reinforces the already-mentioned idea that the village of Canadá is very remote ("He lives in a remote village called Canadá.")

Distractor Explanations: Choice B is incorrect because the underlined portion talks about how far Canadá is from the nearest city ("a three–day trip by motorboat") and does not mention the Amazonas state at all. **Choice C** is incorrect because the underlined portion does not mention Baniwa's life. **Choice D** is incorrect because the river network of the Amazon is not discussed in the underlined sentence.

Text 1

An iceberg is free–floating freshwater ice that is over 15 meters long that has calved—broken off—from a glacier or ice shelf. Since most of an iceberg is underwater, they can pose great hazards for marine traffic. Due to the sinking of the RMS *Titanic*, the International Ice Patrol was formed in 1914 to help monitor the locations of these dangerous obstacles.

Text 2

Iceberg calving is a frequent event as climate change is warming the earth. It is hard to generalize the impact of melting icebergs because they vary greatly in size and makeup. The freshwater floats on the saltwater of the ocean, and minerals such as iron can create blooms of phytoplankton. Large icebergs can also disrupt wave patterns in the surrounding waters that also affect wildlife.

Which choice would the authors of both texts most likely agree on?

A) Efforts to warn ships about icebergs should be strengthened.

B) The number of icebergs that calve has increased over time.

C) Icebergs can be difficult to monitor because most parts are not visible.

D) Large icebergs have the potential to cause serious problems.

Text 1

Air travel is a luxury that should be seriously questioned, as it consumes large amounts of fossil fuels merely for the pleasure of visiting a new place in person. One of the fastest growing sources of greenhouse gasses that contribute to climate change is passenger jets. In addition, jets are a serious source of noise pollution.

Text 2

Tourism forms about 10.3% of the world's GDP and is an effective tool for bolstering a region. Tourism creates new jobs and creates economic diversity so that a region is not reliant on only one industry. Tourism also brings in outside money that can be taxed by the government to provide essential public services like schools, law enforcement, and health benefits.

Based on the texts, how would the author of Text 1 respond to the argument in Text 2?

A) By pointing out that the drawbacks of tourism might outweigh the benefits

B) By saying that essential public services can be paid for in ways other than tourism

C) By questioning whether the data supporting Text 2 is actually true

D) By countering that most regions have enough economic diversity without tourism

155

Text 1

The Guinea worm is a parasite contracted primarily by drinking unpurified water. It lives in the digestive tract for about a year, where it can grow to about a meter long. There is no vaccine and no treatment for the pain when the adult parasite moves towards the skin, forms a blister, and finally erupts. Often victims suffer from debilitating secondary infections, but fortunately this condition is almost eradicated: there were only 15 reported cases in 2021.

Text 2

About forty percent of the known species in the world are parasitic. Parasites are organisms that survive to the detriment of others, and range from microbes to plants to insects and worms. However, parasites often have a very limited habitat that is restricted by the host, but they play multiple essential roles in the ecosystem such as maintaining populations. Therefore, it is important to study and preserve them.

How would the author of Text 2 most likely respond to the last sentence in Text 1?

A) With understanding, because some parasites are too dangerous to survive

B) With sadness, because the worm does not really cause people injury

C) With trepidation, because there could be unforeseen repercussions

D) With appreciation, because a painful parasite is almost gone

156

Text 1

Astronomers from the University of California–Berkeley worked out there could be as many as 40 billion Earth–sized exoplanets in the so-called "habitable zone" around their star, where temperatures are mild enough for liquid water to exist on the surface. There's even a potentially Earth–like world orbiting our nearest neighboring star, Proxima Centauri. At just four light years away, that system might be close enough for us to reach using current technology. The ancient question, "Are we alone?" has graduated from being a philosophical musing to a testable hypothesis. We should be prepared for an answer.

Text 2

Our observations suggest increasingly that earth–size planets orbiting within the habitable zone may be common in the galaxy. But are any of them inhabited? With no ability to send probes there to sample, we will have to derive the answer from the light and other radiation that come to us from these faraway systems. We also might not be able to detect biospheres even if they exist. Life has flourished on Earth for perhaps 3.5 billion years, but the atmospheric "biosignatures" that, today, would supply good evidence of life to distant astronomers have not been present for all of that time.

Based on the texts, how would the author of Text 2 most likely respond to the claim in Text 1: that encountering extraterrestrial life is now a testable hypothesis?

A) It is farfetched, as there is no method of exploring places where life might exist.

B) It is fallacious, as the only planet with a detectable biosphere is Earth.

C) It is plausible, as many planets could contain life in subsurface regions.

D) It is inconceivable, as there is no evidence that extraterrestrial life exists.

Text 1

Shoo–fly pie is a traditional molasses–based dessert made by the Pennsylvania Dutch. The first version was originally crustless and called the Centennial Cake, as it was developed for the 100th anniversary of the signing of the Declaration of Independence. The sweet pie got its common name because it forms a pool of molasses on top, so the housewives who made it always complained about "shooing" the flies away.

Text 2

The earliest known shoo–fly pie recipes were baked with no eggs, so historians speculate that they were made and eaten primarily in winter when the rich, sweet molasses would have been readily available and hens rarely laid eggs. As there are few flies in winter, the name actually refers to a popular circus animal called Shoo–fly the Boxing Mule.

Based on the texts, how would the author of Text 2 respond to the claim in the last sentence of Text 1?

A) By saying that the pie does not form a pool of molasses sweet enough to attract flies

B) By pointing out that there is a flaw in the theory about the common name

C) By claiming that the earliest shoo–fly pie recipes predate the Centennial Cake

D) By admitting that eggs would have stopped the problem of a pool of molasses forming

Text 1

Towering cumulus clouds are a form of isolated cloud that is changing into a thunderstorm. These clouds form in periods of atmospheric instability when low, large clouds have a significant amount of vertical movement. If there is enough moisture and lift, then the clouds can develop into a mature thunderstorm with strong rain and electrical discharges that manifest as thunder and lightning.

Text 2

Stratus clouds are uniform and flat, covering the sky with a very low–lying gray layer that has either no precipitation or only periodic drizzle. By contrast, nimbostratus are much thicker stratus clouds that are dense and dark, though they are at a similar level in the sky. These clouds produce steady, sometimes heavy, rain or snow.

Based on the texts, what do towering cumulus clouds and stratus clouds have in common?

A) They both occur during periods of atmospheric instability.

B) They both cover the sky in a thick layer, though the density is different.

C) They are both a form of cloud that is not found high in the sky.

D) They both result in strong rain, but stratus clouds do not produce thunder.

Text 1

In Costa Rica, there are about 300 stone spheres ranging in size from a few inches to over six feet across. The perfect symmetry of these sculptures indicate that they were carved by an advanced civilization with mathematical skills. It would have taken a significant effort to pound the shapes with larger stones than polish them with sand for the smooth finish they now have. Even more impressive was moving them, as the nearest source for the rocks—some up to 15 tons—was about 30 miles away.

Text 2

It is a fallacy to consider the stone spheres of Costa Rica as created by hand, as it is hardly possible for a society with no writing from around 200 B.C. to calculate and follow through with the process of shaping the virtually round rocks. About 50 miles away is a river, the Terraba, which could easily have produced the shapes in its current form, and all that was needed was to transport them to the current location with rafts.

With which of the following points would the authors of Text 1 and Text 2 both agree?

A) For the rocks to have their present shape, there was a need for some refining.

B) Moving the rocks to their present location would have been difficult at the time.

C) At the time the rocks were formed, the people in Costa Rica were extremely advanced.

D) No matter how they were formed, the rocks had to be transported a great distance.

Text 1

The global oceans are an important sink for human–released CO_2, absorbing nearly a quarter of the total CO_2 emissions every year. Of all ocean regions, the Southern Ocean below the 35th parallel south plays a particularly vital role. "Given the importance of the Southern Ocean to the global oceans' role in absorbing atmospheric CO_2, we must continue to expand our measurements in this part of the world despite the challenging environment," says lead investigator Colm Sweeney.

Text 2

It was an audacious idea: To send an unmanned research vehicle called a *saildrone* on a 13,670–mile journey around Antarctica alone, at the mercy of the most hostile seas on the planet. In winter. Despite a run-in with an iceberg that wrecked some of its sensors, Saildrone 1020 completed its mission on August 3, 2019, having successfully collected oceanic and atmospheric carbon dioxide measurements. "It was a high-risk, high reward kind of deployment," NOAA oceanographer Adrienne Sutton said. "We weren't sure it was going to make it."

How would Sweeney in Text 1 most likely respond to Sutton's claim at the end of Text 2?

A) By saying that the imperative for more concrete data justified the risks taken

B) By saying that the resulting conclusions were not commensurate with the dangers

C) By saying that the research was redundant after previous studies

D) By saying that the data could have been gathered using less risky methods

Text 1

Ball lightning is a rare atmospheric effect that has been reported multiple times over the centuries, but which has not been scientifically explained. Part of the problem is that the event is unpredictable, so it is impossible to set up a controlled experiment that incorporates all of the relevant variables. Eyewitness accounts vary, but describe balls of light associated with lightning storms that travel in unpredictable trajectories for several seconds before exploding or vanishing, often amid the odor of sulfur.

Text 2

The Serbian–American inventor Nikola Tesla, apparently out of curiosity, decided to recreate the effect known as ball lightning. He managed to produce balls of light with the same appearance as ball lightning multiple times in laboratory settings, but it is unclear whether such balls actually form in the same fashion as the actual phenomenon does.

Based on the texts, how would the author of Text 1 most likely respond to the claim in Text 2 that Tesla produced ball lightning?

A) By doubting the accuracy of the report

B) By claiming that such results are irreplicable

C) By conceding that the argument in Text 1 is flawed

D) By agreeing that such a demonstration is possible

Text 1

The tomb of the Egyptian King Tutankhamun was opened in 1922 by a team led by Howard Carter. Subsequently, the deaths of at least five people have been attributed to a curse associated with the excavations. Though there was actually no curse directly written on any of the walls or ornaments within the tomb, there is a belief that handling mummies will bring bad luck, illness, or death upon anyone involved.

Text 2

Very few Egyptian graves have a written curse associated with them, and most are from the Old Kingdom; one of the most notable is that of the 6th dynasty ruler Kentika Ikhekhi. Despite that fact, many deaths have been attributed to a "pharaoh's curse" that protects ancient tombs from desecration. In reality, many such deaths may indeed be related, but they have scientific causes rather than spiritual ones. For example, early explorers did not know to protect themselves against bacterial infections or radiation.Based on the texts, how would the author of Text 2 most likely respond to the claim in Text 1 that "the deaths of at least five people have been attributed to a curse?"

A) By admitting that it is possible that the deaths were linked to a curse because some tombs contained them

B) By pointing out that the people must have died of natural causes that were unrelated to their field of study

C) By arguing that there were probably causes associated with the tomb that contributed to the deaths

D) By saying that there is no basis for making such a claim because curses only existed on a few tombs

Text 1

The Salar de Uyuni in Bolivia contains about 17 percent of the world's lithium reserves, so the region needs to enter in the market to meet the demand for lithium for the production of rechargeable batteries. Rechargeable batteries are essential technology for reducing greenhouse gas emissions because they are now being effectively adapted for use in electric vehicles.

Text 2

While it is true that there are huge lithium reserves under the Salar de Uyuni in Bolivia, tapping those reserves is a controversial issue. The process of refining the element requires a significant amount of water, and if groundwater is extracted for that purpose, then it could place pressure on farmers whose livelihoods depend on water to raise food crops for the region's population.

Based on the texts, how would the author of Text 2 respond to the argument in Text 1?

A) By claiming that rechargeable batteries are not as essential as Text 1 says they are

B) By stating that certain factors need to be considered before enacting Text 1's plan

C) By pointing out that Text 1 makes faulty calculations about the demand for lithium

D) By conceding that local needs might be subordinated to the greater benefits stated

Text 1

Parasitic infections, caused by intestinal helminths and protozoan parasites, are among the most prevalent infections in humans in developing countries. In developed countries, protozoan parasites more commonly cause gastrointestinal infections compared to helminths. Intestinal parasites cause significant morbidity and mortality in endemic countries.

Text 2

The most common protozoan parasites are *G. intestinalis, Entamoeba histolytica*, and *Cryptosporidium spp. G. intestinalis* is the most prevalent parasitic cause of gastrointestinal diseases like diarrhea in the developed world, and this infection is also very common in developing countries.

Which choice would the authors of both texts agree on?

A) Efforts to destroy parasitic infections must be increased.

B) The frequency of parasitic infections is increasing.

C) Endemic countries are at risk of intestinal parasites.

D) Protozoan parasites can frequently cause gastrointestinal infections, resulting in diarrhea.

165

Text 1

"Continental drift" describes one of the earliest ways geologists thought continents moved over time. Today, the theory of continental drift has been replaced by the science of plate tectonics. The theory of continental drift is most associated with the scientist Alfred Wegener. In the early 20th century, Wegener published a paper explaining his theory that the continental landmasses were "drifting" across the earth, sometimes plowing through oceans and into each other. He called this movement *continental drift*.

Text 2

One of the elements lacking in the theory of continental drift was the mechanism for how it works — why did the continents drift and what patterns did they follow? Wegener suggested that perhaps the rotation of the earth caused the continents to shift towards and apart from each other. (It doesn't.) Today, we know that the continents rest on massive slabs of rock called *tectonic plates*. The plates are always moving and interacting in a process called "plate tectonics."

What would the author of text 2 most likely respond to the author of text 1?

A) With understanding because Wegener's theory was correct

B) With disagreement because scientists did not accept Wegener's theory of continental drift

C) With hesitance because alternate theories disproved Wegener's theory

D) With appreciation because Wegener was one of the earliest geologists

153. **Level:** Medium | **Skill/Knowledge:** Cross–Text Connections

Key Explanation: Choice D is the best answer because both authors refer to problems, though the effects are different. Text 1 refers to the danger of icebergs to marine traffic; the serious problem of sinking ships is great enough to have formed a group to monitor the locations of icebergs. Text 2 also refers to serious problems from melting: freshwater on top of seawater, phytoplankton blooms, and altered wave patterns.

Distractor Explanations: Choice A is incorrect because Text 1 says that a group has been created to monitor icebergs, but does not say that such efforts are not enough and should be "strengthened" or "made more rigorous." Also, Text 2 does not refer to ships at all. **Choice B** is incorrect because Text 2 obliquely indicates that more icebergs are calving, but there is no mention of that in Text 1. **Choice C** is incorrect because Text 2 does not say that icebergs are difficult to monitor due to visibility; it only says that the effects are hard to "generalize" or "apply to every case."

154. **Level:** Hard | **Skill/Knowledge:** Cross–Text Connections

Key Explanation: Choice A is the best answer because the author of Text 1 says that "Air travel is a luxury that should be seriously questioned," meaning that the author has doubts that air travel should be exist at all; the author feels it is a "luxury" rather than a necessity and causes environmental harm. Therefore, the author would say that the benefits of tourism might not "outweigh" or "be worth more" than the "drawbacks" or "problems."

Distractor Explanations: Choice B is incorrect because the author of Text 1 does not discuss how public services should be paid for. The author could feel that these services will suffer, but that the risk is worth eliminating air traffic. **Choice C** is incorrect because the author of Text 1 does not "question" or "doubt" that the data is true. The author does not discuss the related data at all. **Choice D** is incorrect because the author of Text 1 does not address economic diversity. The author could feel that diversity will decrease, but that it is worth eliminating air travel.

155. **Level:** Hard | **Skill/Knowledge:** Cross–Text Connections

Key Explanation: Choice C is the best answer because "trepidation" means "concern." The author of Text 2 says that parasites "play essential roles in the ecosystem" and that "it is important to study and preserve them." In other words, there may be roles that are unknown, and eliminating the Guinea worm could lead to "repercussions" or "consequences" that are "unforeseen" or "not yet predicted."

Distractor Explanations: Choice A is incorrect because the author of Text 2 does not say that some parasites should be eliminated; the author says that they should be studied because they play many roles. **Choice B** is incorrect because the author of Text 2 does not deny that the Guinea worm can harm people. **Choice D** is incorrect because the author of Text 2 says that parasites should be "preserved" or "kept." Therefore, the author would not be glad that a parasite is gone.

156. **Level:** Medium | **Skill/Knowledge:** Cross–Text Connections

Key Explanation: Choice A is the best answer because "farfetched" means "very unlikely." The author of Text 2 says that there is "no ability to send probes there to sample," so there is no way of "encountering" or "meeting" extraterrestrial life in person. Instead, Text 2 indicates we can only learn about life through second–hand methods such as scanning the "light and other radiation" from systems that may contain life, and the "biosignature" searched for in such testing might not reveal life even if it exists. Therefore, the author of Text 2 would say it is not "testable" now to meet or identify specific types of life, though it may be possible to detect signs of life.

Distractor Explanations: Choice B is incorrect because "fallacious" means "based on a mistaken belief." The author of Text 2 might say the idea was fallacious because it is impossible to go somewhere to meet the organisms, but it indicates that it is possible that other planets are similar to Earth in being able to host life. **Choice C** is incorrect because "plausible" means "reasonable" or "likely." However, the author of Text 2 does not delve into where life might be found on the planets. However, if life can only be detected from afar, it probably is harder to find under the surface. **Choice D** is incorrect because the author of Text 2 indicates that life could exist, though we do not have evidence of it yet. Therefore, meeting life is not "inconceivable" or "not possible," just "not likely."

157. **Level:** Easy | **Skill/Knowledge:** Cross–Text Connections

Key Explanation: Choice B is the best answer because the claim in the final sentence of Text 1 is that the name of the shoo–fly pie comes from housewives who shooed the flies away. However, Text 2 directly says that the name comes from a different source, a circus animal, because

there were no flies to shoo away when the pie was usually eaten. Hence, there is a "flaw" or "problem" with the theory in Text 1.

Distractor Explanations: Choice A is incorrect because the author of Text 2 refers to "rich, sweet molasses," so probably would agree about the taste. There is no discussion in Text 2 about whether a pool forms or not. **Choice C** is impossible to determine from Text 2 because there is no specific date associated with "the original recipes." **Choice D** is incorrect because the author of Text 2 does not discuss a pool, so it is unclear from the text whether that problem existed or how it could be solved.

158. **Level:** Medium | **Skill/Knowledge:** Cross–Text Connections

Key Explanation: Choice C is the best answer because Text 1 says that towering cumulus forms from "low, large clouds." Text 2 says that stratus clouds form "a very low–lying gray layer." Therefore, both are low rather than high in the sky.

Distractor Explanations: Choice A is incorrect because Text 2 does not refer to atmospheric instability at all. **Choice B** is incorrect because Text 1 says that towering cumulus clouds are "isolated" or "alone" rather than a thick layer. **Choice D** is incorrect because stratus clouds have "either no precipitation or only periodic drizzle," so they do not form strong rains.

159. **Level:** Medium | **Skill/Knowledge:** Cross–Text Connections

Key Explanation: Choice D is the best answer because Text 1 says that "nearest source for the rocks…was about 30 miles away," which made moving them "impressive," so it was a long distance. Text 2 also says that the distance was far because they probably came from a river "about 50 miles away."

Distractor Explanations: Choice A is incorrect because "refining" refers to "finishing" or "polishing" something. Text 1 says that the rocks were polished with sand, but Text 2 implies that there was no need to shape them after taking them from the river. **Choice B** is incorrect because in Text 2, the phrase "all that was needed" implies that it was easy; only rafts were required. **Choice C** is incorrect because Text 1 refers to advanced civilizations, but Text 2 does not. Text 2 refers to "a society with no writing" that could not calculate how to shape the spheres.

160. **Level:** Medium | **Skill/Knowledge:** Cross-Text Connections

Key Explanation: Choice A is the best answer because Sweeney claims that "we must continue to expand our measurements in this part of the world despite the challenging environment." In other words, the data needs to be collected even though the environment is "challenging" or "dangerous." He would therefore most likely say that the risks were "justified" or "acceptable" because there was an "imperative" or "great need" for more measurements.

Distractor Explanation: Choice B is incorrect because "commensurate" means "corresponding in degree." However, Sweeney acknowledges both the great need for data and the potential great danger. Therefore, he would consider them both to have a similar degree. **Choice C** is incorrect because Sweeney would not call additional research "redundant" or "repetitive and not needed." He points out that "we must continue to expand our measurements," meaning he thinks more measurements are needed beyond those from previous studies. **Choice D** is unsupported by any evidence because Sweeney does not compare various methods of collecting data. Therefore, it is impossible to tell his opinion of the risk level of the saildrone project.

161. **Level:** Hard | **Skill/Knowledge:** Cross-Text Connections

Key Explanation: Choice D is the best answer because the author of Text 1 says that setting up a laboratory experiment that "incorporates all of the relevant variables" or "includes every factor related to ball lightning" is impossible. However, the author does not say that experiments that replicate some of the variables, such as Tesla's replication of the "appearance" of the balls, cannot be done.

Distractor Explanations: Choice A is incorrect because there is no indication that the author of Text 1 would "doubt" or "not believe" that Tesla could make something which looked like ball lightning. He would just say that it was not true ball lightning. **Choice B** is incorrect because "irreplicable" refers to not being able to do something more than once. However, Tesla demonstrated the balls of light "multiple times," and the author of Text 1 does not say that lab experiments cannot be done more than once. **Choice C** is incorrect because the information in Text 2 is compatible with that in Text 1, so there is no need to "concede" or "admit" that his own argument is "flawed" or "has mistakes in it."

162. **Level:** Hard | **Skill/Knowledge:** Cross-Text Connections

Key Explanation: Choice C is the best answer. The author of Text 2 points out that "many such deaths may indeed be related, but they have scientific causes rather than spiritual ones." In other words, the deaths have "causes associated with the tomb" such as bacteria found inside.

Distractor Explanations: Choice A is incorrect because the author of Text 2 uses the transition "in reality" to show that the previous discussion, the idea that there really are curses protecting the tombs, is not real. Instead, the author of Text 2 offers scientific reasons rather than spiritual ones like a curse. **Choice B** is incorrect because the causes that the author of Text 2 discusses, such as bacterial infections or radiation, are related to the study of the tombs. **Choice D** is incorrect because the author of Text 2 does say there are only a few curses, but does not deny that people died after opening Egyptian tombs. The author gives scientific reasons for the deaths, so there is a "basis" or "foundation" for the claim that people died in association with handling the mummies.

163. **Level:** Medium | **Skill/Knowledge:** Cross–Text Connections

Key Explanation: Choice B is the best answer because Text 2 points out that "tapping" or "mining" the lithium is a "controversial issue," which means that there are disagreements about the plan. Text 2 then continues to explain one side that needs to be "considered" or "thought about" before the plan is "enacted" or "pursued": the problem of the groundwater needs to be solved so that farmers can still pursue their "livelihoods" or "careers" and the region still has food.

Distractor Explanations: Choice A is incorrect because Text 2 does not discuss the value of batteries, only the problem of using too much groundwater to mine the lithium. **Choice C** is incorrect because there is no indication that Text 1 made "faulty calculations" or "erroneous measures." **Choice D** is incorrect because the author of Text 2 does not "concede" or "admit" that the needs of the farmers should be "subordinated" or "made less important" than the need for car batteries.

164. **Level:** Medium | **Skill/Knowledge:** Cross–Text Connections

Key Explanation: Choice D is the best answer as both texts mention that protozoan parasites can cause infections like diarrhea. Text 1 mentions "protozoan parasites more commonly cause gastrointestinal infections" and text 2 mentions "*G. intestinalis* is the most prevalent parasitic cause of gastrointestinal diseases like diarrhea." The first sentence in text 2 mentions that *G. intestinalis* is a common protozoan parasite.

Distractor Explanations: Choices A and **B** are incorrect because neither of the two texts mention that efforts to destroy parasitic infections must be increased or that the frequency of parasitic infections is increasing. **Choice C** is incorrect because text 1 only mentions that "intestinal parasites cause a significant morbidity and mortality in endemic countries" and not that endemic countries are at risk.

165. **Level:** Hard | **Skill/Knowledge:** Cross–Text Connections

Key Explanations: Choice B is the correct answer as text 2 talks about what the theory of continental drift lacked. It also disapproves Wegener's theory of continental drift. Therefore, we can infer that scientists did not accept Wegener's theory of continental drift.

Distractor Explanations: Choice A is incorrect because text 2 explains how Wegener's theory was incorrect. **Choice C** is incorrect because there is no information about alternate theories. Only one other theory is mentioned, (*i.e.*, plate tectonics). **Choice D** is incorrect because text 2 does not mention anything about Wegener being one of the earliest geologists.

Chapter 5

Expression of Ideas

This chapter includes questions on the following topics:

- Rhetorical Synthesis
- Transitions

When researching a topic, a student has taken the following notes:

- *A Sunday Afternoon on the Island of La Grande Jatte* is the most famous painting by French artist Georges Seurat and is one of the archetypal pictures in the neo–impressionist style.

- *Sunday Afternoon* was painted between 1884 and 1886 from a series of oil sketches that Seurat made in the park and it now hangs in the Art Institute of Chicago.

- Seurat used a type of painting called pointillist, though he preferred the term divisionism at the time, which involved putting small dots of color next to each other that optically blend into an image.

- *Sunday Afternoon* is about 6.6 by 9.9 feet (2 × 3 meters) and was painted with many extremely bright colors including the new zinc yellow, which started oxidizing and becoming darker even during Seurat's lifetime.

The student wants to explain the present condition of *Sunday Afternoon*. Which choice most effectively uses relevant information from the notes to accomplish this goal?

A) The most famous painting by Georges Seurat, *Sunday Afternoon*, is a classic of the neo–impressionist style and uses tiny dots of bright colors to create a whole image.

B) Between 1884 and 1886, Georges Seurat used a style of painting now called pointillism, which consists of tiny dots of bright colors close together, in the *Sunday Afternoon*.

C) Georges Seurat's *Sunday Afternoon* is currently in the Art Institute of Chicago, though some of the colors are darker than in 1886 when Seurat completed the painting.

D) *Sunday Afternoon*, Georges Seurat uses a style that he called divisionism but which is now called pointillism to create optical effects that were brighter than mixed colors

When researching a topic, a student has taken the following notes:

- Rathcroghan is an archaeological site in county Roscommon, Ireland, that contains burial mounds, forts, standing stones, and other structures.

- Rathcroghan covers over two square miles and contains at least 240 sites that are about 5,500 years old, but none have been excavated.

- There are no urban centers, so Rathcroghan was not a town, but instead the residence of nobility or a gathering place for festivals.

- There is a cave which is said to be the entrance to the underworld.

- The holiday of Samhain, which over time turned into Halloween, is thought to have originated at Rathcroghan.

The student wants to explain the archaeological significance of Rathcroghan. Which choice most effectively uses relevant information from the notes to accomplish this goal?

A) Rathcroghan is an area of 240 unexcavated sites in Ireland with 5,500–year–old structures such as mounds, forts, and standing stones that may be associated with a noble's residence or a gathering place for festivals.

B) Rathcroghan in Roscommon, Ireland, has a cave which people believed was the entrance to the underworld, and this place is possibly the origin of the holiday Samhain, which evolved into Halloween.

C) In Roscommon, Ireland, there is a site called Rathcroghan with structures about 5,500 years old, including burial mounts, forts, and standing stones, which may be associated with the holiday of Samhain.

D) Though it was not a town, Rathcroghan in Roscommon, Ireland, could have had many other uses in relation to the holiday of Samhain, but because it contains over 240 sites that have not been excavated, it is hard to determine.

When researching a topic, a student has taken the following notes:

- The Sun's average temperature is over 5,000 degrees Celsius and the surface has constantly changing magnetic fields.

- A solar flare is a fast burst of radiation that can cause serious repercussions on Earth, such as impeding communications.

- A solar prominence is an arc of plasma that has an electric charge that can form in less than a day.

- A solar prominence can last for many months and remains attached to the Sun's corona.

- A solar prominence looks like a black line when silhouetted against a sunspot.

The student wants to explain the difference between a solar flare and a solar prominence to an audience that has basic knowledge about the Sun. Which choice most effectively uses relevant information from the notes to accomplish this goal?

A) A solar flare is a fast burst of radiation and a solar prominence can last many months.

B) A solar prominence, unlike a solar flare, looks black when it is silhouetted against a sunspot.

C) Unlike a solar flare, a fast burst of radiation, a solar prominence lasts longer and remains as a plasma arc attached to the Sun.

D) Solar prominences do not cause repercussions on Earth, whereas solar flares can cause problems to communication.

When researching a topic, a student has taken the following notes:

- Cheddar cheese is made from cows' milk that is cultured, which means that bacteria is added to acidify it.

- The taste varies depending on how long it is aged: mild (2–3 months), sharp (6–9 months), or extra–sharp (1–2 years).

- The texture changes from creamy to hard as the cheese ages, and the color may be white, its natural color, or orange.

- The orange color associated with the cheese is because cows in the past had a diet rich in beta–carotene, which tainted the milk orange.

- Modern cheddar cheese uses colorants, often annatto, which is the fruit of the achiote tree that is native to tropical regions in the Americas.

The student wants to answer the question of why cheddar cheese is often orange. Which choice most effectively uses relevant information from the notes to accomplish this goal?

A) In the past, cheddar cheese was orange because the cows ate beta–carotene to give it color, but today a different process is used since the cheese is white in its natural form.

B) Cheddar cheese comes from cows' milk that is aged at different lengths of time to give it different flavors, textures, and colors, so the younger cheese is white and older cheese is orange.

C) Cheddar cheese is made from cows' milk that is cultured, and depending on what the cows consume, the cheese can vary from white to orange.

D) Although natural cheddar cheese is white, it is sometimes colored with additives such as annatto from the tropical achiote tree, because historically, the cheese was slightly orange from beta–carotene in the cows' food.

When researching a topic, a student has taken the following notes:

- Carl Friedrich Gauss (1777–1855) is considered to be one of the most important mathematicians of all time.

- A child prodigy, he corrected a math error in his father's account books when he was 3 years old.

- He proved many mathematical theorems which were only conjectural, including ones by Fermat, Descartes, and Kepler.

- In 1801, an astronomer found and tracked the dwarf planet Ceres for about a month before it got lost behind the Sun and did not reappear where expected. Gauss used the data and correctly predicted where it could be found later that year.

- Gauss was active in adding important practical applications of math to many fields, including magnetics and geological surveys.

- Between 1989 and 2001, a picture of Gauss was on the German 10–mark banknote.

The student wants to explain who Gauss is to someone who has never heard of the person. Which choice most effectively uses relevant information from the notes to accomplish this goal?

A) From a very young age, Carl Friedrich Gauss (1777–1855) showed proficiency in mathematics and proved the theorems of mathematicians like Fermat, Descartes, and Kepler.

B) The German mathematician Carl Friedrich Gauss (1777–1855) was one of the most important people in his field and contributed greatly to other fields, including astronomy, magnetics, and geological surveys.

C) Carl Friedrich Gauss (1777–1855) was such a good mathematician that he was able to predict the location of the dwarf planet Ceres in 1801 after some astronomers were unable to find it.

D) A child prodigy solving math problems starting at age 3, Carl Friedrich Gauss (1777–1855) worked in the fields of astronomy, magnetics, and geological surveys, including predicting where to find the dwarf planet Ceres in 1801.

When researching a topic, a student has taken the following notes:

- The coldest place in North America is Mt. Denali in Alaska, which reached −73 degrees Celsius; it is the second–coldest place on Earth.

- Satellite data shows that the Dome Argus and Dome Fuji areas on the Eastern Antarctic Plateau might have air temperatures as low as −94 degrees Celsius, the coldest on Earth.

- Vostok Research Station in Antarctica had the lowest recorded surface temperature ever in July, 1983, at −89.2 degrees Celsius.

- Vostok Research Station has only 20 millimeters of precipitation per year.

- The coldest permanently inhabited location is Oymyakon, Siberia in Russia, with the lowest temperature being −67.7 degrees Celsius.

- Oymyakon has a population under 500, and schools remain open unless the temperature drops below −55 degrees Celsius.

The student wants to emphasize how cold the coldest temperatures on Earth are relative to other places. Which choice most effectively uses relevant information from the notes to accomplish this goal?

A) Oymyakon in Siberia is the coldest permanently inhabited place, and it is so cold that fewer than 500 people live there and children still go to school in weather as cold as −55 degrees Celsius.

B) The coldest temperatures in North America, on Mt. Denali in Alaska, are nothing compared to the freezing conditions in the Dome Argus and Dome Fuji areas in Antarctica.

C) Antarctica has the coldest temperatures on Earth, as low as −94 degrees Celsius, as compared to the next coldest location, Mt. Denali in Alaska, which only gets down to −73 degrees Celsius.

D) People are unable to live year–round in the coldest places of the Earth, but less than 500 live in Oymyakon, Siberia, which has gotten as low as −67.7 degrees Celsius.

When researching a topic, a student has taken the following notes:

- The Stratemeyer Syndicate was founded by Edward Stratemeyer and lasted from 1899 to 1981 when it was sold.

- The Syndicate packaged adventure book series designed for children and after 1911, focused on mysteries.

- The series included popular protagonists such as Nancy Drew, The Hardy Boys, The Dana Girls, and The Rover Boys.

- Stories were written by ghostwriters who used the same pseudonym for each series.

- The first ghostwriter for Nancy Drew was Mildred Wirt Benson, who wrote the first seven books under the name Carolyn Keene.

- The Nancy Drew series continued for 175 volumes written by dozens of authors.

The student wants to describe the Stratemeyer Syndicate production process for someone who knows the Nancy Drew book series. Which choice most effectively uses relevant information from the notes to accomplish this goal?

A) The Stratemeyer Syndicate, formed by Edward Stratemeyer, wrote adventure books such as Nancy Drew during its existence from 1899 to 1981, after which it was sold.

B) Edward Stratemeyer formed a syndicate with his name in order to hire people to write Nancy Drew and other stories such as The Hardy Boys, The Dana Girls, and The Rover Boys.

C) Ghostwriters wrote the remaining 175 volumes of the Nancy Drew series after Carolyn Keene wrote the first seven for the Stratemeyer Syndicate.

D) The Nancy Drew series is an example of the production style used by the Stratemeyer Syndicate (1899–1981), since dozens of ghostwriters starting with Mildred Wirt Benson all wrote adventure books under the name Carolyn Keene.

When researching a topic, a student has taken the following notes:

- Blue whales are the largest animal to ever live on Earth and can grow up to 100 feet and weigh 219 tons.

- Whale sharks are the largest species of fish and can grow up to 61.7 feet and 47,000 pounds.

- Blue whales are mammals and whale sharks are sharks that are not related to whales at all.

- Blue whales are filter feeders that actively grab mouthfuls of plankton and krill and then expel the water through fine teeth called a baleen.

- Whale sharks swim and passively consume plankton and other small creatures that enter their mouths.

- Whale sharks live in water over 70 degrees Fahrenheit, but blue whales live in all the oceans.

The student wants to highlight a similarity between blue whales and whale sharks. Which choice most effectively uses relevant information from the notes to accomplish this goal?

A) Though one is a mammal and one is a fish, blue whales and whale sharks are both filter feeders that eat plankton and other small foods from the water.

B) Blue whales and whale sharks are both extremely large animals, growing up to 100 feet and 61.7 feet, respectively.

C) Blue whales and whale sharks both have "whale" in their names, but they are not related and eat food in different ways.

D) Both blue whales and whale sharks are both extremely large and live in water that is over 70 degrees Fahrenheit.

When researching a topic, a student has taken the following notes:

- In Jakarta, Indonesia, over 40% of the land is below sea level.

- Global warming increases the level of the ocean by about 1/8 of an inch per year.

- In some districts of Jakarta such as Demak Regency, over 1,000 acres per year, about 0.5% of the area, is reclaimed by the ocean.

- Many residents do not have the financial ability to move, even though their homes are often flooded during high tide.

- Indonesia sinks at a rate of up to 4 inches per year, in part due to pumping of reserves of groundwater when the monsoons season was delayed.

The student wants to emphasize the difficulties that climate change can cause for people. Which choice most effectively uses relevant information from the notes to accomplish this goal?

A) Since over 40% of the land in Jakarta, Indonesia, is below the sea level, a 1/8 increase in the ocean level per year due to global warming can have serious repercussions for the people who live there.

B) Climate change causes serious problems such as a rising ocean and delayed monsoons that have forced residents of Jakarta, Indonesia, to pump their reserves of groundwater and lower the land.

C) Many districts in Jakarta, Indonesia, are rapidly becoming submerged as the ocean rises and the land sinks due to global warming, but residents cannot afford to move from flooded housing.

D) Jakarta, Indonesia is seriously affected by climate change because the rising sea levels encroach on the land at a rate of over 1,000 acres per year in some areas such as Demak Regency.

When researching a topic, a student has taken the following notes:

- Leonardo da Vinci (1452–1519) was an architect, engineer, sculptor, theorist and painter during the Italian Renaissance.

- The *Mona Lisa* is da Vinci's most famous painting and probably the most famous painting in the world.

- Da Vinci wrote thousands of pages of sketches and notes on such wide–ranging topics as botany, engineering, and cartography, and all were written in reversed or mirrored writing.

- Lisa Gherardini of the Giocondo family was the subject of the *Mona Lisa*, but da Vinci did not give the painting to the family.

- The painting is most noted for its subtle shadows around the mouth and eyes that make the expression enigmatic.

- The *Mona Lisa* was painted in oil on white Lombardy poplar.

- It was painted between 1503 and 1506.

The student wants to add more information about the *Mona Lisa* to a paper that has already introduced da Vinci. Which choice most effectively uses relevant information from the notes to accomplish this goal?

A) Da Vinci painted the *Mona Lisa* with its famous enigmatic expression on white Lombardy poplar between 1503 and 1506 using Lisa Gherardini of the Giocondo family for a subject.

B) The most famous painting in the world, the *Mona Lisa*, was painted by Leonardo da Vinci during the Italian Renaissance and is notable for its enigmatic expression.

C) Lisa Gherardini of the Giocondo family was the subject of Leonardo da Vinci's *Mona Lisa*, but the painter did not give the picture to her, possibly because it was his most famous picture.

D) Along with the *Mona Lisa*, which was painted between 1503 and 1506, da Vinci wrote thousands of pages of notes and sketches on wide–ranging topics like botany and engineering.

When researching a topic, a student has taken the following notes:

- Doberman dogs were bred in 1890 by a tax collector named Karl Doberman who wanted a dog for protection.

- There are now two kinds of Doberman dogs, American and European, named for the place where they were developed.

- American Dobermans are 24–28 inches tall and European Dobermans are 25–29 inches tall.

- American Dobermans are good family dogs or watchdogs that weigh about 60–100 pounds. They are sleek and have a narrow head.

- European Dobermans are good work dogs and wary of strangers. They usually weigh 65–105 pounds because they are very muscular and have a broad head.

The student wants to explain the difference between American and European Doberman dogs to someone who has a general familiarity with the breed. Which choice most effectively uses relevant information from the notes to accomplish this goal?

A) American and European Dobermans are related and came from a dog bred in Germany in 1890, though they have different names based on the place they were raised.

B) There are some similarities between American and European Dobermans, but the main difference is that the European breed is larger.

C) Though originating from the same breed, American Dobermans are sleek and good family pets, while European Dobermans are slightly heavier, muscular, and better working dogs.

D) Named for the place where they were developed, American Dobermans are good family pets and European Dobermans are larger working dogs that do not like strangers.

When researching a topic, a student has taken the following notes:

- The necropolis of Nuri is in the North Sudan desert, but has been flooded with groundwater from the Nile River.

- The necropolis is a pyramid built for the Kushite king Nastasen, who ruled for about two decades approximately 2,300 years ago.

- Pearce Paul Creaseman, who is an archaeologist, conducted the excavations, which were the first to occur in a pyramid underwater.

- The excavation techniques were different from underground and notes were taken on waterproof pads.

- Scuba tanks did not fit in the spaces so air was pumped through hoses for the people who performed the tasks underwater.

The student wants to emphasize Pearce Paul Creaseman's accomplishments regarding this archaeological dig. Which choice most effectively uses relevant information from the notes to accomplish this goal?

A) Pearce Paul Creaseman did the first excavation of a pyramid underwater at the 2,300–year–old temple of Nuri, using special techniques like pumping air through hoses for the workers.

B) The temple of Nuri, built about 2,300 years ago for the Kushite king Nastasen, was excavated by Pearce Paul Creaseman, even though it was flooded by water from the Nile River.

C) In order to excavate the temple of Nuri that was built about 2,300 years ago, Pearce Paul Creaseman had to use special tools like waterproof pads.

D) Pearce Paul Creaseman was a pioneer in exploring a North Sudanese temple built 2,300 ago for a Kushite king because that temple had many obstacles that made it different from a regular excavation.

When researching a topic, a student has taken the following notes:

- Hippopotamus, often called just "hippos," are large mammals that spend most of their lives in aquatic environments.

- Hippos have a special skin that needs to be kept wet or they dehydrate, but they also secrete mucus that helps retain moisture and protects them from sunburn.

- Their eyes have membranes that allow them to see underwater.

- Their nostrils can close, and hippos can stay underwater for about five minutes without breathing.

- Hippos are too dense to swim, but they gallop along the bottoms of rivers or lakes by pushing off the ground with webbed feet.

The student wants to explain the ways that a hippopotamus is adapted to live in an aquatic environment. Which choice most effectively uses relevant information from the notes to accomplish this goal?

A) Although a hippopotamus is too dense to swim, it has membranes on its eyes, nostrils that close, and webbed feet that help it spend most of its life in water.

B) If a hippopotamus does not stay wet, its skin can dehydrate, so it must remain in an aquatic environment and has special mucus that helps protect it.

C) A hippopotamus can gallop in aquatic environments because it has webbed feet, even though it is too heavy to swim otherwise.

D) Since a hippopotamus can see underwater and hold its breath for five minutes, it does not need to be able to swim but instead gallops using webbed feet.

When researching a topic, a student has taken the following notes:

- When herrings are smoked and salted, they turn red and have a very strong smell.

- The term "red herring" was used as early as 1420 to refer to smoked herrings.

- In 1686, a British men's magazine suggested dragging red herrings across the path of a fox hunt to prolong the chase.

- In 1807, William Cobbett wrote a story that used the same technique to stop a fox from chasing a rabbit.

- The phrase now refers to a false clue that is plausible but totally irrelevant to the solution of a mystery story.

The student wants to explain the meaning of "red herring" to an audience who has not heard the phrase before. Which choice most effectively uses relevant information from the notes to accomplish this goal?

A) The phrase "red herring" has been used since 1420 and refers to the red color of a smoked and salted herring.

B) Over time, the meaning of the phrase "red herring" has changed as people have suggested using smoked and salted herrings for many purposes.

C) William Cobbett created the modern use of the word "red herring," which is a clue in a mystery story.

D) A "red herring" is a clue in a mystery that, just like the smell of a real smoked and salted herring, is distracting but does not relate to the solution.

180

When researching a topic, a student has taken the following notes:

- There are over 200,000 glaciers on Earth, covering about one fourth of the planet.

- Glaciers are an essential source of fresh water in places such as the Andes and in Asia.

- Global warming is accelerating the melting process, and manmade greenhouse gasses might be responsible for all of the glacial ice loss since 1850.

- Between 2000 and 2019, the world's glaciers were melting at a rate of about 267 billion metric tons of water per year.

- The sea level has risen about half an inch since 2000, due to the extra water from glaciers.

The student wants to explain how fast the glacial ice is melting. Which choice most effectively uses relevant information from the notes to accomplish this goal?

A) Covering about a fourth of Earth's surface, the 200,000 glaciers have been melting due to greenhouse gasses since 1850.

B) Since 1850, greenhouse gasses have contributed to glacial melting, causing glaciers to disappear at the rate of about 267 billion metric tons of water every year.

C) About 267 billion metric tons of water have been melting from glaciers annually since 2000, enough to make the ocean levels rise by half an inch.

D) As glacial ice melts, people in the Andes and Asia will not have as much fresh water and people by the oceans will have problems as the sea level rises.

When researching a topic, a student has taken the following notes:

- The Philippines has some of the most active social media users in the world.

- The average use of social media in the Philippines is four hours per day.

- False content is extremely common in Philippine social media.

- The population of the Philippines is about 110 million.

- The most prevalent example of false information was prior to the 2022 presidential election of Ferdinand "Bongbong" Marcos, Jr. and it may have swayed some of the votes.

- Ferdinand "Bongbong" Marcos, Jr., is the son of the deposed president, Marcos.

The student wants to stress a concern about the extensive false information on Philippine social media. Which choice most effectively uses relevant information from the notes to accomplish this goal?

A) False content has increased in the Philippines since the 2022 presidential election because the population of about 110 million is among the most active social media users.

B) False content is extremely common in the Philippines, and that is a serious concern because the average person uses social media four hours per day.

C) Ferdinand "Bongbong" Marcos, Jr., used false content on social media to win the 2022 presidential election in the Philippines, highlighting a problem of social media.

D) Since the Philippines's population of 110 million includes some of the world's most active social media users, false content can cause serious problems such as biasing election results.

When researching a topic, a student has taken the following notes:

- There are only four species in the family that include hyenas, which are carnivorous mammals from Africa.

- Hyenas look a lot like dogs, but unlike dogs and most other social mammals, they are matriarchal.

- Female hyenas can weigh up to 190 pounds and are on average about 10 percent heavier than males.

- Hyena clans can be over 100 animals and they have complex societies that are kept by forming alliances with females.

- Hyenas in the wild can live 10 to 12 years, though some in captivity have lived as long as 21 years.

The student wants to explain the role of the female in hyena society. Which choice most effectively uses relevant information from the notes to accomplish this goal?

A) Hyena clans, which can have over 100 members, are matriarchal, and the organization is maintained through associations with female allies.

B) Female hyenas are about 10 percent heavier than males and can weigh up to 190 pounds, and they are social animals that form hierarchies in clans that can have over 100 animals.

C) Wild female hyenas can weigh 190 pounds and live up to 12 years, and they join with other females for power in complex societies which may contain more than 100 animals.

D) Hyenas are carnivorous mammals from Africa that live in clans of over 100 animals and have a lifespan of up to 12 years, though females are larger than males.

When researching a topic, a student has taken the following notes:

- Geodes are rocks that have cavities with crystals growing inside.

- Under Pulpi, Spain, a 390–cubic–foot geode was found in an abandoned mine in 1999. It has remarkably long, 7–foot–long spires of crystal.

- A geode forms when gypsum dissolved in liquid within the stone crystalizes; in the case of the Pulpi geode, the water seeped in from above.

- University of Almeria researcher Fernando Gasquez is performing tests to determine if tourists to the cave are altering the crystal formations.

- The crystals in the Pulpi geode formed between 164,000 and 60,000 years ago.

The student wants to present information about the Pulpi geode to an audience that knows what geodes are. Which choice most effectively uses relevant information from the notes to accomplish this goal?

A) There is a geode, a cavity with crystals, under Pulpi, Spain, that University of Almeria researcher Fernando Gasquez is studying to confirm that it is not being damaged by tourists.

B) Gypsum that had been dissolved in liquid in an abandoned mine under Pulpi, Spain, formed between 164,000 and 60,000 years ago into a geode that was 390 cubic feet.

C) In 1999, a 390–cubic–foot geode with 7–foot crystal spires that formed between 164,000 and 60,000 years ago, was found in an abandoned mine under Pulpi, Spain.

D) Fernando Gasquez, a researcher from the University of Almeria, found a 390–cubic–foot geode with 7–foot crystal spires in 1999 in an abandoned mine under Pulpi, Spain.

When researching a topic, a student has taken the following notes:

- The cane toad (*Bufo marinus*) is native to South America, where there are many predators such as caimans, snakes, birds and fish.

- In the 1930s, farmers in Australia were having problems with beetle infestations in their sugarcane fields and wanted to find a solution.

- In 1935, 101 cane toads were imported to eat the beetles, but the population quickly expanded due to a lack of predators, since they contain a toxin that makes them unpalatable.

- Now there are over 200 million cane toads in Australia.

- The Australian government is seeking ways to control the pest without further harming local wildlife.

The student wants to use the cane toad as an example of an invasive species. Which choice most effectively uses relevant information from the notes to accomplish this goal.

A) Since cane toads (*Bufo marinus*) have predators in South America, farmers thought their toxin could control beetle infestations, but unfortunately, the population exploded to over 200 million in Australia.

B) Native to South America, 101 cane toads (*Bufo marinus*) were introduced to Australia in 1935 and the population exploded to over 200 million because there are no predators or effective solution to keep the population in check

C) Unpalatable to most predators, the cane toad (*Bufo marinus*) population has grown in Australia even though farmers assumed it would be beneficial in eating beetles that were infesting sugar cane fields.

D) The cane toad (*Bufo marinus*) has predators in South America but not in Australia, where its populations have grown to over 200 million as predators there find it unpalatable.

When researching a topic, a student has taken the following notes:

- Giant oarfish are deep–sea fish that live about 1,000 meters deep in the ocean, though they are evenly distributed among tropical and temperate waters.

- They move by undulating their dorsal fins and often swim vertically in the water column.

- The giant oarfish is the longest bony fish in the world, reaching lengths of over 8 meters.

- The giant oarfish filters krill, small fish, and squid from the water because it does not have teeth, but instead, special bony structures for eating.

- The giant oarfish is most likely the origin of sea serpents and other legends about monsters that attacked sailors in ancient times.

The student wants to explain to someone who saw a picture of a giant oarfish that the fish are not dangerous to humans. Which choice most effectively uses relevant information from the notes to accomplish this goal?

A) The movement of giant oarfish is unique because they undulate their dorsal fins and swim vertically, catching fish and squid to eat.

B) Giant oarfish live about 1,000 feet deep in the ocean and can reach over 8 meters in length, but they do not harm humans.

C) Although giant oarfish grow over 8 meters long, they are filter feeders with no teeth, so they pose no threat to humans.

D) Giant oarfish are extremely long and often swim vertically, so ancient sailors created legends of sea serpents and monsters about them.

When researching a topic, a student has taken the following notes:

- Muhammad Yunus was born in British India, in an area which is now Bangladesh, in 1940.

- He is the only Nobel Prize winner from Bangladesh, and he won the award in the division of Peace in 2006.

- The award was given for his efforts to establish economic and social benefits for the underprivileged.

- He received an education in Bangladesh and the U.S. and returned to teach as professor of economics at the University of Chittagong in 1970.

- In 1974, a famine motivated him to do more than teach, so he started giving small loans with easy repayment terms —called microloans—so people could start their own businesses.

- He then founded the Grameen Bank to extend the project.

The student wants to explain why Muhammad Yunus earned the 2006 Nobel Peace Prize. Which choice most effectively uses relevant information from the notes to accomplish this goal?

A) Muhammad Yunus won the Nobel Peace Prize in 2006, and he is the only winner from his country, Bangladesh, where there was a severe famine in 1974 that he helped people get through.

B) Muhammad Yunus won the 2006 Nobel Peace Prize for establishing a bank to give microloans that allowed underprivileged people gain economic and social benefits by starting their own businesses.

C) A Bangladesh banker named Muhammad Yunus won the 2006 Nobel Peace Prize because he gave microloans with easy repayment terms starting in 1974.

D) Muhammad Yunus from Bangladesh was honored because he changed his job from being a professor of economics, and in order to help people through a severe famine in 1974, he started a bank.

When researching a topic, a student has taken the following notes:

- The Bell–Beaker culture had no written language, but many cultural similarities, and is named after a specific shape of drinking vessel.

- The culture was widespread in Europe, and lasted from 2800 B.C. to 2300 B.C. in most places, but only until 1800 B.C. in Britain.

- The Bell–Beaker people did metalwork in gold and copper, exchanged over large distances, had archery technology, and were socially stratified.

- There were local variations in housing, economics, ceramics, and burial customs.

- There are enough regional variations in populations that some scientists dispute that the Bell–Beaker culture was unified.

- Genetic studies show that the Bell–Beaker people were genetically diverse.

The student wants to put forward a counterargument against the critics who say the Bell–Beaker culture is not unified. Which choice most effectively uses relevant information from the notes to accomplish this goal?

A) People of the Bell–Beaker culture had differences in genetics, but they were otherwise alike in their social customs across a wide area in Europe between 2800 B.C. and 2300 B.C. in most places, and until 1800 B.C. in Britain.

B) The Bell–Beaker culture was obviously unified because it extended across a large area and lasted hundreds of years in Europe, and even longer in Britain.

C) The notion of a Bell–Beaker culture is flawed because regions had differences in housing, economics, ceramics, and burial customs, let alone differences in genetic makeup.

D) Despite regional and genetic differences, the Bell–Beaker culture had many unifying features such as gold and copper metalworking skills, long–distance exchange, archery technology, and social stratification.

When researching a topic, a student has taken the following notes:

- Tapirs are mammals with short snouts, eat fruit, and spread seeds via their dung.

- Tapirs live in the lowland forest areas of Brazil.

- Tapirs are one of the few larger mammals to not go extinct during the megafauna extinctions during the last ice age.

- Tapirs tend to defecate in degraded forests more than pristine forests, which increases the rate of reseeding in those areas.

- The International Union for Conservation of Nature lists tapirs as vulnerable or endangered, depending on the species.

- Habitat loss, hunting, and vehicle strikes contribute to the decreasing population sizes.

The student wants to explain the ecological value of tapirs to an audience that knows what the animals are. Which choice most effectively uses relevant information from the notes to accomplish this goal?

A) Since tapirs spread the seeds of the fruit they eat in their dung, they accelerate the rate of reseeding in the degraded forests in Brazil where they prefer to defecate.

B) Tapir populations in Brazil are now, depending on the species, vulnerable or endangered due to habitat loss, hunting, and vehicle strikes.

C) Large mammals that survived the megafauna extinctions of the last ice age, tapirs have short snouts and eat fruit, but they are now categorized as endangered or vulnerable.

D) Though tapir populations are declining due to habitat loss, hunting, and vehicle strikes, they still eat fruit and spread seeds in Brazil.

When researching a topic, a student has taken the following notes:

- The corvid family has 133 species, including jays, rooks, crows, ravens, magpies, and nutcrackers.

- Corvids, like other birds, have no cerebral cortex, but they have a high concentration of neurons.

- Some corvids are considered among the smartest creatures in the world.

- New Caledonian crows have been documented making and using tools to catch prey.

- Magpies can recognize themselves in mirrors and try to remove spots on themselves that are visible in the mirror but not directly by eye.

The student wants to emphasize the intelligence of corvids to an audience that already has a general knowledge of the family. Which choice most effectively uses relevant information from the notes to accomplish this goal?

A) Corvids, which contain jays, rooks, crows, ravens, magpies, and nutcrackers, have no cerebral cortex but are still among some of the smartest creatures in the world.

B) New Caledonian crows make and use tools, showing that corvids are among the smartest creatures in the world.

C) Corvids have a high concentration of neurons that help them complete complex tasks such as making tools and taking action in response to things they see in mirrors.

D) The 133 species of the corvid family are extremely intelligent and can accomplish tasks like making and using tools and responding to things they see in mirrors.

While researching a topic, a student has taken the following notes:

- The Malahai is a historical headgear originating in present–day Kazakhstan, which was worn throughout the Russian Empire from the mid–18th to mid–19th centuries.

- It is a fur hat with a noticeably high conical, cylindrical, or quadrangular crow and four long flaps. The side flaps or "ears" (naushi) were tied together either on top of the wearer's chin or under the chin, with leather straps or ribbons sewn on the flaps. The wide rear flap covered the wearer's neck and shoulders.

- Worn by men in winter to protect themselves against the cold and withstand the elements on the road, the headgear also served as a soft protective helmet against bladed weapons.

- Among Old Believers—Eastern Orthodox Christians who maintain the liturgical and ritual practices of the Russian Orthodox Church—wearing Malahai was forbidden because the wearer of the headgear cast a silhouette that allegedly resembled that of a horned demon.

The student wants to explain the significance of the Malahai. Which choice most effectively uses relevant information from the notes to accomplish this goal?

A) The Malahai was a fur hat, worn throughout Russia from the mid–18th to mid–19th centuries by men who used it as a protection from natural elements, as well as a protective headgear.

B) The Old Believers had prohibited the wearing of the Malahai since it created a silhouette of a devil with its side flaps or naushi.

C) The Malahai was essentially a fur cap that protected men from the cold and from head injuries.

D) Although it was banned, the Malahai was exceedingly popular among Russian men.

While researching a topic, a student has taken the following notes:

- To make the naming of plants more precise and universal, an international system of naming plants is used by scientists and plant professionals. Known as the "International Code of Botanical Nomenclature," the code is based on a two–name (binomial) system developed by the famous botanist Linnaeus.

- Each plant is given a first name and last name, generally based in Latin, that is unique to each species. This name is recognized for that plant throughout the world, no matter what the native language might be.

- The first name of a botanical binomial is the genus name. The second name of a botanical binomial is called the species name. This narrows down the identity to a specific species of plant.

- Among horticultural plants, it is common for new variations of species to be produced by means of cultivation techniques, hybridization, or even encouragement of mutations. This type of variation is called a *cultivar* or cultivated variety.

- While it may sometimes seem a bit daunting to pronounce these botanical names, gardeners should endeavor to at least know how to find a reference to such names, particularly when trying to acquire new plants.

The student wants to explain how a plant is named to those unfamiliar with the International Code of Botanical Nomenclature. Which choice most effectively uses relevant information from the notes to accomplish this goal?

A) Narrowing down the species name is the first step in the process of naming a plant, according to the famous botanist Linnaeus.

B) The names of plants are decided by the "International Code of Botanical Nomenclature" which is headed by the famous botanist Linnaeus.

C) Because the "International Code of Botanical Nomenclature" is based on a two–name (binomial) system, the name of the plant is divided into its genus name (first name) and its species name (last name). These names are based in Latin and are standardized across the world.

D) Cultivated varieties of plants are rare and take longer to name. This is especially because they are a new variation on an existing horticultural plant species, making it the process all the more daunting.

166. **Level:** Medium | **Skill/Knowledge:** Rhetorical Synthesis

Key Explanation: Choice C is the best answer because the question is asking about the "present condition" or "current status" of the painting. **Choice C** gives specific facts about the painting as it is today, where it now is and what the appearance is. The date that the painting was finished is a useful detail for the reader to understand that the colors have been darkening for over 100 years, so might be quite dark in places.

Distractor Explanations: None of the other choices adequately describe the "condition" or "state" of the painting now. **Choice A** only says it is a classic. **Choice B** describes the painting when it was made, not how it is now. **Choice D** explains what the art style is now called, but not anything about the painting.

167. **Level:** Medium | **Skill/Knowledge:** Rhetorical Synthesis

Key Explanation: Choice A is the best answer because the question asks about the "archaeological significance of Rathcroghan." In other words, the student needs to explain why it is important historically. **Choice A** gives many pieces of valuable information from the notes to achieve this goal. For example, it points out the number of sites and that those sites are unexcavated, the age and location of them, a list of different objects, and the possible actual use of the site.

Distractor Explanations: None of the other choices offer as many useful details for understanding what Rathcroghan is and why scientists are interested in it. **Choice B** only refers to the cave, so the reader has no idea that there is an entire complex of other structures which

may have different uses. **Choice C** describes the structures and a speculation about the site, but does not include relevant details like the number of sites, what they contain, the fact that they are unexcavated, or what they might be for. **Choice D** is incorrect because it offers very few facts. The reader knows it is not a town, but does not know what scientists believe the site might be, nor how old it is, not what the sites contain.

168. **Level:** Easy | **Skill/Knowledge:** Rhetorical Synthesis

Key Explanation: Choice C is the best answer because it offers three facts that differentiate solar flares from solar prominences: the length they last, the fact that prominences remain attached whereas flares burst, and the plasma arc compared to a burst of radiation.

Distractor Explanations: Choice A explains a difference between flares and prominences, but since there is only one fact, it is less complete than **Choice C**. **Choice B** explains what a prominence looks like in one situation, but does not contrast that with the appearance of the flare. **Choice B**, therefore, only says that they are different but does not help an audience visualize how the two look. **Choice D** is incorrect because it adds information not found in the notes: there is no evidence that prominences do not cause problems on Earth.

169. **Level:** Medium | **Skill/Knowledge:** Rhetorical Synthesis

Key Explanation: Choice D is the best answer because the student wants to explain why cheddar cheese is often orange. **Choice D** explains that the cheese is not naturally orange, but it gets that color due to additives, and even says what the additives usually are. **Choice D** further offers a reason for adding the additives: to replicate the historical appearance of the cheese.

Distractor Explanations: Choice A can be eliminated because it only says that a "different process" is used to color the cheese than was used in the past; a reader does not really know how the cheese gains its colors now. **Choice B** is incorrect because the notes say that additives give the cheese color, not the aging process. **Choice C** is incorrect because it only describes what made the cheese orange in the past; it does not explain why cheddar cheese is orange today.

170. **Level:** Medium | **Skill/Knowledge:** Rhetorical Synthesis

Key Explanation: Choice B is the best answer because it shows that Gauss was a German, which is pertinent information to share for someone who had not heard of the person. In addition, it explains that he was one of the best in the world in his career field (mathematics) and that he helped other fields. These are broad statements so that the audience has a general idea of who Gauss was.

Distractor Explanations: Choice A is incorrect because it only says that Gauss was good at math as a youth "and proved" makes it appear that proving theorems also occurred when Gauss was young, which may or may not be the case. **Choice C** is incorrect because it only gives one detail about what Gauss did, but it doesn't tell the reader anything about how much he is still respected today or how much he influenced other fields than astronomy. **Choice D** is incorrect because it only says that Gauss was good at math; it does not show that he actually was a mathematician or that he made any major contributions in the fields he worked in.

171. **Level:** Medium | **Skill/Knowledge:** Rhetorical Synthesis

Key Explanation: Choice C is the best answer because it gives the actual difference between the coldest temperatures in the first and second coldest places on Earth, so the student successfully emphasizes the "relative" or "comparative" difference: there are about 20 degrees Celsius difference between those places. The reader can, therefore, see that the coldest place really is very cold compared to other regions which are cold.

Distractor Explanations: Choices A and **D** are incorrect because they focus on the coldest place that people live year-round on Earth, but they do not give any clue about the place with the coldest temperatures. **Choice B** is incorrect because it only explains where the coldest places are; it does not explain how much difference there is or what the actual temperatures are.

172. **Level:** Medium | **Skill/Knowledge:** Rhetorical Synthesis

Key Explanation: Choice D is the best answer. The student wants to explain the "process" or "production method" of the company. If the reader knows Nancy Drew but not any of the background, **Choice D** clearly states the company that published the books and the fact that different people wrote the series using the same pseudonym.

Distractor Explanations: Choice A is incorrect because it does not give any clues that explain the method of writing the books; it only describes what company published them. **Choice B** is incorrect because it is vague. It is unclear what the syndicate was really called (it could be the Edward Syndicate) and it does not say that the writers used the same pseudonym. **Choice C** is incorrect because it erroneously states that Carolyn Keene wrote the first seven books, but in reality, that was a name used by Birt. In addition, the total number of volumes was 175, not seven plus the remaining 175.

173. **Level:** Hard | **Skill/Knowledge:** Rhetorical Synthesis

Key Explanation: Choice A is the best answer. The student wants to highlight a similarity, and **Choice A** indicates that blue whales and whale sharks both catch food the same way and have the same diet despite being from different classes of animals.

Distractor Explanations: Choice B is incorrect because it doesn't stress the similarity between the animals; it says that they are large, but not that they are the largest in a category, and the sizes appear widely different rather than similar. **Choice C** is incorrect because it only mentions a similarity in the name that the reader can easily identify without an explanation; it does not show any similarities between the actual animals. **Choice D** is incorrect because, while true, it does not accurately express the range of the blue whale, which can swim in any temperature. The reader may think that the similarity is that the range is exactly the same.

174. **Level:** Medium | **Skill/Knowledge:** Rhetorical Synthesis

Key Explanation: Choice C is the best answer because the student's goal is to show how climate change affects people, and **Choice C** illustrates a serious repercussion of climate change: people have flooded housing but cannot move. The reason for the flooding is also given: the ocean rises and the land sinks due to global warming.

Distractor Explanations: Choice A says that there are "serious repercussions" due to the rising

sea level, but the reader does not know how serious those repercussions are. One–eighth inch does not sound like very much, so the reader might not realize the true extent of the problem for residents, or might think that people have time to move elsewhere. **Choice B** is incorrect because it only says that the land is lowered due to using underground reserves, but there is no hint about how serious that problem might be. **Choice D** is incorrect because it only shows that land is being lost; like **Choice A**, the reader might think that the process is slow enough that people can move away as needed.

175. **Level:** Medium | **Skill/Knowledge:** Rhetorical Synthesis

Key Explanation: Choice A is the best answer because it gives the average reader many facts about the Mona Lisa painting: that da Vinci painted it, it has a famous enigmatic expression, it is on white Lombardy poplar, it was painted between 1503 and 1506, and Lisa Gherardini of the Giocondo family was the subject.

Distractor Explanations: Choice B is incorrect because it does not include much new information for the average reader; if the painting is the most famous in the world, the reader might already know it was by da Vinci and that it has an enigmatic expression. **Choice C** is incorrect because the reason for not giving the picture to the family is speculation that is outside the scope of the notes. **Choice D** is incorrect because it focuses more on the notes than on the Mona Lisa, which is the topic that the student wants to explain.

176. **Level:** Medium | **Skill/Knowledge:** Rhetorical Synthesis

Key Explanation: Choice C is the best answer because the student wants to explain the difference between the two dog breeds. **Choice C** includes both physical differences (sleek compared to heavier and muscular) and behavioral differences (good family pets compared to working dogs). It also includes the fact that they are from the same breed to avoid any confusion.

Distractor Explanations: Choice A is incorrect because it only shows a difference in names, but does not distinguish that there is any physical or behavioral difference between the dogs. **Choice B** is incorrect because it only refers to size, but the notes identify other differences in characteristics. **Choice D** is incorrect because it only refers to behavioral differences and the name, so the reader is unaware that there are also physical differences between the animals.

177. **Level:** Medium | **Skill/Knowledge:** Rhetorical Synthesis

Key Explanation: Choice A is the best answer because the student wants to emphasize Creaseman's accomplishments. The fact that Creaseman was the first person to excavate a pyramid underwater is the biggest point which makes him stand out from other researchers; the special techniques such as pumping air hint at the difficulty of the task compared to other excavations.

Distractor Explanations: Choice B is incorrect because it does not show what Creaseman did that was special or different from the work of other archaeologists. **Choice B** focuses on the temple rather than the person. **Choice C** says that Creaseman used special tools, but does not explain why. The fact that it was flooded is important because they could just have been

working in a rainy and humid environment where regular paper got damp. **Choice D** is incorrect because it only says that there were "obstacles," but the reader has no idea what they were or why Creaseman was "pioneering" or "a leader in the field."

178. **Level:** Easy | **Skill/Knowledge:** Rhetorical Synthesis

Key Explanation: Choice A is the best answer because it gives three separate ways that a hippo is adapted to life in water: eye membranes, closing nostrils, and webbed feet. **Choice A** also gives another interesting fact about life in the water, hippos cannot swim.

Distractor Explanations: Choice B is incorrect because it only says that the hippo needs to stay in water; it does not explain how it is adapted to live in such an environment. The fact that mucus "protects it" does not clarify in what way the hippo uses the mucus. **Choice C** can be eliminated because it only discusses one adaptation rather than many. **Choice D** is incorrect because it does not indicate how the hippo is adapted to see underwater and hold its breath; furthermore, there is no indication that those are the reason it does not swim.

179. **Level:** Medium | **Skill/Knowledge:** Rhetorical Synthesis

Key Explanation: Choice D is the best answer because a person who does not know what "red herring" means can imagine a smelly smoked fish distracting someone in the same way as a clue that is not relevant to the solution of a mystery.

Distractor Explanations: Choice A is incorrect because it describes the origin of the phrase but not the current meaning, so the reader would not know how it is used. **Choice B** is incorrect because it only refers to the fact that the meaning changed, but not to the current meaning. **Choice C** explains that the "red herring" is a clue, but does not explain what type it is.

180. **Level:** Medium | **Skill/Knowledge:** Rhetorical Synthesis

Key Explanation: Choice C is the best answer because it most clearly expresses how fast the glacial ice is melting: it gives the amount in metric tons, and also helps the reader envision the amount by showing that the water has raised the sea level a measurable amount.

Distractor Explanations: Choice A is incorrect because it only says there are a lot of glaciers and they cover a large area; the reader does not get a sense of how fast they are melting. **Choice B** is incorrect because it erroneously implies that the rate of 267 billion metric tons of water every year has occurred since 1850, but in reality, that rate has only occurred since 2000. **Choice D** is incorrect because it discusses problems caused by melting glaciers rather than how fast they are melting.

181. **Level:** Medium | **Skill/Knowledge:** Rhetorical Synthesis

Key Explanation: Choice D is the best answer because the student's goal is to stress a concern about false information, and **Choice D** points out a specific problem: it could "bias" or "sway" results of an election. Including the fact that so many people use social media and they are extremely active using it stresses that the bias could affect a lot of people, not just a small percentage of the population.

Distractor Explanations: Choice A is incorrect because it says that false content increased "since" or "after" the election, but the notes point out that the increase was "prior to" or "before" the election. **Choice B** is weak because it says that many people use social media and that there is false content, but it does not explain a problem or reason that the false content can cause harm. **Choice C** is incorrect because it says that Marcos used the false content, but the notes do not say that. The notes say the election may have been swayed, but do not report who posted the false content.

182. **Level:** Medium | **Skill/Knowledge:** Rhetorical Synthesis

Key Explanation: Choice A is the best answer because the question is to explain the "role" or "part played" by the female hyena. **Choice A** shows that the clans are "matriarchal" or "female–ruled," as well as pointing out that the "alliances" or "relationships" with other females within the clan help form the organization, which presumably is important if there are over 100 members.

Distractor Explanations: Choice B is incorrect because it describes the physical attributes rather than the role of females; **Choice B** says they are social, but not what the role is. **Choice C** is incorrect because it also focuses on the physical qualities; the only reference to female roles is "joining for power," but that could mean that they have a very low position in the clan. **Choice D** focuses on describing the hyena in general rather than the role of the female; **Choice D** only says that they are bigger than males.

183. **Level:** Medium | **Skill/Knowledge:** Rhetorical Synthesis

Key Explanation: Choice C is the best answer because it includes many pertinent details about the specific geode in Pulpi: when it was found, how large it is, the size of the crystals, the time it formed, and the current location.

Distractor Explanations: Choice A is incorrect because the audience already knows what a geode is, so the definition is not needed; more importantly, there is no detail about the geode itself, only a discussion of the person who is studying it. **Choice B** gives some details about the geode, but does not include the massive size of the crystals, which is "remarkable" or "notable." **Choice D** is incorrect because it reports that Gasquez found the geode, but the notes do not say that he did.

184. **Level:** Medium | **Skill/Knowledge:** Rhetorical Synthesis

Key Explanation: Choice B is the best answer because the student's goal is to show an example of an "invasive species," which refers to species that are not native to an area. **Choice B** includes the facts that the species is not native to Australia and there is no way to "keep the population in check" or "control the number of toads." As a result, there is a huge number, and the reader can clearly see the increase.

Distractor Explanations: Choices A and **D** are incorrect because they do not adequately show how much the population grew or over what time period. Though there are a lot of the toads now, it could be because there were a lot in Australia, or that they had centuries to reach that number. **Choice C** is incorrect because it does not show that the toad came from somewhere else, so the reader does not know it is invasive.

185. **Level:** Medium | **Skill/Knowledge:** Rhetorical Synthesis

Key Explanation: Choice C is the best answer because the fact that the giant oarfish has no teeth and filters food establishes that they really will not harm or attack humans despite being large.

Distractor Explanations: Choice A is not necessarily reassuring to a person who has seen a picture of the fish because based on that sentence, they could attack people as well as eat fish and squid with giant teeth. **Choice B** is incorrect because it only says they do not harm humans; a choice with evidence about why they cannot bite is more effective at convincing the reader. **Choice D** is incorrect because it offers no reason why giant oarfish are not dangerous; the myths could be based on the oarfish attacking the sailors.

186. **Level:** Easy | **Skill/Knowledge:** Rhetorical Synthesis

Key Explanation: Choice B is the best answer because it most clearly states why Yunus won the Nobel Prize, as well as explaining that the prize was for peace and in which year it was awarded. **Choice B** shows his efforts included giving microloans to help people start their own businesses.

Distractor Explanations: Choice A is incorrect because it does not explain how Yunus helped the people of his country; **Choice A** focuses more on where he lived. **Choice C** is incorrect because it erroneously implies that Yunus had always been a banker, but it is also notable that he changed careers in order to help others. Furthermore, **Choice C** is weak because it appears that all the microloans have repayment terms that started in 1974, not that he started giving them in 1974. **Choice D** is incorrect because it is very vague; the reader does not know what award Yunus got, when he got it, or how starting a bank helped people get through a famine.

187. **Level:** Medium | **Skill/Knowledge:** Rhetorical Synthesis

Key Explanation: Choice D is the best answer because it acknowledges the stance of the critics in the first clause "despite...differences," then gives an argument listing many features in common that could qualify as uniting the culture.

Distractor Explanations: Choice A is incorrect because although it acknowledges part of the critics' argument, it then errs in saying that the Bell–Beaker people were "otherwise alike." The fourth bullet point specifically lists ideas that are not identical from area to area. **Choice B** is incorrect because it only says that the culture is unified, but does not explain why; if there is no reason that the people are unified, then it is ineffective to say that the culture existed for a certain length of time. If anything, the difference in ending time might reflect differences within the population. **Choice C** is incorrect because it supports rather than offers a "counterargument" or "rebuttal" to the view of the critics.

188. **Level:** Medium | **Skill/Knowledge:** Rhetorical Synthesis

Key Explanation: Choice A is the best answer because the student wants to highlight the "ecological value" or "why they are important to the environment." **Choice A** shows one essential reason: they help forests that are "degraded" or "damaged" to regrow because they spread seeds.

Distractor Explanations: All of the other choices are true, but do not accomplish the goal of explaining why tapirs are important to the environment. **Choice B** only shows that the populations are getting smaller. **Choice C** describes the animals, but the audience already knows what tapirs are. **Choice D** explains that tapirs eat fruit and spread seeds, but does not give details about how the seeds are spread or what type of environment they prefer.

189. **Level:** Medium | **Skill/Knowledge:** Rhetorical Synthesis

Key Explanation: Choice C is the best answer because it gives a reason for the intelligence—a high concentration of neurons—and also explains some of tasks that are often considered very complicated. Therefore, someone who does not know much about the family has specific details to show that the birds are smart.

Distractor Explanations: Choice A is incorrect because it only says that the birds are smart. The audience already knows what corvids are, so it is not necessary to discuss the species; it is more important to establish they are intelligent. **Choice B** is incorrect because it only shows that New Caledonian crows are smart; it does not establish that other members of the family are also intelligent. The audience must take that information at the student's word. **Choice D** inaccurately attributes the skills of the New Caledonian crows and magpies to the entire corvid family. However, there is no proof that the other species can perform the same tasks.

190. **Level:** Medium | **Skill/Knowledge:** Rhetorical Synthesis

Key Explanation: Choice A is the best answer because the question asks for the significance of the Malahai. **Choice A** encompasses the significant parts of the notes, such as it being a "fur hat," "worn throughout Russia," and "protection from natural elements."

Distractor Explanations: All the other choices do not offer enough evidence of the significance of the Malahai. **Choice B** only talks about why the Old Believers had prohibited the wearing of the Malahai. **Choice C** describes the Malahai but does not mention why it became significant. **Choice D** is incorrect because the notes do not offer any evidence to support this claim.

191. **Level:** Medium | **Skill/Knowledge:** Rhetorical Synthesis

Key Explanation: Choice C is the best answer as it provides a comprehensive summary of the process of naming a plant. It mentions the "International Code of Botanical Nomenclature" is based on a two–name (binomial) system, and that the plant name is divided into genus and species.

Distractor Explanations: All the other choices are incorrect as they do not provide accurate information on how a plant is named.

192

Even though the sport originated from traditional martial arts in Japan, judo has spread around the world. _____ there are about 800,000 people who practice judo in France, as opposed to 200,000 in Japan.

Which choice completes the text with the most logical transition?

A) Likewise,

B) In fact,

C) Nevertheless,

D) Accordingly,

193

The early Italian Renaissance painter Sandro Botticelli was a respected painter with his own workshop and apprentices, but after his death, his work was mostly disregarded. It was only in the late 19th century that the Pre–Raphaelites rediscovered its beauty. _____ his work has been given its rightful position in the history of art.

Which choice completes the text with the most logical transition?

A) Subsequently,

B) To illustrate,

C) Lastly,

D) Meanwhile,

194

There are over 1,200 known ice caves in the Austrian Alps; the largest is Eisriesenwelt. The giant and beautiful ice formations in the caves attract casual visitors and scientists from all over the world. _____ many of the caves which had perennial ice now completely melt during the summer due to global warming.

Which choice completes the text with the most logical transition?

A) Consequently,

B) Accordingly,

C) Therefore,

D) Unfortunately,

195

Charismatic megafauna such as pandas, tigers, and polar bears tend to dominate the spotlight when it comes to discussions of endangered species. _____, nearly forty percent of the known animal species are parasites. Although scientists estimate that between ten and thirty percent of those will go extinct within the next fifty years, these species seldom are mentioned at all.

Which choice completes the text with the most logical transition?

A) In reality,

B) Furthermore,

C) Likewise,

D) Alternatively,

196

St. Joseph Atoll in the Seychelles was made a marine protected area in 2020 because it contains large seabird colonies and has a large amount of marine biodiversity. _____ it is home to one of the healthiest inland shark populations in the Indian Ocean.

Which choice completes the text with the most logical transition?

A) Furthermore,

B) Similarly,

C) Conversely,

D) Nonetheless,

197

Ahmes, an Egyptian who lived from approximately 1680 to 1620 B.C., wrote one of the oldest known mathematical documents, a papyrus divided into multiple sections which has become one of the main sources of information about ancient Egyptian mathematics. _____ Ahmes claims in the preface that he was not the author but merely a scribe who copied calculations from centuries before.

Which choice completes the text with the most logical transition?

A) Consequently,

B) However,

C) Subsequently,

D) Likewise,

198

JIT is the abbreviation for "Just in Time" management, which refers to a method of handling inventory so that the goods are received from the supplier only when needed. _____ the goal of the system is to increase turnover and reduce the costs of storing product that is not in use.

Which choice completes the text with the most logical transition?

A) Ultimately,

B) Conversely,

C) Nevertheless,

D) For instance,

199

Ishtaboli is a traditional game played by Choctaw Native Americans who lived in an area that is now Oklahoma. A form of stickball, the game has players that hit or pass a ball with sticks into a goal, but there are virtually no rules. _____ the game was suppressed by the U.S. government, but now Choctaws play ishtaboli as an expression of culture and take pride in their heritage.

Which choice completes the text with the most logical transition?

A) Simultaneously,

B) Previously,

C) For instance,

D) Furthermore,

200

Poison dart frogs have bright coloration to warn potential predators of their toxins. _____ they are active during the day when their colors are most visible, unlike most frogs, which are nocturnal.

Which choice completes the text with the most logical transition?

A) Consequently,

B) In conclusion,

C) By contrast,

D) Alternatively,

201

George Orwell wrote the classic dystopian novel *1984* in 1949. _____ some of the details are dated or seem quaint when looking back on what actually happened in that year, the book contains important messages that are still relevant today.

Which choice completes the text with the most logical transition?

A) However,

B) Because

C) Since

D) Although

202

Paleoclimatologist Tanguy Racine of the University of Innsbruck spends much of his time underground in caves picking out twigs and pine needles from melting ice. The information he retrieves from carbon dating these small objects gives valuable information about the formation, waxing, and waning of the ice. _____ he can tease out details about the changes in the climate over hundreds of years.

Which choice completes the text with the most logical transition?

A) By contrast,

B) In turn,

C) Nevertheless,

D) In any case,

203

Four of Jupiter's moons were identified in 1610 by the astronomer Galileo: Io, Europa, Ganymede, and Calisto. Subsequently, other moons have been identified, with the count at 59 officially named moons. _____ there are also now 23 more celestial bodies pending formal identification and naming.

Which choice completes the text with the most logical transition?

A) In conclusion,

B) In reality,

C) On one hand,

D) To be specific,

204

The first modern credit card was issued by Bank of America in 1958. _____ the idea of a credit card predates that event by over 150 years: the term was first used in the 1887 book *Looking Backward* by Edward Bellamy.

Which choice completes the text with the most logical transition?

A) However,

B) Specifically,

C) Consequently,

D) Furthermore,

205

Whoopi Goldberg is the stage name of Caryn Elaine Johnson, a talented actress and comedian. As well as being only one of 17 people to earn all four major performance awards in the United States (the Emmy, Grammy, Oscar, and Tony), she is a human rights activist who has supported many causes. _____ she moderated the 2008 Alliance of Youth Movements Summit showing how to fight violent extremism with social networks.

Which choice completes the text with the most logical transition?

A) In other words,

B) For example,

C) On the other hand,

D) Inevitably

206

Edvard Munch's iconic image, *The Scream*, was first painted in 1893, though he actually completed two paintings, two pastels, and about 40 lithographs, some hand–colored, of the same design. Both of the paintings have been stolen, one in 1994 and one in 2004. _____ both were found and returned to the museums where they had been on display.

Which choice completes the text with the most logical transition?

A) Therefore,

B) Subsequently,

C) Specifically,

D) Consequently,

207

Obesity is a complex subject, and scientists have isolated over 244 genes in mice that are related to obesity. These genes are not just ones that regulate fat storage, _____ They cover a wide range of metabolic processes including food intake and the drive to do exercise.

Which choice completes the text with the most logical transition?

A) though.

B) therefore.

C) consequently.

D) accordingly.

208

A flamingo is a filter feeder that holds the top of its mouth underwater until it fills with water, then shuts its mouth and pushes out the liquid through comb–like structures. _____ the bird has to stand with its head upside–down to eat this way.

Which choice completes the text with the most logical transition?

A) Consequently,

B) However,

C) Finally,

D) To illustrate,

209

As human rights are becoming more inclusive, transgender athletes are gaining more public awareness and acceptance. _____ four transgender players participated in the 2020 Tokyo Olympic games, which were postponed to 2021.

Which choice completes the text with the most logical transition?

A) Likewise,

B) For example,

C) In addition,

D) Furthermore,

210

William Butler Keats is considered one of the foremost poets of the 20th century and was very influential in the Irish Literary Revival. He was also deeply fascinated by mysticism and astrology. _____ many of his poems are deeply symbolic and have allusive imagery.

Which choice completes the text with the most logical transition?

A) Howbeit,

B) Likewise,

C) Notwithstanding,

D) Consequently,

211

Gauntlet buttons are the closures on the slit on a casual shirt such as a button–down Oxford. They are found between the elbow and wrist, and are designed to keep the gap from opening too wide and showing the forearm. _____ the buttons are not necessary, as a well–tailored shirt will remain shut without gapping.

Which choice completes the text with the most logical transition?

A) In reality,

B) Consequently,

C) Furthermore,

D) In other words,

212

Wildebeest herds, which can number over a million animals, have no leader for their annual migrations that extend from Kenya to Tanzania. _____they follow trails made by previous animals, demonstrating an impressive form of group memory.

Which choice completes the text with the most logical transition?

A) For instance,

B) In addition,

C) Instead,

D) Likewise,

213

A tax collector named Karl Doberman developed the breed of dog named after him in the 1890s. Most people imagine Dobermans as black dogs with tan markings on the face, legs, and belly. _____ the dogs also come in chocolate brown (also called red or rust), blue (a mutation of black), and Isabella or fawn (a mutation of chocolate).

Which choice completes the text with the most logical transition?

A) Specifically,

B) For instance,

C) However,

D) Furthermore,

214

In the district of Demak Regency in Jakarta, Indonesia, over 1,000 acres of land are lost to the ocean each year. One contributing cause is the fact that global warming is making the sea level rise by about an eighth of an inch per year. _____ delayed monsoon seasons and tourism have led to draining of the underground water, causing the land to sink at a rate of up to four inches per year.

Which choice completes the text with the most logical transition?

A) Secondly,

B) Therefore,

C) Consequently,

D) Specifically,

215

In 2020, a review of 83 urban wildlife studies that were conducted on six continents revealed that 93 percent of the animal species studied had distinct behavioral differences from their rural counterparts. This striking result is now prompting researchers to pursue a new line of study. _____ are the changes merely behavioral, or are there genetic alterations as well?

Which choice completes the text with the most logical transition?

A) Furthermore,

B) Consequently,

C) Namely,

D) Likewise,

216

Venus is the only planet to rotate clockwise, which means that it is in effect, spinning upside-down compared to Earth. In addition, the rotational period is the slowest of all the planets, taking 243 Earth days to make one complete Venusian day. _____ astronomers believe that the planet probably was involved in a collision in the distant past.

Which choice completes the text with the most logical transition?

A) Conversely,

B) Meanwhile,

C) Hence,

D) Thereafter,

217

The potato, a staple food crop around the world, originated in the South American Andes mountains and was domesticated about 8,000 years ago, but was not introduced in North America until thousands of years later. _____ it was first brought to Europe in the mid–1500s, then spread westward to North America.

Which choice completes the text with the most logical transition?

A) Ironically,

B) Therefore,

C) Furthermore,

D) Subsequently,

218

Dendrochronology is the science of dating objects based on the growth of tree rings, which vary in size due to climatic changes such as temperature or availability of water. Scientists are able to compare the growth across trees to compile a map that can be compared to an unidentified piece of wood, such as one from a historic building, and accurately determine when the tree was harvested. _____ the map is so comprehensive that scientists can now date wooden objects in the northern hemisphere to any period within the past 13,910 years.

Which choice completes the text with the most effective transition?

A) In fact,

B) Therefore,

C) Nonetheless,

D) By contrast,

219

Slavery was officially abolished in 1865 with the Thirteenth Amendment to the U.S. Constitution. _____ equality was not legally established until almost exactly a hundred years later, with the Civil Rights Act of 1964, in which discrimination based on race, color, religion, sex or national origin was prohibited.

Which choice completes the text with the most effective transition?

A) Likewise,

B) Nevertheless,

C) Consequently,

D) Furthermore,

220

Christopher Pissarides was born in Nicosia, Cyprus, to a family that came from a small village in the Agaros mountains. It might be expected that someone with that humble background would have a modest career, _____ Pissarides went on to earn the 2010 Nobel Prize in Economics for his theories governing search frictions and macroeconomics.

Which choice completes the text with the most effective transition?

A) and

B) but

C) since

D) for

221

At 6,190 meters above sea level, Mt. Denali in Alaska is the highest point in North America. _____the lowest point in North America is Death Valley in Eastern California; it is 86 meters below sea level. Death Valley is also the hottest place in the world in the summer.

Which choice completes the text with the most effective transition?

A) Nonetheless,

B) To illustrate,

C) Conversely,

D) Indeed,

222

In December of 1783, John Wordsworth, returning home from a business trip, lost his way and was forced to spend a cold night in the open. _____, he was very ill when he reached home, and died December 30.

Which of the following words best completes the text with the most logical transition?

A) Subsequently

B) Consequently

C) But

D) However

223

Nurtured by a loving mother and father, Dodgson began writing at an early age. _____ at the Richmond School in 1845, Dodgson composed *Useful and Instructive Poetry*, his first family magazine, for the edification of his seven–year–old brother, Wilfred Longley Dodgson, and his five–year–old sister, Louisa Fletcher Dodgson.

Which choice completes the text with the most logical transition?

A) So

B) While

C) Therefore

D) Meanwhile

224

The use of superlatives—"furthest" and "saddest"—reflects the heightening of the speaker's emotions. _____, the speaker's despair and sorrow seem never–ending; although the speaker continues to progress on the walk, the speaker doesn't actually go anywhere on a figurative and emotional level. This sense of despair and sorrow is inescapable, like the night itself.

Which choice completes the text with the most logical transition?

A) Likewise

B) In case

C) Therefore

D) In fact

192. Level: Easy | **Skill/Knowledge:** Transitions

Key Explanation: Choice B is the best answer because it is used to emphasize a point by adding more details. In this context, the point that judo has spread around the world from Japan is emphasized by showing that a large number of people practice judo in a country other than Japan.

Distractor Explanations: Choice A is incorrect because it is used to identify a similarity between two ideas rather than give an example. **Choice C** is incorrect because it is used to show that something happened despite something else, not because of something else. **Choice D** is incorrect because it is used to show that the following is fitting or appropriate in a given situation. However, it is not necessarily "appropriate" that France has more judo players than Japan does.

193. Level: Easy | **Skill/Knowledge:** Transitions

Key Explanation: Choice A is the best answer because it establishes a time sequence; the following information comes chronologically after the previous claim. In this context, the rediscovery of Botticelli's paintings occurred before the work got its rightful position. That order is possible to confirm by the verbs: "rediscovered" is in the past tense, whereas "has been given" is a present passive form.

Distractor Explanations: Choice B is incorrect because it is used to give an example, not a result. **Choice C** is used to indicate the last item in a list, not a result of an action that is still continuing. **Choice D** is used to show that the following idea occurs at the same time as the preceding idea, but the verb tenses are not the same, so the actions are sequential.

194. Level: Easy | **Skill/Knowledge:** Transitions

Key Explanation: Choice D is the best answer because it is used to indicate that something is sad or causes regret. The text refers to beautiful ice formations that attract visitors of all types, but the following portion points out that the formations do not exist year–round; they are no longer "perennial" or "permanent." That could be considered a sad circumstance, and **Choice D** highlights the loss.

Distractor Explanations: Choices A and **C** are used to describe the logical result of an argument, but the fact that the ice is gone part of the year due to global warming is not necessarily a logical result of people coming to see the ice. **Choice B** is used to point out that the following claim is appropriate or fitting given the preceding discussion, but it is not "fitting" that the ice has melted due to a separate cause.

195. Level: Easy | **Skill/Knowledge:** Transitions

Key Explanation: Choice A is the best answer because it is used to show what the actual situation is. It fits the context of pointing out that while some animals get a lot of attention about conservation, a much larger percentage of animals receive no attention but are in serious danger.

Distractor Explanations: Choice B is incorrect because it is used to indicate there are additional points that support the previous idea, but the following idea changes the topic from charismatic species to parasites. **Choice C** is incorrect because it is used to highlight a similarity rather than a difference. **Choice D** is used to show a second choice or possible explanation for a finding after a first choice or possibility is discussed; it is not used to show two sides of a situation which exists.

196. **Level:** Medium | **Skill/Knowledge:** Transitions

Key Explanation: Choice A is the best answer because it is used to add more information on the same topic. **Choice A** fits the context because the first sentence explains why the St. Joseph Atoll became a marine protected area, and the following sentence gives another reason why it is an important natural area.

Distractor Explanations: All of the other choices can be eliminated because they are not used to add more specific detail about the same topic. **Choice B** is used to highlight a similar feature of two different cases, such as comparing why two areas were both named marine protected areas. **Choice C** is used to show the opposite of a previous claim. **Choice D** is used to show that something happens despite the first claim.

197. **Level:** Easy | **Skill/Knowledge:** Transitions

Key Explanation: Choice B is the best answer because it is used to show a contrast in ideas or introduce something that might be considered surprising. In the context, the first sentence points out the important role that Ahmes plays in understanding Egyptian mathematics: he wrote one of the most important documents. The following sentence is surprising or unexpected, though, because it says that although Ahmes wrote the document, he did not come up with the ideas in it.

Distractor Explanations: Choice A is incorrect because it is used to show the result of an argument. However, the fact that Ahmes claims that he did not write the document is not a result of his document becoming famous. **Choice C** is incorrect because it establishes that the following idea comes later in time. Although "claims" is

in the present tense, the action of claiming was far in the past, as Ahmes died about 1620 B.C. Therefore, the act of his document becoming a main source of information happened after he wrote the preface in which he claimed he was not the author. **Choice D** is incorrect because it is used to show similarities between two ideas, but the second sentence emphasizes a difference or potential misunderstanding about the first sentence.

198. **Level:** Easy | **Skill/Knowledge:** Transitions

Key Explanation: Choice A is the best answer because it is used to introduce the end result or most basic principle of something. It therefore fits the context of introducing the primary goal of the JIT method.

Distractor Explanations: Choice B is incorrect because it is used to show a contrast between opposite ideas, not show the goal of the previous idea. **Choice C** is incorrect because it is used to show that something happens despite something else, but in this case, the preceding sentence is the result of the goal in the second sentence. **Choice D** is used to give a specific example that illustrates an earlier claim, not the motivations behind the claim.

199. **Level:** Easy | **Skill/Knowledge:** Transitions

Key Explanation: Choice B is the best answer because it refers to something that happened before something else. It introduces the first half of the sentence, which says that the game was "suppressed" or "not allowed." By contrast, the second half of the sentence says that now Choctaws play the game to show cultural pride. Therefore, **Choice B** clearly establishes a time sequence in which the game was not allowed but which is now played again.

Distractor Explanations: Choice A is incorrect because it introduces something that happens at the same time as a previous action, but the previous discussion is not a specific action but rather a general discussion of rules. **Choice C** is incorrect because it is used to give a specific example of a previous claim, not change to another aspect of the discussion. **Choice D** is incorrect because it is used to elaborate on the same topic, in this case, rules of the game.

200. **Level:** Medium | **Skill/Knowledge:** Transitions

Key Explanation: Choice A is the best answer because it is used to introduce the result of an earlier claim or argument. In this text, the result that the poison dart frogs are active during the day is a result of bright coloration that needs to be visible.

Distractor Explanations: Choice B is incorrect because it is used to summarize what has been discussed rather than present the results of a claim. **Choices C** and **D** are incorrect because they are used to show that the following idea is different from the preceding idea. The following idea has a contrast: regular frogs are nocturnal, but poison dart frogs are not. However, that contrast is consistent with the preceding idea about coloration, so those transitions do not signal the difference between sentences.

201. **Level:** Easy | **Skill/Knowledge:** Transitions

Key Explanation: Choice D is the best answer because the sentence contrasts two ideas, the fact that some ideas are dated and that they are also relevant. **Choice D** has the meaning of "in spite of the fact" and is used to subordinate a clause, so it fits the context and the grammar.

Distractor explanations: Choice A is incorrect because it is used to show a contrast, so it fits the logic of the paragraph, but it is a transition word that does not subordinate a clause. Therefore, the resulting sentence is a comma splice. **Choices B** and **C** are both used to show a cause–and–effect relationship, so do not fit the context of showing that the book is both dated and relevant. In addition, **Choice C** does not subordinate a clause and therefore creates a comma splice.

202. **Level:** Medium | **Skill/Knowledge:** Transitions

Key Explanation: Choice B is the best answer because it is used to show that something is the result of another claim. It fits the context of showing that teasing out details of the climate are a result of carbon dating twigs and pine needles.

Distractor Explanations: None of the other choices adequately show how the idea of getting information from carbon dating relates to finding details about climate change. **Choice A** is used to show that the following claim is opposite or different from the previous claim. **Choice C** is used to show that the following claim happens despite the first claim. **Choice D** is used to show that something would happen in any possible event or situation, but finding details about climate change would not happen without the specific action described.

203. **Level:** Easy | **Skill/Knowledge:** Transitions

Key Explanation: Choice B is used to explain the actual situation. It fits the context of saying that there are 59 official moons, but that 23 other objects might be considered official moons as well because they are "pending" or "awaiting" the process of being "formally" or "officially" identified and named. Therefore, the number 59 is not as accurate as the real number of moons.

Distractor Explanations: Choice A is incorrect because it introduces a result or summary of the previous discussion rather than brings up new facts. **Choice C** is incorrect because it is used to show the first of two opposing options, but only one example is given after that phrase. **Choice D** is incorrect because it is used to add more detail that clarifies the previous claim, such as stating that 23 of the 59 moons are pending identification. However, the following sentence adds new information about moons that are not in the original 59 in the discussion.

204. **Level:** Medium | **Skill/Knowledge:** Transitions

Key Explanation: Choice A is the best answer because it is used to introduce something that is unexpected or contrasting. **Choice A** fits the context because the preceding sentence refers to the first time that credit cards were used, and the second brings up the unexpected or contrasting point that the idea had been around for a long time before they were actually invented.

Distractor Explanations: Choice B is incorrect because it is used to clarify a preceding claim with more detail, not introduce an idea that is not included in the preceding portion. **Choice C** is incorrect because it is used to show the result of an action or argument, but the following portion refers to something that occurred at an earlier time. **Choice D** is incorrect because it is used to elaborate on the same topic, not change the idea with something unexpected.

205. **Level:** Easy | **Skill/Knowledge:** Transitions

Key Explanation: Choice B is the best answer because it is used to give a specific case that illustrates a general claim. In the text, the preceding sentence is the general claim that

Goldberg supported many causes, and the following sentence gives a specific cause that she supported.

Distractor Explanations: Choice A is incorrect because it is used to paraphrase the previous idea for clarity, not give additional facts. **Choice C** is incorrect because it is used to show something that is opposite the previous claim, not a continuation of it. **Choice D** is used to show that something was destined to happen, but Goldberg did not have to moderate the summit; she could have been involved in other movements or even just busy that day.

206. **Level:** Medium | **Skill/Knowledge:** Transition

Key Explanation: Choice B is the best answer because it is used to show that something occurred later in a chronological order. **Choice B** effectively establishes that both paintings were stolen, but that later, both were found and returned to the museums.

Distractor Explanations: Choices A and **D** can be eliminated because they are used to introduce the logical result of an argument. However, it is not necessarily a given that the paintings would be returned after being stolen, so it is not the only reasonable conclusion given the information to that point. **Choice C** is incorrect because it is used to clarify a previous general claim using details or examples.

207. **Level:** Easy | **Skill/Knowledge:** Transitions

Key Explanation: Choice A is the best answer because it is used to show that a statement may be unexpected or contrary to what has been said already. It fits the context of saying that there are genes related to obesity, but there is an unexpected idea because the genes are not all related to fat storage.

Distractor Explanations: Choices B and **C** can be eliminated because they introduce the logical conclusion to an argument, but the fact that the genes are not just ones that regulate fat storage is not the end of the discussion. **Choice D** is incorrect because it shows that something is fit or proper in a given context, but it is not necessarily appropriate that obesity is controlled by genes that perform different metabolic processes than storing fat.

208. **Level:** Medium | **Skill/Knowledge:** Transition

Distractor Explanations: Choice B is used to bring up something that is contradictory to the previous discussion. Though the fact that the flamingo eats with its head upside–down is odd, it is not contradictory to the idea that it has to hold the top of its mouth underwater. **Choice C** is incorrect because it is used to introduce the last item in a series of three or more items, but the previous and following information are two aspects of the same discussion. **Choice D** is incorrect because it is used to give a specific example of a general case, not summarize a discussion.

209. **Level:** Easy | **Skill/Knowledge:** Transition

Key Explanation: Choice B is the best answer because it is used to give a specific case that illustrates a general claim. It fits the context of adding the fact about four transgender athletes in the Olympics to the general idea that such athletes are "gaining more public awareness and acceptance."

Distractor Explanations: Choice A is incorrect because it is used to highlight a similarity between two different things, not give a specific example of the same thing. **Choices C** and **D** are incorrect because they are used to add more detail on the same topic, such as another argument for the overall development of the thesis, not give a specific case.

210. **Level:** Medium | **Skill/Knowledge:** Transition

Key Explanation: Choice D is the best answer because it is used to show that the following idea is the result of the previous idea. It clearly establishes the relationship in which the interest in "mysticism and astrology" led to Keats writing poems that were very symbolic.

Distractor Explanations: Choices A and **C** are incorrect because they are used to show that the following is a contrast or different in some way from the previous claim, but the ideas of mysticism and symbolism are closely related. **Choice B** highlights a similarity between two things, but does not fit the context because is not used to show cause and effect.

211. **Level:** Easy | **Skill/Knowledge:** Transition

Key Explanation: Choice A is used to highlight the difference between what is true and something that is previously stated. It fits the context of showing that the gauntlet buttons are claimed to be used for something, but the true situation is that they are not needed.

Distractor Explanations: Choice B is used to show the logical result of an argument, not offer contrasting information. **Choice C** is used to continue the argument on the same topic, not reverse the idea. **Choice D** is used to paraphrase the same idea in a different form for clarity.

212. **Level:** Medium | **Skill/Knowledge:** Transition

Key Explanation: Choice C is the best answer because the text starts with a statement that the wildebeests have no leader on their migration, then continues with the alternative that they use: they follow trails. **Choice C** fits the context because it is used to introduce an alternative that fills the place of something else.

Distractor Explanations: None of the other choices clearly identifies the relationship between the preceding sentence that there is no wildebeest leader and the following sentence that the wildebeests follow trails. **Choice A** is used to give a specific example of the previous claim. **Choice B** is used to add more information on the same idea, not give an alternative. **Choice D** is used to highlight a similarity rather than a difference.

213. **Level:** Medium | **Skill/Knowledge:** Transition

Key Explanation: Choice C is the best answer because it indicates that the following information might be unexpected based on what has already been said. The preceding portion says that most people think Dobermans are black, but the following portion states that they actually come in four different colors. That information is probably a surprise based on the common expectation.

Distractor Explanations: Choices A and **B** are incorrect because they are used to add an explanation that clarifies or gives an example of the previous claim. However, the following information contradicts the previous part by offering different colors rather than expanding on the common view. **Choice D** is incorrect because it is used to add more information that continues on the same topic in the same tone, so would typically introduce more information about people's expectations.

214. **Level:** Medium | **Skill/Knowledge:** Transition

Key Explanation: Choice A is the best answer because the previous idea is "one contributing factor" about why land in Demak Regency is lost to the ocean. The following idea is another reason. **Choice A** is a transition that is used to identify an item in position number two in a list, so fits the context well.

Distractor Explanations: None of the other choices indicates that the following item is another idea in a list. **Choices B** and **C** are used to introduce the conclusion or result of an argument. **Choice D** is used to give a precise detail that expands on a previous, more general claim.

215. **Level:** Easy | **Skill/Knowledge:** Transition

Key Explanation: Choice C is the best answer because the previous sentence says that the researchers want to "pursue a new line of study" or "do research about something new." The following sentence shows what that "something" is: they want to find out if there are genetic "alterations" or "changes." Therefore, the following sentence clarifies a detail of the previous sentence. **Choice C** fits the context because it is used to introduce a specific example or explanation.

Distractor Explanations: None of the other choices effectively establishes the relationship between the previous sentence's general claim and the specific information in the following sentence. **Choice A** is used to introduce another, related point to expand on an argument. **Choice B** is used to show the result of a previous claim. **Choice D** is used to highlight a similarity between two things.

216. Level: Medium | **Skill/Knowledge:** Transition

Key Explanation: Choice C is the best answer because the first two sentences give unusual facts about the planet Venus. The final sentence is a claim that could be responsible for those facts. **Choice C** is used to introduce the logical conclusion of an argument, so fits well in the context.

Distractor Explanations: Choice A is used to show something which is opposite or different from something else, so does not fit the context of giving a reason for some facts. **Choice B** is used to show that something happens at the same time as something else. Though the facts are indeed both occurring now, they are not simultaneous in that the planet's orbit has been around for millions of years more than scientists believed. **Choice D** is incorrect because it is used to show things which happen one after another, but Venus's orbit and rotational period have not ended.

217. Level: Medium | **Skill/Knowledge:** Transition

Key Explanation: Choice A is the best answer because it is used to show that something is rather paradoxical. In this case, it fits the context of showing the rather odd fact that the potato was transported from South America to Europe and back to North America rather than just moving the comparatively short distance through the Americas.

Distractor Explanations: None of the other choices establishes the correct relationship between the ideas. **Choice B** is used to show the logical conclusion of the previous argument, not an unexpected fact. **Choice C** is used to add a new point to building an argument rather than give more specific detail on the same point. **Choice**

D is used to show that the following idea comes after the previous idea in time. It breaks up the order because the previous sentence mentions that potatoes were brought to North America, but the following sentence shows an event—the transport to Europe—that happened before the action in the previous sentence.

218. Level: Easy | **Skill/Knowledge:** Transition

Key Explanation: Choice A is the best answer because it is used to emphasize a point that might come as a surprise. The previous sentence discusses the idea that dendrochronology can be used to date wood, and the following sentence offers the potentially surprising detail that the wood can be dated to be thousands of years old. **Choice A**, therefore, accentuates the point that the map is "so comprehensive."

Distractor Explanations: Choice B is incorrect because it is used to show a logical conclusion to a discussion, but it is not obvious from the discussion that the map extends so far back in time; that is surprising new information. **Choice C** introduces something that happens despite what has been stated, not something which happens because of the previous information. **Choice D** is incorrect because it introduces something opposite of what has been stated.

219. Level: Easy | **Skill/Knowledge:** Transition

Key Explanation: Choice B is the best answer because it is used to show that something happens despite something else. It fits the context of showing that equality was not legally enforced for almost 100 years even though slavery was abolished.

Distractor Explanations: None of the other ideas effectively show the contrast between the preceding idea that slavery was abolished and the following idea that equality was not legally established. **Choice A** is used to highlight a similarity, but "not" in the second sentence shows that the author is not highlighting the similarity between two laws, but rather showing a contrast. **Choice C** is used to show the logical result of an action. **Choice D** is used to add more information on the same idea, not create a change in tone.

220. **Level:** Easy | **Skill/Knowledge:** Transition

Key Explanation: Choice B is the best answer because it is used to establish a contrast. It fits the context of showing that the first idea, that Pissarides has a modest background, contrasts greatly with the fame he accomplished.

Distractor Explanations: None of the other choices establishes a contrast between two ideas that are very distinct: what "might be expected" did not happen. **Choice A** is used to show that two things happened, but does not indicate contrast. **Choices C** and **D** are used to show that the following is the reason for the former, which does not fit the context.

221. **Level:** Easy | **Skill/Knowledge:** Transition

Key Explanation: Choice C is the best answer because it is used to introduce an idea that contrasts or is the opposite of a previous claim. It fits the context of describing the lowest place in North America after describing the highest place, based on sea level.

Distractor Explanations: Choice A is incorrect because it is used to show that something happens despite something else, but there is no reason that

the two facts should not occur simultaneously. **Choice B** is used to introduce a specific example of a general claim, not offer a contrast. **Choice D** is used to emphasize the previous statement by adding more information that supports it rather than bringing up a different subject.

222. **Level:** Medium | **Skill/Knowledge:** Transition

Key Explanation: Choice B is the best choice because "consequently" means "as a result of." In this context, it implies that because John Wordsworth was forced to spend a cold night in the open, he became ill.

Distractor Explanations: Choice A is incorrect because "subsequently" means "after something happened." Therefore, this does not emphasize the fact that Wordsworth fell ill because of the night he spent out in the cold. **Choice C** is incorrect because one would usually use "but" when trying to say something that is different from what has been said before (for example: He dressed warmly, but he still caught a cold.) **Choice D** is incorrect because "however" is also used as a conjunction to mean "in whatever way or degree." This does not fit the context here.

223. **Level:** Medium | **Skill/Knowledge:** Transition

Key Explanation: Choice B is correct because it is used to emphasize a point more strongly by adding additional details. Thus, while he was at school, he composed "Useful and Instructive Poetry," thereby emphasizing the point made in the first sentence ("Dodgson began writing at an early age.")

Distractor Explanations: Choice A is incorrect because "so" is a connecting conjunction that does not usually appear at the beginning of a sentence.

Choice C is incorrect because "therefore" is used when talking about a result of a situation or circumstance. **Choice D** is incorrect because "meanwhile" is used to describe an incident that is happening at or during the same time.

224. **Level:** Medium | **Skill/Knowledge:** Transition

Key Explanation: Choice D is the correct answer because "in fact" emphasizes and gives more information about "the heightening of the speaker's emotions." The speaker's emotions are so heightened that they seem to never end.

Distractor Explanations: Choice A is incorrect because "likewise" is usually used when a comparison is being made and the situations or things being compared are similar. Here, no comparison is being made. **Choice B** is incorrect because "in case" points to the probability of something happening, which does not make sense in this context. **Choice C** is incorrect because "therefore" is used to denote a conclusion is being reached.

This page is intentionally left blank

Chapter 6

Standard English Conventions

This chapter includes questions on the following topics:

- Boundaries
- Form, Structure, and Sense

225

Global warming has led _____ melting ice has granted scientists access to fresh material for study that has previously been trapped deep within glaciers.

Which choice completes the text so that it conforms to the conventions of Standard English?

A) to one unexpected benefit

B) to: one unexpected benefit

C) to: one unexpected benefit,

D) to one unexpected benefit:

226

In 2021, cracks opened on the Cumbre Vieja ridge in the Canary _____ off 2,000–foot–high lava fountains and glowing streams of lava that destroyed nearby marine ecosystems.

Which choice completes the text so that it conforms to the conventions of Standard English?

A) Islands; setting

B) Islands; and these set

C) Islands, they set

D) Islands, setting

227

Eurasian _____ among the world's most intelligent creatures, despite the fact that they do not have a cerebral cortex.

Which choice completes the text so that it conforms to the conventions of Standard English?

A) magpies, (birds of the Corvidae family) are considered:

B) magpies (birds of the Corvidae family), are considered

C) magpies (birds of the Corvidae family), are considered:

D) magpies (birds of the Corvidae family) are considered

228

The 1957 Broadway hit *The Music Man*, with both music and lyrics by Meredith Wilson, was an unrivaled _____ 5 Tonys (including Best Musical) and ran for 1,375 performances.

Which choice completes the text so that it conforms to the conventions of Standard English?

A) success, it won

B) success: it won

C) success: winning

D) success:

229

The invention of the pizza as it is known today occurred in _____ although flatbreads with various toppings were consumed in the Egyptian, Greek, and Roman cultures many centuries earlier.

Which choice completes the text so that it conforms to the conventions of Standard English?

A) Naples Italy

B) Naples, Italy

C) Naples Italy,

D) Naples, Italy,

230

Chess is thought to have derived from a two–person Indian board game called _____ which was carried by Persian traders to Europe around 1000 A.D.

Which choice completes the text so that it conforms to the conventions of Standard English?

A) *chatarung*

B) *chatarung,*

C) *chatarung ;*

D) *chatarung—*

231

The geological record shows that the Earth's magnetic field reverses every million years or so, but that astounding event has not been associated with any mass _____ to occur about every hundred million years.

Which choice completes the text so that it conforms to the conventions of Standard English?

A) extinctions, those appear

B) extinctions, which appear

C) extinctions (appearing

D) extinctions; which appear

232

Endemic to Congo, the okapi is a _____ a tongue that is 18 inches long that allows the herbivorous creature to feed on over 100 different species of plants.

Which choice completes the text so that it conforms to the conventions of Standard English?

A) striped, large, mammal with,

B) striped, large, mammal with

C) striped, large mammal with

D) striped large mammal with,

233

Mercury is not only the smallest planet in the solar _____ the fastest, as it travels around the Sun in a period of only 88 days.

Which choice completes the text so that it conforms to the conventions of Standard English?

A) system but also

B) system, but also:

C) system but also:

D) system, but also

234

"The sword of Damocles" is a common phrase that refers to looming _____ in a parable written by the Roman orator Cicero in 45 B.C. in a book called *Tusculum Disputations*.

Which choice completes the text so that it conforms to the conventions of Standard English?

A) danger. It originated

B) danger, it originated

C) danger; originating

D) danger and originating

235

Little is known about the life of Heraclitus, a Greek philosopher who wrote only one book, but who is remembered for his famous _____ is nothing permanent except change."

Which choice completes the text so that it conforms to the conventions of Standard English?

A) saying "there

B) saying, "there

C) saying: "There

D) saying, "There

236

Sixty–five countries have gained their independence _____ when the United States declared that it no longer wanted to be under English rule.

Which choice completes the text so that it conforms to the conventions of Standard English?

A) from: the British Empire after 1776

B) from the British Empire after 1776,

C) from, the British Empire, after 1776

D) from the British Empire, after 1776:

237

In the 1930s, George and Versa Boyington had a small hot dog stand at Rockaway Beach in Oregon. Upset by how the coastal rains ruined the buns, they invented a coating that could be cooked as _____ invented the first corn dog.

Which choice completes the text so that it conforms to the conventions of Standard English?

A) needed: they

B) needed: They

C) needed, they

D) needed;

238

As preposterous as it may sound, fish are capable of getting sunburn. In particular, koi and other ornamental fish in shallow ponds do not have the protection of dirty water and shady _____ can develop fatal sores from exposure to ultraviolet rays.

Which choice completes the text so that it conforms to the conventions of Standard English?

A) retreats; so they

B) retreats, so they

C) retreats, they

D) retreats,

239

Recently, the Event Horizon Telescope captured an elusive image of something that astronomers have predicted the existence of but which until now has been _____ the supermassive black hole within the center of the Milky Way galaxy.

Which choice completes the text so that it conforms to the conventions of Standard English?

A) only, theoretical, Sagittarius A*,

B) only theoretical Sagittarius A*:

C) only theoretical: Sagittarius A*,

D) only—theoretical Sagittarius A*—

240

"Soft drinks" is a general term used by the beverage industry to refer to non–alcoholic drinks made of water mixed with a sweetener and often flavorings. However, even within the United States, there are many regional variations on what such drinks are called, including soda, pop, _____ tonic.

Which choice completes the text so that it conforms to the conventions of Standard English?

A) coke and,

B) coke, and

C) coke and,

D) coke, and,

241

The painter and teacher Robert _____ greatly inspired by Impressionist paintings when he was in Paris and determined to create a movement that was even more modern upon his return to New York.

Which choice completes the text so that it conforms to the conventions of Standard English?

A) Henri (1865–1929) was

B) Henri, (1865–1929) was,

C) Henri (1865–1929), was

D) Henri, (1865–1929) was

242

Recently in the United States there has been a rise in the popularity of a traditional Native American game _____ in which players change horses while riding horses bareback at a gallop.

Which choice completes the text so that it conforms to the conventions of Standard English?

A) called "Indian relay"

B) called, "Indian relay"

C) called "Indian relay,"

D) called, "Indian relay,"

243

Majuscule letters are often _____ because in the past, printers would ask their apprentices to bring the letters from the top box when typesetting pages of print.

Which choice completes the text so that it conforms to the conventions of Standard English?

A) called "upper case letters"

B) called, "upper case letters"

C) called "upper case letters";

D) called, "upper case letters,"

244

The tallest building in the world, the Burj Khalifa in Dubai, stands 829.8 _____ and is the center of a successful mixed–use development area that was designed to diversify the city.

Which choice completes the text so that it conforms to the conventions of Standard English?

A) meters (2,722 feet) tall

B) meters, (2,722 feet), tall

C) meters (2,722 feet), tall,

D) meters, (2,722 feet) tall,

245

David Harris faced a significant amount of prejudice on his _____ the first Black man to pilot a commercial airliner in the United States.

Which choice completes the text so that it conforms to the conventions of Standard English?

A) journey to become

B) journey, to become

C) journey to: become

D) journey to become:

246

In March 2022, scientists found the remains of the Endurance, which sank off the coast of Antarctica in 1915. The brass lettering on the stern was extremely well-preserved due to the lack of light, _____ almost freezing temperatures.

Which choice completes the text so that it conforms to the conventions of Standard English?

A) low oxygen, and

B) low oxygen and,

C) low oxygen, and,

D) low, oxygen, and

247

In Caracas, Venezuela, the pet trade for birds is so extensive that now a flock of approximately 400 blue-and-yellow macaws—as well as many other escaped _____ within the city limits.

Which choice completes the text so that it conforms to the conventions of Standard English?

A) parrots thrive

B) parrots thrive—

C) parrots, thrive

D) parrots—thrive

248

"Forest _____ and appreciating the gentle beauty of nature—can reduce stress and thus improve mental and physical health.

Which choice completes the text so that it conforms to the conventions of Standard English?

A) bathing," walking in

B) bathing"—walking in

C) bathing" walking in—

D) bathing"—walking in—

249

In a Zurich, Switzerland, laboratory, scientists are exploring technology that uses solar radiation to create compounds from the air that can be refined _____ that are suitable for fuel.

Which choice completes the text so that it conforms to the conventions of Standard English?

A) into kerosene or methane

B) into kerosene, or methane

C) into: kerosene or methane,

D) into: kerosene, or methane,

250

Only about two percent of Europe's forested area is _____ the areas that still exist have trees over 800 years old.

Which choice completes the text so that it conforms to the conventions of Standard English?

A) undisturbed old growth but

B) undisturbed old growth, but

C) undisturbed, old growth but,

D) undisturbed, old, growth, but

251

Aji _____ a professional photographer who has worked on articles for the prestigious magazine *National Geographic*, is now documenting the changes taking place in his home country of Indonesia as the ocean levels rise and irrevocably alter the coastline.

Which choice completes the text so that it conforms to the conventions of Standard English?

A) Styawan—

B) Styawan,

C) Styawan, he is

D) Styawan, whose

252

On May 12, 2022, eight Nepali guides led seven climbers to the top of the world's tallest _____ a notable feat as it was the first all–Black expedition to reach the summit.

Which choice completes the text so that it conforms to the conventions of Standard English?

A) mountain, Mt. Everest, (29,032 feet),

B) mountain, Mt. Everest (29,032 feet),

C) mountain Mt. Everest, (29,032 feet)

D) mountain Mt. Everest (29,032 feet)

253

Not all penguins live on ice in the _____ endangered Galapagos penguin lives in the tropics on some of the Galapagos Islands, though it is the only penguin to live north of the equator.

Which choice completes the text so that it conforms to the conventions of Standard English?

A) Antarctic; the

B) Antarctic; and the

C) Antarctic, the

D) Antarctic, however, the

254

Medlar is a member of the rose family that has been cultivated for over 3,000 years and which was an important part of the Medieval _____ it has grown out of favor because it looks rotten when it is actually ready to eat.

Which choice completes the text so that it conforms to the conventions of Standard English?

A) diet, however

B) diet however,

C) diet however—

D) diet. However,

255

In the Meradalir _____ is about a one–hour drive from Reykjavik in Iceland, a volcano which has been dormant for about 800 years suddenly burst forth with rivers of lava on August 3, 2022.

Which choice completes the text so that it conforms to the conventions of Standard English?

A) Valley,

B) Valley, it

C) Valley, which

D) Valley, that

256

The thermal state of frozen ground and its changes are important for understanding environmental change and supporting related applications to the Earth's Third Pole, which is a hotspot area for scientific research. However, challenges remain in data and modeling _____ especially for the entire Third Pole region.

Which choice completes the text so that it conforms to the conventions of Standard English?

A) , meaning that much information is unavailable,

B) –meaning that much information is unavailable.

C) meaning that much data is unavailable,

D) . Meaning that much data is unavailable

257

Japan is an island country in East Asia. It is a part of the Ring of Fire and spans an archipelago of 6852 islands covering _____ are Hokkaido, Honshu (the "mainland"), Shikoku, Kyushu, and Okinawa.

Which choice completes the text so that it conforms to the conventions of Standard English?

A) 145,937 square miles; the five main islands

B) 145,937 square miles – the five main islands

C) 145,937 square miles and the five main islands

D) 145,937 square miles but the five main islands

258

The Indian peacock has iridescent blue and green plumage_____ but the green peacock has green and bronze body feathers. In both species, females are a little smaller than males in terms of weight and wingspan, but males are significantly longer due to the "tail," also known as a "train."

Which choice completes the text so that it conforms to the conventions of Standard English?

A) mostly metallic blue and green;

B) , mostly metallic blue and green,

C) – mostly metallic blue and green

D) mostly metallic blue and green:

259

Originating from the highlands of the _____ potatoes were introduced to Europe in the sixteenth century. They were initially popular in Spain because they provided cheap sustenance for the poor.

Which choice completes the text so that it conforms to the conventions of Standard English?

A) Andes South America,

B) Andes, South America

C) , Andes, South America,

D) Andes, South America,

260

When the egg whites have the consistency of _____ stop whipping and add the vanilla essence.

Which choice completes the text so that it conforms to the conventions of Standard English?

A) shaving foam,

B) shaving foam

C) shaving foam;

D) shaving foam:

225. **Level:** Medium | **Skill/Knowledge:** Boundaries

Key Explanation: Choice D is the best answer because a colon should follow a complete idea that can stand on its own as a sentence. The following portion is information that clarifies the whole preceding idea.

Distractor Explanations: Choice A is incorrect because it is a run–on sentence that joins two independent clauses. **Choices B** and **C** are incorrect because a colon should follow a complete idea, but "to" is left dangling, so the first idea cannot stand alone.

226. **Level:** Easy | **Skill/Knowledge:** Boundaries

Key Explanation: Choice D is the best answer. An "–ing" form of a verb can be used after a comma to add an additional action of the subject of the sentence. In this case, the subject "cracks" set off lava fountains and streams of lava as well as the main action of opening on the ridge.

Distractor Explanations: Choices A and **B** are both incorrect because a semicolon needs to be both preceded and followed by independent clauses. In the sentence, the first part is a clause, but the second part cannot stand on its own as a sentence. **Choice C** is incorrect because it is a comma splice between two independent clauses.

227. **Level:** Medium | **Skill/Knowledge:** Boundaries

Key Explanation: Choice D is the best answer because parenthetical ideas are treated as part of the word they refer to. In this case, the parenthetical idea is more detail describing "Eurasian magpies," so needs to be treated like the subject. There should be no comma between the subject and its verb, "are considered." There also is

no need for punctuation between the verb and its object.

Distractor Explanations: All of the other choices can be eliminated because they contain commas. In **Choice A**, the comma separates the subject from the parenthetical information related to it, and in **Choices B** and **C**, the comma separates the subject from the verb. **Choices A** and **C** are also incorrect because a colon should come after a complete clause, but instead it divides the verb "are considered" from its object.

228. **Level:** Medium | **Skill/Knowledge:** Boundaries

Key Explanation: Choice B is the best answer because a colon is correctly used after an independent clause to add more detail explaining the entire clause.

Distractor Explanations: Choice A is incorrect because it is a comma splice between two independent clauses. **Choice C** is incorrect because "–ing" verbs that modify a clause need to be placed after a comma rather than a colon; in addition, "winning" is not parallel with the other verb joined by "and," which is "ran." **Choice D** is incorrect because a colon can follow a clause, but the following portion is not parallel; "and" should join two ideas that are the same grammatical structure. Since "ran for 1,375 performances" has a verb and object, the first portion also needs a verb.

229. **Level:** Medium | **Skill/Knowledge:** Boundaries

Key Explanation: Choice D is the best answer because when a city and country name are included in a text, there needs to be a comma after the city. There also needs to be a comma after "Italy" in this sentence because the following portion, "although…earlier" is a dependent clause. A dependent clause needs to be divided from the main sentence with a comma.

Distractor Explanations: Choices A and **C** are incorrect because they do not have a comma separating the city, Naples, from the country, Italy, and therefore do not follow Standard English conventions. **Choices A** and **B** are incorrect because there should be a comma separating the dependent clause "although…earlier" from the main idea of the sentence.

230. **Level:** Easy | **Skill/Knowledge:** Boundaries

Key Explanation: Choice B is the best answer. "Which" is the start of a relative clause that refers to the preceding noun, in this case *chatarung.* Since the information includes additional facts about the noun, there should be a comma separating the relative clause from the rest of the sentence.

Distractor Explanations: Choice A is incorrect because there should be a comma separating the main sentence from the additional words that describe chatarung. **Choices C** and **D** are incorrect because the information following a semicolon or dash should not be a relative clause starting with "which." After those forms of punctuation in this context, "which" should be replaced with the pronoun "it."

231. **Level:** Medium | **Skill/Knowledge:** Boundaries

Key Explanation: Choice B is the best answer. "Which" starts a relative clause, so needs to be separated from the noun it modifies, in this case "mass extinctions," with a comma.

Distractor Explanations: Choice A is incorrect because it is a comma splice between two sentences that can stand on their own. **Choice C** is incorrect because a parenthesis needs an end parenthesis later in the sentence. **Choice D** is incorrect because "which" creates a dependent clause, but a semicolon needs to be followed by an independent clause that can stand on its own as a sentence.

232. **Level:** Medium | **Skill/Knowledge:** Boundaries

Key Explanation: Choice C is the best answer because two adjectives modifying the same noun should be divided with a comma, so "striped" and "large" should be separated. No other punctuation is needed here.

Distractor Explanations: Choices A and **B** are incorrect because there should be no comma between the final adjective in a list and the noun it refers to, so there should be no comma after "large." **Choices A** and **D** are incorrect because there should be no comma separating "with" and its object, "a tongue." **Choice D** is also missing a necessary comma after "striped."

233. **Level:** Medium | **Skill/Knowledge:** Boundaries

Key Explanation: Choice A is the best answer because the idiom "not only…but also…" does not need any punctuation unless they are complete clauses. "The fastest" is not a complete clause because it has no verb and cannot stand on its own as a sentence.

Distractor Explanations: All of the other choices can be eliminated because they contain unnecessary punctuation. **Choices B** and **D** are incorrect because there should be no comma after "system" dividing the parts of the idiom.

Choices **B** and **C** are incorrect because a colon should follow a complete clause, but "but also" is dangling.

234. **Level:** Easy | **Skill/Knowledge:** Boundaries

Key Explanation: Choice A is the best answer because a period correctly divides two independent clauses into distinct sentences.

Distractor Explanations: Choice B is incorrect because it is a comma splice between two independent clauses. **Choice C** is incorrect because a semicolon should divide two independent clauses, but the following portion has no subject and active verb. **Choice D** is incorrect because the resulting sentence is not parallel; verbs relating to the same subject need to be in the same form, but "is" and "originating" are different.

235. **Level:** Medium | **Skill/Knowledge:** Boundaries

Key Explanation: Choice D is the best answer because a quote that contains a full clause should be separated from the rest of the sentence using a comma. The first word in the quote is made capital.

Distractor Explanations: Choices A and **B** are incorrect because the first letter of a quotation should be capitalized if the quotation is a full clause that can stand on its own as a sentence. **Choice A** is also incorrect because there should be a comma after "saying" to divide the quote from the main clause. **Choice C** is incorrect because there should be no colon after "saying." A colon should follow a complete clause, but "saying" has no object.

236. **Level:** Medium | **Skill/Knowledge:** Boundaries

Key Explanation: Choice B is the best answer. "When…rule" is a clause that refers to the date "1776." It is possible to identify the year without the added information, so there should be a comma separating the clause from the word it modifies. No other punctuation is necessary here.

Distractor Explanations: Choice A is incorrect because a colon should follow a complete clause, but "from" is dangling without an object. In addition, **Choices A** and **C** are incorrect because there should be a comma separating "1776" and the clause that adds detail to it. **Choice C** is incorrect because a comma should not separate "from" from its object. **Choices C** and **D** are incorrect because there should not be a comma after "Empire" because the date is necessary for understanding the main clause. **Choice D** should also not have a colon after "1776" because "when" starts a dependent clause that needs to be joined to the word that modifies it with a comma.

237. **Level:** Medium | **Skill/Knowledge:** Boundaries

Key Explanation: Choice A is the best answer. A colon is preceded by a complete clause and can be followed by a clause, as long as the information expands on the claim in the entire first sentence. In this case, the following information clarified that the Boyington's desire for a more practical bun led to the invention of the corn dog.

Distractor Explanations: Choice B is incorrect because a colon is not the end of a sentence, so the following word needs to be lower case. **Choice C** is incorrect because it creates a comma splice between two independent clauses. **Choice D** is incorrect because a semicolon should be followed by a complete clause, but in this case, the following portion has no subject.

238. **Level:** Easy | **Skill/Knowledge:** Boundaries

Key Explanation: Choice B is the best answer because "so" subordinates the second half of the sentence. A subordinate clause needs a comma in front of it.

Distractor Explanations: Choice A is incorrect because a semicolon must be followed by an independent clause, but "so" subordinates the clause so it cannot stand on its own as a sentence. **Choice C** is incorrect because it is a comma splice between two clauses. **Choice D** is incorrect because the idea after the comma has no subject, so it is unclear what "can develop" is referring to.

239. **Level:** Medium | **Skill/Knowledge:** Boundaries

Key Explanation: Choice C is the best answer because a colon is used after a complete clause to add more information that refers to the content of the sentence. It fits the context of naming and describing the hypothetical thing that the scientists have been searching for.

Distractor Explanations: Choice A is incorrect because there should be no comma between "only" and the word it modifies, "theoretical." **Choice B** is incorrect because there should be punctuation dividing "theoretical" from the name of the black hole to indicate the end of the clause and the beginning of added details. It is also incorrect because "Sagittarius A*" is tacked onto the end of the part before the colon with no explanation. **Choice D** is incorrect because hyphens should frame additional information, but in this case divides "only" from the word it modifies, "theoretical."

240. **Level:** Medium | **Skill/Knowledge:** Boundaries

Key Explanation: Choice B is the best answer because the standard punctuation for a list that is joined by "and" is to place a comma after each item in the list, but no comma after "and."

Distractor Explanations: All of the other choices can be eliminated because there should not be any comma after "and" when writing a list.

241. **Level:** Easy | **Skill/Knowledge:** Boundaries

Key Explanation: Choice A is the best answer because ideas in parentheses are to be considered as a grammatical part of the word that they refer to. In this text, the dates that Henri was alive should be treated as part of the subject, "Robert Henri." Therefore, no other punctuation is necessary.

Distractor Explanations: Choices B and **D** can be eliminated because they contain a comma that divides the subject "Robert Henri" from the parenthetical words that describe it, "(1865–1929)." **Choice B** is also incorrect because it includes a comma after "was" that divides the passive past–tense verb "was inspired." **Choice C** is incorrect because the comma after the parentheses separates the subject from its verb.

242. **Level:** Easy | **Skill/Knowledge:** Boundaries

Key Explanation: Choice C is the best answer because words between quotation marks that are not independent clauses are treated as if they did not have quotation marks in a sentence. In this context, "Indian relay" is the object of the verb "called," so does not need to be separated by a comma. "[I]n which…gallop" is a relative clause that refers to "Indian relay," so there should be a comma after "relay." In American English, the comma goes inside the quotation mark.

Distractor Explanations: Choices A and **B** are incorrect because there needs to be a comma separating the relative clause, "in which…gallop," from the words that it modifies. **Choices B** and **D** are incorrect because there is only a comma before a quotation that is a complete independent clause, but "Indian relay" has no verb.

243. Level: Medium | **Skill/Knowledge:** Boundaries

Key Explanation: Choice A is the best answer because no punctuation is needed in the blank. "Upper case letters" is not a complete clause, so should be treated as if it were a standard object with no quotation marks.

Distractor Explanations: Choices B and **D** are incorrect because a comma is only necessary after "called" if the part in quotations is a full clause; in **Choice D**, the second comma is optional. **Choice C** is incorrect because a semicolon should be followed by an independent clause, which is not the case.

244. Level: Easy | **Skill/Knowledge:** Boundaries

Key Explanation: Choice A is the best answer because words in parentheses are to be treated as part of the word that they modify. In this case, "(2,722 feet)" refers to "meters," so there should be no punctuation between "meters" and the word it modifies, "tall." No commas are needed.

Distractor Explanations: Choices B and **D** are incorrect because there should be no comma dividing "(2,722 feet)" and the word it describes, "meters." **Choices B** and **C** are incorrect because the parenthetical aside is considered part of

"meters," and there should be no comma between "meters" and the word it describes, "tall." **Choices C** and **D** are incorrect because there should be no comma after tall because "and" joins two verbs ("stand" and "is") that go with the same subject, the Burj Khalifa. No comma should come between the subject and verb.

245. Level: Easy | **Skill/Knowledge:** Boundaries

Key Explanation: Choice A is the best answer because "to become" is necessary for understanding what journey is being discussed, so it should not be divided from the main clause with any punctuation.

Distractor Explanations: All of the other choices are incorrect because they contain unnecessary punctuation that divide essential parts of the sentence from each other. In **Choice B**, the comma separates "journey" from the words that explain what the journey is. In **Choices C** and **D**, colons should be preceded by independent clauses, but the preceding part cannot stand on its own as a sentence.

246. Level: Easy | **Skill/Knowledge:** Boundaries

Key Explanation: Choice A is the best answer because a list joined by "and" has a comma after each item in the list and no comma after "and."

Distractor Explanations: Choices B and **C** are incorrect because there is no comma after "and" in a list; **Choice B** is also missing the comma after "oxygen." **Choice D** is incorrect because "low" is one adjective modifying "oxygen," and no comma is used if there is only one adjective.

247. Level: Medium | **Skill/Knowledge:** Boundaries

Key Explanation: Choice D is the best answer because information added to a sentence with two dashes should be non–essential to the main sentence. If the portion is removed, the sentence still makes sense: "400 blue–and–yellow macaws thrive within the city limits."

Distractor Explanations: Choices A and **C** are incorrect because if there is a single dash in a sentence, the preceding portion must be a complete idea, but there is no active verb in the relative clause that starts with "that." **Choice B** is incorrect because when the portion between the dashes is removed, including "thrive," the remaining portion does not have an active verb.

248. Level: Easy | **Skill/Knowledge:** Boundaries

Key Explanation: Choice B is the best answer. Information added to a sentence between hyphens should not affect the grammatical structure of the main sentence. If the added information is removed, the main sentence still makes sense: "Forest bathing" can reduce stress…" The added information is a definition that helps a reader not familiar with the topic.

Distractor Explanations: All of the other choices are incorrect because the main sentence is not complete if the parts between the dashes are removed. In **Choice A**, the first portion is only a noun and the part after the dash starts with a verb. In **Choice C**, "…walking in can…" has no object for "in." In **Choice D**, there are two dashes, so it is unclear what is supposed to be the main sentence and what is the added portion

249. Level: Easy | **Skill/Knowledge:** Boundaries

Key Explanation: Choice A is the best answer because "kerosene or methane" is the object of the preposition "into." No punctuation should separate these elements of a sentence from each other.

Distractor Explanations: Choices B and **D** are incorrect because no comma should divide two nouns joined by "or." **Choices C** and **D** are incorrect because a colon should follow a complete clause, but "into" is hanging. **Choices C** and **D** are also incorrect because "that" introduces an essential idea that restricts the meaning of the noun it refers to. In this case, "that" shows that the kerosene or methane is of a quality for fuel, as opposed to lower grades. Essential parts of a sentence should not be divided from the main clause with any punctuation.

250. Level: Medium | **Skill/Knowledge:** Boundaries

Key Explanation: Choice B is the best answer because a comma needs to divide two clauses, and the second clause starts with "but." No other punctuation is needed here.

Distractor Explanations: Choice A is incorrect because a comma is needed to divide the two clauses "only about…growth" and "but the… years old." **Choice C** is incorrect because the comma should not follow "but" because it leaves that word dangling at the end of the preceding clause. In addition, no comma is needed between "undisturbed" and "old growth" because "old growth" is treated as a single idea rather than an adjective and noun. **Choice D** is incorrect because when there is a series of adjectives that modify a noun, no comma is placed after the last adjective.

Boundaries (Answers)

251. **Level:** Easy | **Skill/Knowledge:** Boundaries

Key Explanation: Choice B is the best answer because "a…*Geographic*" describes the subject, Aji Styawan. Such details need to be separated from the main clause using the same punctuation at the start and end. Since "*Geographic*" is followed by a comma, "a professional" should be preceded by one.

Distractor Explanations: Choice A is incorrect because information added to a sentence must have the same punctuation at the start and end, and there is a comma after "*Geographic.*" **Choice C** is incorrect because it creates a complete independent clause inside the main clause that is not subordinated in any way. **Choice D** is incorrect because "whose" shows possession, but Styawan does not own "a professional photographer."

252. **Level:** Easy | **Skill/Knowledge:** Boundaries

Key Explanation: Choice B is the best answer because "the world's tallest mountain" can only refer to one thing, so the name is additional information rather than essential details for explaining which mountain is being described. As a result, the added information must be set off from the main sentence with commas at both ends. Information in parentheses is considered as part of the word they refer to. In this case, the exact height refers to the mountain. The comma after the name must therefore go after the second parenthesis.

Distractor Explanations: Choices A and **C** are incorrect because there should be no comma dividing "Mt. Everest" from the parenthetical information that refers to it. **Choices C** and **D** are incorrect because there needs to be a comma after

the parenthesis to show where the next portion of the sentence begins. The following portion is an appositive which refers to the main clause. **Choices C** and **D** are incorrect because there needs to be a comma after "mountain" because the name is additional information rather than essential.

253. **Level:** Easy | **Skill/Knowledge:** Boundaries

Key Explanation: Choice A is the best answer because the text contains two independent clauses, "not all…Antarctic" and "the endangered…Islands." A semicolon accurately divides two ideas when one is not subordinated to the other in any way.

Distractor Explanations: Choice B is incorrect because a semicolon should join two independent clauses, but "and" subordinates the second idea so it cannot stand on its own. **Choice C** is incorrect because it is a comma splice between two independent clauses. **Choice D** is also a comma splice because "however" does not subordinate an idea; it only acts as an independent comment to the reader.

254. **Level:** Easy | **Skill/Knowledge:** Boundaries

Key Explanation: Choice D is the best answer because there are two independent clauses, "medlar is…diet" and "it has…eat." "However" is a transition word that does not subordinate either clause, so the two ideas should be divided with a period and the H should be capitalized. There should be a comma after "however" to separate it from the second clause.

Distractor Explanations: Choices A and **B** are incorrect because they create comma splices between two independent clauses. In addition, "however" is joined to one of the clauses because there is a comma on only one side. **Choice C** is incorrect because a dash should follow a complete clause, but "however" is dangling at the end of the first idea.

255. **Level:** Easy | **Skill/Knowledge:** Boundaries

Key Explanation: Choice C is the best answer because "which" correctly starts a relative clause that refers to the previous noun, "Meradalir Valley."

Distractor Explanations: Choice A is incorrect because "is" needs to have a subject, but there is no subject after the comma in the portion of the sentence containing "is." **Choices B** and **D** are incorrect because they create a complete independent clause that is not subordinated in any way from the main sentence. Note that for **Choice D**, "that" can be used at the start of a relative clause, but in that usage, it cannot be preceded by a comma.

256. **Level:** Hard | **Skill/Knowledge:** Boundaries

Key Explanation: Choice A is the correct answer. Commas are used to mark non–defining clauses. A pair of commas must be used in the middle of a sentence to set off clauses, phrases, and words that are not essential to the meaning of the sentence. In this case, the sentence will make sense even without "meaning that much information is unavailable." Therefore, if a phrase does not add essential meaning to the sentence, two commas must be used at the beginning and end of the phrase to separate it from the rest of the sentence.

Distractor Explanations: Choice B is incorrect because when using a dash to add extra information, if the main sentence resumes, a

second dash must be added at the end of the added information. For example, if the sentence reads, "However, challenges remain in data and modeling–meaning that much information is unavailable–especially for the entire Third Pole region," it would be grammatically correct. **Choice C** is incorrect because two commas are required to break the clauses in the sentence and **Choice C** lacks the initial comma. **Choice D** is incorrect because if a period is added, the last sentence will not make sense on its own.

257. **Level:** Hard | **Skill/Knowledge:** Boundaries

Key Explanation: Choice A is correct. When using a semi–colon, it must be preceded and followed by independent clauses, meaning that both parts of the sentence must make sense independently.

Distractor Explanations: Choice B is incorrect because when using a dash to add extra information, if the main sentence resumes, a second dash must be added at the end of the added information. **Choice C** is incorrect because while joining three independent clauses in a compound sentence, a comma must be inserted before the conjunction. **Choice D** is incorrect because "but" is used when trying to say something that is different from what has been said before.

258. **Level:** Medium | **Skill/Knowledge:** Boundaries

Key Explanation: Choice B is correct because two commas are required to mark non–defining clauses in a sentence. Non–defining clauses give the reader extra information about the noun in the sentence. It is not necessary information, and the sentence will make sense even without the extra information.

Distractor explanations: Choice A is incorrect because when using a semi–colon, it must be preceded and followed by independent clauses, meaning that both parts of the sentence must make sense independently. **Choice C** is incorrect because when using a dash to add extra information, if the main sentence resumes, a second dash must be added at the end of the added information. **Choice D** is incorrect because a colon is usually used to introduce a list or between sentences when the second sentence explains or justifies the first sentence.

259. **Level:** Medium | **Skill/Knowledge:** Boundaries

Key Explanation: Choice D is correct because when the name of a place is followed by the country or region it exists in, a comma must separate the name of the place and the name of the region. A comma also must be added after "South America" as "Originating from the highlands of the Andes, South America" is an introductory clause. Introductory clauses are dependent clauses that provide background information or "set the stage" for the main part of the sentence, the independent clause. A comma must be used after an introductory clause.

Distractor Explanations: Choice A is incorrect because no comma separates the name of the place from the region. **Choice B** is incorrect because no comma follows South America. A comma must be used after an introductory clause. **Choice C** is incorrect because a comma is not required before "Andes."

260. **Level:** Easy | **Skill/Knowledge:** Boundaries

Key Explanation: Choice A is correct because when the dependent clause ("When the egg whites have the consistency of shaving foam") starts with a subordinating conjunction ("when"), a comma is needed.

Distractor Explanations: Choice B is incorrect because it does not have a comma to offset the clause at the beginning of the sentence. **Choice C** is incorrect because a semicolon is used to separate two main clauses. **Choice D** is incorrect because a colon is only used to introduce a list, direct speech, or to indicate a subdivision of a topic.

261

A resident of Canada and Alaska, the wood frog is one of the only amphibians that lives north of the Arctic Circle. It is able to survive the frigid winters because _____ contain a substance that acts like antifreeze.

Which choice completes the text so that it conforms to the conventions of Standard English?

A) it's cells

B) it's cell's

C) its cells

D) its cell's

262

Scientists who live aboard the International Space Station _____ conduct experiments that demonstrate that flames form orb shapes rather than a long taper in an environment with no gravity.

Which choice completes the text so that it conforms to the conventions of Standard English?

A) regular

B) regularity

C) regulate

D) regularly

263

Designers of the ambitious 2,000–mile–long Ring Road in Afghanistan would be disheartened to observe _____ condition today: incomplete in some places and destroyed in others.

Which choice completes the text so that it conforms to the conventions of Standard English?

A) it's

B) its

C) their

D) they're

264

Some monkeys and apes can recognize themselves in a mirror and other actions which demonstrate self–awareness, _____

Which choice completes the text so that it conforms to the conventions of Standard English?

A) humans develop this trait at about 18 months old.

B) about 18 months old is when this trait develops in humans.

C) a trait that develops at about 18 months old in humans.

D) it is a trait that develops at about 18 months old in humans.

265

Yangchen, which means "salt city," is a city in China that _____ salt flats which historically have produced much of the salt used for trade in the region and now are stopping places during migrations of rare bird species.

Which choice completes the text so that it conforms to the conventions of Standard English?

A) had

B) has

C) has had

D) is having

266

Meat alternatives form a multi–billion–dollar market that continues to grow. For all the pleasant flavors and _____ , many consumers feel that meat cannot be adequately simulated.

Which choice completes the text so that it conforms to the conventions of Standard English?

A) nutritional benefits

B) they have nutritional benefits

C) the benefits are in the nutrition

D) also nutritional benefits as well

267

Scientists are now debunking many theories about the superiority of humans over other species in the animal kingdom. For example, once considered an emotion exclusive to humans, _____

Which choice completes the text so that it conforms to the conventions of Standard English?

A) pilot whales and orcas have demonstrated grief over a dead calf.

B) a dead calf has caused demonstrations of grief in pilot whales and orcas.

C) grief has been demonstrated by pilot whales and orcas over a dead calf.

D) pilot whales and orcas which have a dead calf will demonstrate grief.

268

Jane Goodall is best known for her groundbreaking research on chimpanzees in the 1960s. She demonstrated that primates not only used found objects _____ tools to complete specific tasks.

Which choice completes the text so that it conforms to the conventions of Standard English?

A) and were making

B) but they make

C) but also made

D) and also made

269

In 1922, archaeologist Howard Carter discovered the tomb of the ruler known _____ as King Tut. Scientists still debate whether he was active and able–bodied or an invalid, since he was buried with items associated with either lifestyle, including walking sticks and chariot whips.

Which choice completes the text so that it conforms to the conventions of Standard English?

A) familiar

B) familiarly

C) familiarity

D) familial

270

Among all the grim news about coral reef bleaching, Kiribati's Line Islands have provided data stating that protecting herbivorous fish that remove algae can help damaged reefs _____.

Which choice completes the text so that it conforms to the conventions of Standard English?

A) rebound

B) have rebounded

C) rebounded

D) they rebound

271

Researchers at the Max Planck Institute showed videos to chimpanzees in an effort to determine the capacity for emotions such as empathy and determined that when chimpanzees are stressed, their noses, just like those of humans, get colder.

Which choice completes the text so that it conforms to the conventions of Standard English?

A) humans

B) that of humans

C) those human's

D) those of humans

272

Blue cheese is a general term that describes a wide variety of cheeses that have been aged with *Penicillium* cultures to give _____ distinct, greenish–blue spots or veins and complex flavors.

Which choice completes the text so that it conforms to the conventions of Standard English?

A) it

B) it's

C) their

D) theirs

273

The wood frog of North America resides north of the Arctic Circle. To survive the cold winters in hibernation, it allows its cells to freeze rather than _____ into the ground to stay warm.

Which choice completes the text so that it conforms to the conventions of Standard English?

A) buries

B) burying

C) it buries

D) to bury itself

274

Air plants are epiphytes, which means that they live on other plants in the wild, so they _____ adequate moisture, warm temperatures, and indirect sunlight, but have no need for soil.

Which choice completes the text so that it conforms to the conventions of Standard English?

A) require

B) are requiring

C) required

D) have been requiring

275

Tyrian purple, _____ is named after Tyre in Lebanon where it was produced, was a dye used in ancient times that was so expensive to produce that it was often referred to as imperial purple or royal purple.

Which choice completes the text so that it conforms to the conventions of Standard English?

A) it

B) that

C) where

D) which

276

At its height in the second century, _____ and it contained about a fourth of the world's population.

Which choice completes the text so that it conforms to the conventions of Standard English?

A) the Roman Empire spread across three continents

B) three continents were occupied by the Roman Empire

C) there were three continents where the Roman Empire ruled

D) continents under the Roman Empire numbered three

277

The thorny devil lizard of Australia has copious spines to protect _____ from predators, but these hard structures also catch moisture that condenses during the hot, dry weather.

Which choice completes the text so that it conforms to the conventions of Standard English?

A) it

B) itself

C) them

D) one

278

Clap When You Land is a powerful novel for young adults by Elizabeth Acevedo. The tragic story of loss and love is based on an _____ event, the crash of an airplane that was headed from New York City to the Dominican Republic.

Which choice completes the text so that it conforms to the conventions of Standard English?

A) actual

B) actualize

C) actually

D) actuality

279

Born in Okinawa in 1868, _____ though various forms of unarmed combat techniques were used for hundreds of years prior to his birth.

Which choice completes the text so that it conforms to the conventions of Standard English?

A) credit for modern karate was given to its founder, Funakochi Gichin,

B) modern karate has the credit of being founded by Funakochi Gichin,

C) the founding of modern karate is credited to Funakochi Gichin,

D) Funakochi Gichin is credited with being the founder of modern karate,

280

Called the "King of Country," musician George _____ have sold over 120 million copies worldwide, making him one of the top–selling recording artists of all time.

Which choice completes the text so that it conforms to the conventions of Standard English?

A) Straits records

B) Strait's records

C) Strait's records'

D) Straits record's

281

In Greenland, Inughuit Inuits _____ birds called "little auks" every summer for centuries to supplement their diets in a land covered much of the year by snow and ice.

Which choice completes the text so that it conforms to the conventions of Standard English?

A) are harvesting

B) have harvested

C) will harvest

D) harvest

282

Black rhinoceros and white rhinoceros are basically the same color. The head helps in identifying the species: black rhinoceros heads are _____ white rhinoceros heads are.

Which choice completes the text so that it conforms to the conventions of Standard English?

A) short as

B) short than

C) shorter as

D) shorter than

283

Born on Navajo land in Arizona, Quannah Rose Chasinghorse is a Lakota Native American _____ uses her fame as a model to support activism that empowers indigenous peoples.

Which choice completes the text so that it conforms to the conventions of Standard English?

A) she

B) who

C) whom

D) that

284

The complex mosaic patterns on the shell of a wood turtle _____ it to effectively blend in with the leaf debris scattered on the forest floor and hide from creatures that might consider it to be a good meal.

Which choice completes the text so that it conforms to the conventions of Standard English?

A) allow

B) allows

C) is allowing

D) has allowed

285

Although most paleontologists agree that there was likely a massive meteorite impact in the distant past, very few attribute mass extinctions of dinosaurs to such an event. If it were true, then the extinctions _____ place over millions of years, which is what most likely happened.

Which choice completes the text so that it conforms to the conventions of Standard English?

A) would not have taken

B) did not take

C) had not taken

D) would not be taking

286

New York manufacturer Corning has developed flexible ceramics that can be made thinner than a sheet of paper, yet can withstand intense heat. Currently they _____ for use in sensors and batteries.

Which choice completes the text so that it conforms to the conventions of Standard English?

A) had been developed

B) have developed

C) were developed

D) are being developed

287

Actor Bob McGrath was a long–time character on the _____ Sesame Street, but he actually started his career as a singer on a program called *Singing Along with Mitch* between 1960 and 1964.

Which choice completes the text so that it conforms to the conventions of Standard English?

A) children's television series

B) childrens' television series'

C) children's television series

D) children's television series'

288

Although chocolate has been around in various forms for centuries, the company called J.S. Fry & Sons _____ with inventing the first chocolate candy bar in 1846.

Which choice completes the text so that it conforms to the conventions of Standard English?

A) credits

B) is credited

C) are credited

D) were credited

289

The okapi is an animal that has stripes similar to _____, but it is actually more closely related to a giraffe.

Which choice completes the text so that it conforms to the conventions of Standard English?

A) a zebra

B) that of a zebra

C) a zebra's

D) zebras

290

Marion Donovan invented the disposable diaper and greatly simplified one aspect of childcare. Her invention was notable because it not only had absorbent pads _____ snaps that replaced more dangerous safety pins.

Which choice completes the text so that it conforms to the conventions of Standard English?

A) but also

B) and even

C) also

D) and

291

Called the patriarch of modern sculpture, Constantin Brancusi (1876–1957) grew up in Romania, _____ he learned to carve by making farm tools.

Which choice completes the text so that it conforms to the conventions of Standard English?

A) that

B) where

C) there

D) in which

292

Jeannie Raharimampionona is a Malagasy conservationist and biologist who has helped establish dozens of refuges to protect the _____ 1,000 species of orchid in Madagascar from deforestation and habitat loss.

Which choice completes the text so that it conforms to the conventions of Standard English?

A) approximate

B) approximates

C) approximately

D) approximation

293

The planet Jupiter's Great Red Spot is a massive storm that astronomers believe has lasted for at least 350 years. The size has been slowly shrinking over the past few decades, but in 2004, was about three times _____.

Which choice completes the text so that it conforms to the conventions of Standard English?

A) A) Earth

B) B) one of Earth

C) C) the size of Earth's

D) D) the diameter of Earth

294

Opened in 1922, the Lincoln Memorial in Washington, D.C. was envisioned as an imposing monument to the sixteenth president of the United States. Every year, millions of people still _____ the edifice made of 35,000 tons of granite, marble, and limestone.

Which choice completes the text so that it conforms to the conventions of Standard English?

A) visit

B) visited

C) are visiting

D) had visited

295

A young country, _____ in 2008, and half of the population of approximately 1.8 million citizens are under the age of 30.

Which choice completes the text so that it conforms to the conventions of Standard English?

A) the declaration of Kosovo's independence from Serbia was made

B) Kosovo only declared its independence from Serbia

C) independence from Serbia was declared by Kosovo

D) Kosovo's declaration of independence was given to Serbia

296

Hyenas, carnivorous mammals from Africa, have a complex social structure that is matriarchal, and the leader of the clan maintains _____ position through alliances with other females.

Which choice completes the text so that it conforms to the conventions of Standard English?

A) his

B) her

C) their

D) one's

297

The Doppler Shift is a concept first described by Austrian physicist Christian Doppler in 1842 to explain why waves such as sound change in frequency when _____ from a stationary point. A classic example is that ambulance sirens appear to increase in pitch as the vehicle approaches.

Which choice completes the text so that it conforms to the conventions of Standard English?

A) perceive

B) perceived

C) are perceiving

D) have been perceived

298

Since 1971, researchers in Kenya studying the Amboseli baboon population _____ to determine how social behaviors alter the animals' chances of survival.

Which choice completes the text so that it conforms to the conventions of Standard English?

A) work

B) are working

C) had worked

D) have been working

299

In the Blackfoot Siksikaitsitapi language, the word *aatsimoiyihkaan* means "sovereignty." However, the definition is slightly different as it includes not only the freedom to decide personal acts but also _____ maintain balance in the world.

Which choice completes the text so that it conforms to the conventions of Standard English?

A) the responsibility to

B) they are responsible for

C) including the responsibility to

D) includes being responsible for

300

In the original Indian board game involving war strategies that was _____ into chess, the piece next to the king was a male counselor called a *ferz*, but Europeans romanticized the game and made that piece into a queen.

Which choice completes the text so that it conforms to the conventions of Standard English?

A) adaptable

B) adaptation

C) adapted

D) adaptiv

261. **Level:** Easy | **Skill/Knowledge:** Form, Structure, and Sense

Key Explanation: Choice C is the best answer. "Its" is the proper possessive form of the singular "it." "Cells" is a plural noun, so does not need an apostrophe.

Distractor Explanations: Choices A and **B** are incorrect because "it's" is a contraction for "it is," so does not properly indicate that the cells belong to the frog. **Choices B** and **D** are incorrect because "cell's" is the possessive form of the singular word "cell." First, each frog presumably has more than one cell, so the word should be plural. Second, the following word is the verb "contain," so it is not a noun possessed by the cells.

262. **Level:** Easy | **Skill/Knowledge:** Form, Structure, and Sense

Key Explanation: Choice D is the best answer because the blank should modify the verb "conduct." **Choice D** is an adverb, so correctly can refer to a verb.

Distractor Explanations: None of the other choices can be used to modify a verb. **Choice A** is an adjective, so it can modify "experiments," but the blank precedes the verb and therefore refers to the verb. **Choice B** is a noun, and **Choice C** is another verb.

263. **Level:** Easy | **Skill/Knowledge:** Form, Structure, and Sense

Key Explanation: Choice B is the best answer because the blank portion should be a pronoun that indicates what the "condition" belongs to. Since the condition is "incomplete in some places and destroyed in others," the word must refer to the "Ring Road." **Choice B** is a singular possessive form, so accurately fits the context.

Distractor Explanations: Choice A is incorrect because it is a contraction for "it is," so does not indicate possession of the condition. **Choices C** and **D** are plural words so do not describe the singular road; in addition, **Choice D** is not possessive. **Choice D** is a contraction for "they are."

264. **Level:** Medium | **Skill/Knowledge:** Form, Structure, and Sense

Key Explanation: Choice C is the best answer because it is an appositive phrase, meaning it is a noun phrase that correctly describes the previous noun, "self-awareness."

Distractor Explanations: All of the other choices are incorrect because they are independent clauses. Since the part before the comma is also an independent clause, these choices all create comma splices.

265. **Level:** Easy | **Skill/Knowledge:** Form, Structure, and Sense

Key Explanation: Choice B is the best answer because it is a present tense verb and the blank portion is something that is true about the City of Yangchen now. The salt flats still exist because rare birds migrate there.

Distractor Explanations: Choices A and **C** can be eliminated because they are past tense verbs, but the fact that rare birds still visit shows that the salt flats still exist in Yangchen. **Choice D** is a present tense verb, but does not fit the context because the progressive form is used to indicate an action rather than a state of existence.

266. **Level:** Medium | **Skill/Knowledge:** Form, Structure, and Sense

     Key Explanation: Choice A is the best answer because "and" should join two items that are grammatically equivalent. The first item is "the pleasant flavors," a noun. **Choice A** is also a noun.

     Distractor Explanations: Choices B and **C** can be eliminated because they are clauses, so they are not parallel with "the pleasant flavors." **Choice D** is a noun, but "and" gives the same idea as "also" and "as well," so using all three words is redundant.

267. **Level:** Medium | **Skill/Knowledge:** Form, Structure, and Sense

     Key Explanation: Choice C is the best answer. "Once considered an emotion exclusive to humans" is a modifier that describes "an emotion," so it needs to refer to grief. A modifier at the beginning of a sentence must be directly followed by the word that it refers to, and **Choice C** correctly places "grief" at the start of the main clause.

     Distractor Explanations: All of the other choices can be eliminated because the modifier "once… humans" illogically refers to something other than grief. In **Choices A** and **D**, the result is that "pilot whales and orcas" appear to be an emotion. In **Choice B**, the modified word is "dead calf."

268. **Level:** Medium | **Skill/Knowledge:** Form, Structure, and Sense

     Key Explanation: Choice C is the best answer because it correctly uses the idiom "not only XX but also YY." In this pattern, XX and YY must have the same grammatical structure. **Choice**

B maintains the past tense of "used" in the verb "made."

Distractor Explanations: Choices A and **D** are incorrect because they use "and" rather than "but also," deviating from standard conventions. **Choice B** is incorrect because "they make" is not parallel with "used found objects." "Primates" precedes "not only," so the subject should not be repeated. Note that "also" is sometimes eliminated in the idiom, so that is not the reason for eliminating this choice.

269. **Level:** Easy | **Skill/Knowledge:** Form, Structure, and Sense

     Key Explanation: Choice B is the best answer because it is an adverb which can be used to describe a verb. In the context, the "familiar" or "friendly and casual" nature refers to the verb "known."

     Distractor Explanations: Choices A and **D** are adjectives, so cannot be used to refer to a verb such as "known." **Choice C** is a noun, so cannot be used to describe a verb.

270. **Level:** Easy | **Skill/Knowledge:** Form, Structure, and Sense

     Key Explanation: Choice A is the best answer. "Help" should be followed by a noun, in this case "damaged reefs," and a verb in the plain form. **Choice A** is the plain form of "rebound."

     Distractor Explanations: All of the other choices can be eliminated because they are not standard usage with "help." **Choices B** and **C** are past tense verb forms, and **Choice D** includes an extra noun, "they."

271. **Level:** Easy | **Skill/Knowledge:** Form, Structure, and Sense

Key Explanation: Choice D is the best answer because a comparison using "just like" should include two things which are similar in nature. The first thing being compared is "their noses," where "their" refers to the chimpanzees. **Choice D** completes the comparison logically by referring to "those" or "the noses" of humans. Noses can be compared to noses.

Distractor Explanations: All of the other choices are incorrect because they are not comparable items to compare with the noses of chimpanzees. **Choice A** compares the noses to humans, not the noses of humans. **Choices B** has a singular "that" meaning "nose," but "humans" is plural. Humans have more than one type of nose because they are a heterogenous population. **Choice C** is incorrect because "those" modifies "humans," meaning that certain humans are being referred to, but there is no specific referent to show who those people might be. The possessive form, however, would work in the context if "those" were removed.

272. **Level:** Medium | **Skill/Knowledge:** Form, Structure, and Sense

Key Explanation: Choice C is the best answer. The blank portion needs to be a possessive form that shows that the "distinct, greenish–blue spots or veins" and "complex flavors" belong to the "cheeses." **Choice C** is a plural possessive form, so correctly refers to the plural "cheeses."

Distractor Explanations: Choice A is incorrect because it is a singular noun, so does not fit the context of modifying the nouns "spots, veins, and flavors." It also does not work as the object of "give" because the cultures give the cheeses the

spots, veins, and flavors, and "it" is singular and "cheeses" is plural. **Choice D** is incorrect because it is a plural object pronoun, not a possessive pronoun. **Choice D** should be used alone as the object; it should not modify a different noun.

273. **Skill/Knowledge:** Form, Structure, and Sense

Key Explanation: Choice A is the best answer because "rather than" should join two grammatically equivalent verb phrases. The subject is the same pronoun "it" for both verbs. Since the first verb is "allows," **Choice A** is correct because it has the same present tense form.

Distractor Explanations: All of the other choices are incorrect because they do not maintain the parallelism of the sentence. **Choice B** has a gerund rather than an active verb. **Choice C** includes the same subject, but "rather than" with the same subject should only repeat the verb. **Choice D** is incorrect because "to bury" could be parallel with "to freeze," but it does not grammatically fit because the cells are plural and "itself" is singular; **Choice D** does not logically fit because the cells do not bury into the ground, the frog does.

274. **Level:** Easy | **Skill/Knowledge:** Form, Structure, and Sense

Key Explanation: Choice A is the best answer because a general scientific truth should be stated in the simple present tense.

Distractor Explanations: All of the other choices can be eliminated because they are not standard usage when describing a scientific truth in general terms.

275. **Level:** Medium | **Skill/Knowledge:** Form, Structure, and Sense

Key Explanation: Choice D is the best answer because it correctly introduces a relative clause that adds detail to the noun "Tyrian purple."

Distractor Explanations: Choice A is incorrect because it forms an independent clause between the commas rather than subordinates the clause. **Choice B** is incorrect because it is used to add essential information that is necessary to understand the subject, and it does not follow a comma. In the context, it is possible to identify Tyrian purple without the added detail about the origin of the name. **Choice C** is incorrect because it is used to refer to a place. Though there is a place in the relative clause, the clause refers to a color rather than a location.

276. **Level:** Easy | **Skill/Knowledge:** Form, Structure, and Sense

Key Explanation: "At its height in the second century" is a modifier that describes the "Roman Empire." A modifier at the start of a sentence should be followed by the word it refers to.

Distractor Explanations: All of the other choices can be eliminated because the modifier at the start of the sentence illogically refers to a different noun. In **Choice B,** "the height" refers to "three continents." In **Choice C,** it refers to the generic "there," and in **Choice D** it refers to "continents."

277. **Level:** Easy | **Skill/Knowledge:** Form, Structure, and Sense

Key Explanation: Choice B is the best answer because it is used as an object when referring to the subject of the sentence. In the context, the

subject of the sentence is the lizard, and the object that is protected is also the lizard.

Distractor Explanations: Choice A is used when the object is different from the subject, so does not fit the context where the two words refer to the same thing, the lizard. **Choice C** is incorrect because it is plural, but the subject "lizard" is singular. **Choice D** is incorrect because it is used to refer to a general noun that has not previously been mentioned, but "lizard" is specifically stated in the sentence.

278. **Level:** Easy | **Skill/Knowledge:** Form, Structure, and Sense

Key Explanation: Choice A is the best answer because the blank portion refers to the word "event." **Choice A** is an adjective, so can be used to modify a noun.

Distractor Explanations: All of the other choices can be eliminated because they are not used to modify a noun. **Choice B** is a verb, **Choice C** is an adverb, and **Choice D** is a noun.

279. **Level:** Easy | **Skill/Knowledge:** Form, Structure, and Sense

Key Explanation: Choice D is the best answer because a modifier at the start of the sentence needs to be directly followed by the noun it refers to. In the text, "Born in Okinawa in 1868" refers to the person Funakochi Gichin.

Distractor Explanations: All of the other choices can be eliminated because the modifier "Born in Okinawa in 1868" refers to something other than the person; it does not refer to the martial art of karate because the latter part of the sentence refers to "his birth." In **Choice A**, the modifier refers to "credit." In **Choice B**, it refers to "modern karate," and in **Choice C**, it refers to "the founding."

280. **Level:** Easy | **Skill/Knowledge:** Form, Structure, and Sense

Key Explanation: Choice B is the best answer because an apostrophe of possession shows that the "records" are those of "George Strait." No other punctuation is needed here.

Distractor Explanations: Choices A and **D** are incorrect because there needs to be an apostrophe to show that "Strait" made the records. **Choices C** and **D** are incorrect because the records do not own anything, and an apostrophe indicates possession. It does not matter that for **Choice C**, "records" is plural and for **Choice D**, the word is singular.

281. **Level:** Easy | **Skill/Knowledge:** Form, Structure, and Sense

Key Explanation: Choice B is the best answer because it is used to show an action which began in the past and continues to the present, so it fits the context of a hunting style that has been used "for centuries."

Distractor Explanations: All of the other choices can be eliminated because they do not establish the correct time sequence. **Choices A** and **D** are present tense, so do not show that the action occurred in the past as well. **Choice C** refers to something that has not yet happened.

282. **Level:** Easy | **Skill/Knowledge:** Form, Structure, and Sense

Key Explanation: Choice D is the best answer because the sentence is forming a contrast between the heads of black and white rhinoceros. "Than" establishes the comparison, and requires the ending "–er" on "short."

Distractor Explanations: Choices A and **B** are incorrect because "short" is a plain adjective that does not show any comparison with another thing. **Choices A** and **C** are incorrect because "as…as" can be used in a comparison when things are the same size, but the first "as" does not exist in the sentence.

283. **Level:** Easy | **Skill/Knowledge:** Form, Structure, and Sense

Key Explanation: Choice B is the best answer because it is a pronoun that begins a relative clause that describes a person, in this case, Chasinghorse.

Distractor Explanations: Choice A is incorrect because it creates a run–on sentence between two independent clauses. **Choice C** is incorrect because it shows that the word it modifies is the object of the following clause, but in this case, Chasinghorse is the person using her fame, so she is the subject rather than the object. **Choice D** is incorrect because it is used to refer to an object, not a person.

284. **Level:** Easy | **Skill/Knowledge:** Form, Structure, and Sense

Key Explanation: Choice A is the best answer because it is the only plural verb and the subject is the plural "The complex mosaic patterns."

Distractor Explanations: All of the other choices can be eliminated because they are singular verbs, so they do not agree with the plural subject "the complex mosaic patterns." "A wood turtle" and "the shell of a wood turtle" are singular, so the following verb may appear to be singular, but these nouns are joined to the subject with the word "on" and are really just descriptions of the subject.

285. **Level:** Easy | **Skill/Knowledge:** Form, Structure, and Sense

Key Explanation: Choice A is the best answer. A conditional sentence using the possibility word "if" in the first half needs to have the conditional past tense form using "would" in the half starting with "then."

Distractor Explanations: None of the other choices complete the standard usage with the "if… then…" sentence structure. **Choices B** and **C** are past tense forms that are given as certain rather than possible. **Choice D** is a present tense verb, but the sentence is referring to an event in the "distant past."

286. **Level:** Medium | **Skill/Knowledge:** Form, Structure, and Sense

Key Explanation: Choice D is the best answer because it is a present passive form that shows that the act of "developing" is currently happening and is done by something other than the ceramics.

Distractor Explanations: Choice A is incorrect because the verb form is used to show that something happened in the past before another action, but "currently" shows that the action is happening now. **Choices B** and **C** are incorrect because they are active verbs, but the ceramics themselves are not "developing" or "creating" something; scientists at Corning are creating the ceramics.

287. **Level:** Medium | **Skill/Knowledge:** Form, Structure, and Sense

Key Explanation: Choice C is the best answer because to show possession, an apostrophe and "s" are put after a plural noun that does not end with "s." No other punctuation is needed here.

Distractor Explanations: Choice A is incorrect because "childrens" needs an apostrophe to show the "television series" is for "children." **Choices B** and **D** are incorrect because "series" does not own anything, so does not need an apostrophe. **Choice B** is also incorrect because an "s" and apostrophe are only placed after a plural noun that ends in "s," but "children" is plural with no "s."

288. **Level:** Easy | **Skill/Knowledge:** Form, Structure, and Sense

Key Explanation: Choice B is the best answer because "credit" refers to giving acknowledgement for something. It needs to be used in the passive form in this sentence because the credit is given by an unmentioned audience to the company. Although "J.S. Fry & Sons" may appear plural, the subject is the singular "company."

Distractor Explanations: Choice A is incorrect because, although it is singular and agrees with "company," it is active. However, the company does not do the crediting, it receives the credit, so should be passive. **Choices C** and **D** are incorrect because they are plural so do not agree with the singular subject.

289. **Level:** Medium | **Skill/Knowledge:** Form, Structure, and Sense

Key Explanation: Choice C is the best answer because "similar to" indicates that there is a comparison. "The okapi" is a singular animal, and the comparison is between the stripes of that animal and the stripes on a zebra. Since "stripes" is given, all that is needed is the possessive form in **Choice C.**

Distractor Explanations: Choices A and **D** are incorrect because they form an illogical comparison between stripes and the zebras themselves. **Choice B** is incorrect because "stripes" is plural, so does not agree with a singular "stripe;" each zebra has many stripes that are being compared to the stripes on an okapi.

290. **Level:** Easy | **Skill/Knowledge:** Form, Structure, and Sense

Key Explanation: Choice A is the best answer because the sentence includes the idiom "not only…but also…" Therefore, **Choice A** is needed to complete the idiom according to standard conventions.

Distractor Explanations: All of the other choices can be eliminated because they do not follow standard conventions for completing the idiom "not only…but also…"

291. **Level:** Easy | **Skill/Knowledge:** Form, Structure, and Sense

Key Explanation: Choice B is the best answer because it starts a relative clause referring to a place. It fits the context of saying that the place of Romania is where Brancusi learned to carve.

Distractor Explanations: Choice A is incorrect because it is not used after a comma. **Choice C** is incorrect because it is not the start of a relative clause; **Choice C** is a pronoun, so it creates a comma splice between two independent clauses.

Choice D is incorrect because it refers to being inside an object or situation, not a country.

292. **Level:** Easy | **Skill/Knowledge:** Form, Structure, and Sense

Key Explanation: Choice C is the best answer because it is an adverb, so can correctly be used to refer to "1,000," which in the context, is an adjective describing the species. **Choice B** shows that the number is not exact.

Distractor Explanations: None of the other choices fits the grammatical structure of the sentence, as only an adverb can modify an adjective. **Choice A** can be either an adjective or a verb. **Choice B** is a verb, and **Choice D** is a noun.

293. **Level:** Easy | **Skill/Knowledge:** Form, Structure, and Sense

Key Explanation: Choice D is the best answer because "three times" refers to the subject "the size." Therefore, the blank portion needs to refer to a size. **Choice D** gives a specific size, Earth's diameter.

Distractor Explanations: All of the other choices can be eliminated because they do not form a comparison of size. **Choice A** compares the size of the storm to Earth itself, rather than the size of Earth. In **Choice B**, "one" is ambiguous with no clear referent. **Choice C** is incorrect because "the size of" fits the context, but "Earth's" should not be plural. "Of" contains the idea of possession.

294. **Level:** Easy | **Skill/Knowledge:** Form, Structure, and Sense

Key Explanation: Choice A is the best answer because a general action that goes on now is expressed in the present tense.

Distractor Explanations: Choice B is incorrect because "still" shows that the action has not stopped, so the past tense does not fit. **Choice C** is used to show an action that is simultaneous with another stated action, but there is no other action mentioned in the text that happens in the present. **Choice D** is incorrect because it is used to show that something happened before something else in the past, but the people did not "still visit" before the monument was opened.

295. **Level:** Medium | **Skill/Knowledge:** Form, Structure, and Sense

Key Explanation: Choice B is the best answer because "a young country" is a modifier that must be followed by the noun it refers to. Only **Choice B** starts with the young country, Kosovo.

Distractor Explanations: All of the other choices can be eliminated because a modifier at the start of a sentence needs to refer to the first word of the following clause. In **Choices A** and **D**, "a young country" erroneously refers to the "declaration." In **Choice C**, the modifier refers to "independence."

296. **Level:** Easy | **Skill/Knowledge:** Form, Structure, and Sense

Key Explanation: Choice B is the best answer because the blank portion refers to the position of the leader. Since hyenas are "matriarchal," the leader is female. **Choice B** is a female possessive pronoun. Even if the meaning of "matriarchal" is unclear, "other females" indicates that another female has been mentioned; in the context, that referent has to be the leader.

Distractor Explanations: Choice A is incorrect because it is a male pronoun, but the text establishes that the leader is female. **Choice C** is a plural pronoun, so does not agree with the singular "the leader." **Choice D** is a general pronoun used only when there is no clear referent, but the blank portion refers to "the leader."

297. **Level:** Easy | **Skill/Knowledge:** Form, Structure, and Sense

Key Explanation: Choice B is the best answer because "when" shows that the following portion is a time clause that refers to the previous verb, "change," to show the time that the change happens. "When" should be followed by a verb with either the "–ed" or "–ing" ending since the subject of the clause, the ambulance siren, is the object of the verb "to perceive."

Distractor Explanations: None of the other choices are correct verb forms in the context. **Choices A** and **C** are active present tense verbs which makes it appear that the siren is doing the perceiving or listening. **Choice D** is incorrect because it shows that something occurred before rather than simultaneously with another action in the sentence.

298. **Level:** Easy | **Skill/Knowledge:** Form, Structure, and Sense

Key Explanation: Choice D is the best answer because it is used to show that an action started in the past and continues to the present. **Choice D,** therefore, fits the context of saying that the action of working started in 1971 and continues today.

Distractor Explanations: Choices A and **B** are incorrect because they only refer to the present, so do not accurately show that the work began in

1971. **Choice B** discusses an ongoing state, but is used when there is another, simultaneous action in the sentence. **Choice C** is incorrect because it is used to show that an action in the past ended before another action, but there is no second action nor indication that the work has ended.

299. **Level:** Easy | **Skill/Knowledge:** Form, Structure, and Sense

Key Explanation: Choice A is the best answer because the idiom "not only…but also…" needs to be completed with the same grammatical structure in both halves. In the text, "not only" is followed by a noun, "the freedom…." Therefore, the part after "but also" must also be a noun.

Distractor Explanations: All of the other choices can be eliminated because they do not have the same grammatical structure as "the freedom…." **Choice B** is a complete clause and **Choices C** and **D** are verb phrases.

300. **Level:** Easy | **Skill/Knowledge:** Form, Structure, and Sense

Key Explanation: Choice C is the best answer because the blank portion is part of the passive verb showing that an unnamed person did the act of "adapting" or "changing" the Indian game into chess. The passive past tense form of "adapt" is "was adapted."

Distractor Explanations: Choices A and **D** are incorrect because they are adjectives. While an adjective can follow "was," the phrase "into chess" is grammatically correct. **Choice B** also can be eliminated because it is a noun that can follow "was," but "adaptable" is not something that turned into chess.

Chapter 7

Reading and Writing Test

Reading and Writing Test

27 QUESTIONS | 32 MINUTES

DIRECTIONS

The questions in this section address a number of important reading and writing skills. Each question includes one or more passages, which may include a table or graph. Read each passage and question carefully, and then choose the best answer to the question based on the passage(s). All questions in this section are multiple–choice with four answer choices. Each question has a single best answer.

1

The following text is from Amy Tan's 1989 novel, *The Joy Luck Club*.

My mother started the San Francisco version of the Joy Luck Club in 1949, two years before I was born. This was the year my mother and father left China with one stiff leather trunk filled only with fancy silk dresses. There was no time to pack anything else, my mother had explained to my father after they boarded the boat. Still his hands swam frantically between the slippery silks, looking for his cotton shirts and wool pants.

As used in the text, what does the word "swam" most nearly mean?

A) examined

B) dived

C) searched

D) bathed

2

Initially, upon entering the United States in the 1900s, the majority of European immigrants had a lower education level than the U.S. average. However, surveys _____ from 1940–2017, show that European immigrants advanced further in their education by the third generation than United States–born whites.

Which choice completes the text with the most logical and precise word or phrase?

A) managed

B) administered

C) delivered

D) supplied

To avoid conflict with incoming Europeans attempting to colonize North America, the Cherokee nation _____ many of the settler's culture, including language, religion, and economics. Despite this, when gold was discovered in their territory, the Indian Removal Act was passed in 1830 to remove the tribe from their lands and gain access to their resources.

Which choice completes the text with the most logical and precise word or phrase?

A) learned

B) mimicked

C) adopted

D) rejected

Smartwatches and fitness trackers currently available to the public claim to be able to provide data on VO2max, a measurement of an individual's fitness level that indicates heart disease and mortality risk. However, whether or not these measurements are accurate is still unproven. Meanwhile, Cambridge developed a model that can provide more accurate tracking of one's heart rate and can also monitor fitness changes leading to better indications of health risks.

Which choice best states the main purpose of the text?

A) To prove that currently available smartwatches are not an accurate indicator of overall health.

B) To introduce a new fitness tracker model that may provide more accurate data on health than current products.

C) To argue that individuals should not rely on fitness trackers or smartwatches to monitor their health.

D) To summarize the findings of a new fitness tracker model that will be available to the public soon.

5

The following text is from Mark Twain's 1881 novel, *The Prince and the Pauper.*

"In the ancient city of London, on a certain autumn day in the second quarter of the sixteenth century, a boy was born to a poor family of the name of Canty, who did not want him. On the same day another English child was born to a rich family of the name of Tudor, who did want him. All England wanted him too. England had so longed for him, and hoped for him, and prayed God for him, that, now that he was really come, the people went nearly mad for joy. Mere acquaintances hugged and kissed each other and cried."

Which choice best states the function of the underlined sentence in the text as a whole?

A) It establishes a contrast with the previous character description.

B) It introduces a character description continued in the following sentences.

C) It demonstrates the setting that is explored in the rest of the paragraph.

D) It expands upon the characterization in the former sentence.

6

Researchers have found what they believe to be a cause behind mice being motivated to exercise: gut microbes. The specific molecules in these microbes appear to stimulate the desire in the brain to run and continue running. It has been postulated that if this bacteria could be given to people in pill form, they too could experience the same motivation to exercise.

Which choice best states the main purpose of the text?

A) To understand better what makes mice motivated to move.

B) To suggest that the findings in mice could be used to increase human activity.

C) To explain research in mice that will be used to support people.

D) To imply that a lack of motivation to work out is not controllable.

Text 1

In his youth, Benjamin Franklin learned that many considered him so unpleasant they would cross the street to avoid him. Specifically, it was his arrogance and aggressive speech that was off–putting. Franklin determined to focus on self–development by creating a list of thirteen virtues he would practice. Later, he would become an ambassador to France, gaining French support during the American Revolution. Clearly, these habits led to an improved man.

Text 2

The following lists virtues found in *The Autobiography of Benjamin Franklin, Part II* by Benjamin Franklin.

1. Silence
    Speak not but what may benefit others or yourself; avoid trifling conversation.

2. Order
    Let all your things have their places; let each part of your business have its time.

3. Resolution
    Resolve to perform what you ought; perform without fail what you resolve.

4. Frugality
    Make no expense but to do good to others or yourself.

Based on the texts, which virtue of Text 2 would the author or Text 1 theorize was the most influential in Franklin's success as a French ambassador?

A) Silence as it taught Franklin to avoid being loquacious and listen more to develop better French relations.

B) Order since it allowed Franklin to take time to develop his business relations with the French.

C) Resolution because Franklin learned to follow through with his goals for French assistance.

D) Frugality as it led to Franklin becoming economically aware enough to gain French financial support.

The following text is from Sandra Cisnero's 1983 novel entitled, *The House on Mango Street*. In the novel, the narrator is a young girl who lives in a house with her family on Mango Street.

"One day, I will pack my bags of books and paper. One day, I will say goodbye to Mango. I am too strong for her to keep me here forever. One day, I will go away. Friends and neighbors will say, 'What happened to that Esperanza? Where did she go with all those books and paper? Why did she march so far away?' They will not know I have gone away to come back. For the ones I left behind. For the ones who cannot out."

What is the main idea of the text?

A) The narrator is planning on leaving her neighborhood to never return.

B) The narrator hopes to one day become a writer.

C) The narrator will be missed by her neighbors and friends.

D) The narrator explains the reason she will leave her neighborhood.

While Yiddish is no longer spoken in many parts of the world, it was once a very well-known language spoken by Central and Eastern European Jewish communities. The language itself derives predominantly from German and Hebrew, but was also influenced by Aramaic, Slavic, and Romance languages. It is a widely accepted theory that it originated in Germany in the 10th Century and spread throughout European countries as Jews migrated as a result of the Bubonic Plague and the persecution they faced during the Crusades.

Which choice best states the main idea of the text?

A) The Jewish communities would not have developed the Yiddish language without persecution during the Crusades.

B) The Yiddish language originated as a result of several factors including migration, diversity, and challenges.

C) Yiddish is a language that was spoken by Jewish communities for many centuries but is now a dormant language.

D) The Yiddish language is no longer spoken by Jewish communities as a result of the Bubonic Plague and the Crusades.

I Know Why the Caged Bird Sings is a 1969 novel written by Maya Angelou. In the novel, the main character struggles to accept her African American race while growing up in the Southern United States.

Which quotation from *I Know Why the Caged Bird Sings* most effectively illustrates this claim?

A) "The dress I wore was light purple. As I'd watched Momma make it, putting fancy stitching on the waist, I knew that when I put it on I'd look like one of the sweet little white girls who were everyone's dream of what was right with the world."

B) "When people saw me wearing it, they were going to run up to me and say, 'Marguerite [sometimes it was 'dear Marguerite'], forgive us, please, we didn't know who you were,' and I would answer generously, 'No, you couldn't have known. Of course I forgive you.'"

C) "Wouldn't they be surprised when one day I woke out of my black ugly dream, and my real hair, which was long and blonde, would take the place of the kinky mass that Momma wouldn't let me straighten?"

D) "If growing up is painful for the Southern Black girl, being aware of her difference is worse. It is an unnecessary insult."

In her essay entitled, "Slouching Towards Bethlehem," Joan Didion describes her experiences in California during the 1960s and 1970s while proving a darker side of this period existed even though it is often admired for its claimed pursuit of peace and love.

Which quotation from "Slouching Towards Bethlehem" most effectively illustrates the claim?

A) "It was a country of bankruptcy notices and public–auction announcements and commonplace reports of casual killings and misplaced children and abandoned homes and vandals who misplaced even the four–letter words they scrawled."

B) "It was the United States of America in the cold late spring of 1967, and the market was steady and the G.N.P. high and a great many articulate people seemed to have a sense of high social purpose and it might have been a spring of brave hopes and national promise, but it was not, and more and more people had the uneasy apprehension that it was not."

C) "San Francisco was where the missing children were gathering and calling themselves 'hippies.' When I first went to San Francisco in that cold late spring of 1967, I did not even know what I wanted to find out, and so I just stayed around awhile, and made a few friends."

D) "Adolescents drifted from city to torn city, sloughing off both the past and the future as snakes shed their skins, children who were never taught and would never now learn the games that had held the society together."

After 38 years without incident, on November 27, 2022, the Hawaiian volcano Mauna Loa erupted. Mauna Loa and its neighboring volcano, Kīlauea, are monitored for seismic activity and elevation changes to provide warnings for potential eruptions. Despite these observations that are conducted over both the short–term and the long–term, accurate forecasting is still difficult.

Mauna Loa Seismic Activity Prior to Eruption on Nov. 27, 2022

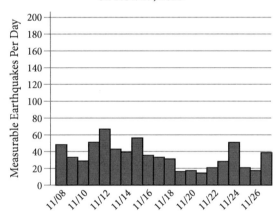

Which choice best describes data from the graph that supports the geologists' conclusion?

A) Seismic activity was higher overall at the beginning of the month than it was later in the month right before the eruption.

B) Seismic activity from 11/08 to 11/15 was at a higher level overall.

C) Seismic activity increased from under 20 per day on 11/26 to nearly 40 on the day the eruption occurred.

D) Seismic activity stayed consistently high from 11/08 to the day of the eruption.

Stereotypical female parts are written into several of William Shakespeare's plays who often behave in manners that are unflattering towards that gender. For instance, the hard–biting nag is represented by Katherina in *The Taming of the Shrew*; the chaste innocent is displayed in *Romeo and Juliet* by the title character, Juliet; and the villain can be seen in roles like Tamora in *Titus Andronicus*. _____

Which choice most logically completes the text?

A) Much of Shakespeare's writing and the writing of his contemporaries were influenced by the social standards of the Elizabethan Era in which he lived.

B) Although Queen Elizabeth was on the throne while Shakespeare was writing these plays, literature during this time did not reflect the changing female roles.

C) Though Shakespeare was an excellent writer appreciated in both his time and the present, female characters that acted in manners outside of these cliches could have made for even more interesting writing.

D) William Shakespeare believed that most women in the Elizabethan era fit into these female stereotypes.

To better understand people living with PTSD, laboratory experiments conducted on mice determined that the brain stores remote fear memories from the past permanently. Due to the connections between memory neurons in the prefrontal cortex, the brain can hold onto distressing experiences from a few months to decades ago. These results are expected to contribute _____

Which choice most logically completes the text?

A) To more effective treatment of individuals suffering from PTSD and other fear–related disorders.

B) To a better understanding of what causes PTSD in the mice that were studied.

C) To the realization that there is a connection between memory neurons in the prefrontal cortex.

D) To additional studies conducted on mice and other lab animals to gain further insights.

The following text is from the short story *Marigolds* written by Eugenia Collier in 1969.

"Miss Lottie's marigolds were perhaps the strangest part of the picture. Certainly, they did not fit in with the crumbling decay of the rest of her yard. Beyond the dusty brown yard, in front of the sorry gray house, rose suddenly and shockingly a dazzling strip of bright blossoms, clumped together in enormous mounds, warm and passionate and sun–golden. The old black witch–woman worked on them all summer, every summer, down on her creaky knees, weeding and cultivating and arranging, while the house crumbled and John Burke rocked. For some perverse reason, we children hated those marigolds. They interfered with the perfect ugliness of the place; they were too beautiful; they said too much that we could not understand; they did not make sense."

According to the text, what is true about Miss Lottie's marigolds?

A) They are the only beautiful part of the neighborhood.

B) The children despise them because they did not understand them.

C) The children are intimidated by them because of their beauty.

D) Miss Lottie cares more about them than the rest of her house.

16

The Greek philosopher Aristotle had ideas that would have substantial influence thousands of years after he taught _____. American Framers would use his philosophies like government moderation, the rule of law, and citizen rights when writing the United States Constitution.

Which choice completes the text so that it conforms to the conventions of Standard English?

A) it.

B) that.

C) this.

D) them.

17

To divorce his first wife and marry Anne Boylyn, King Henry VIII of England separated from the Catholic Church in 1534. He then established his own religion, the Church of England, which would also become known as Protestantism. This decision would send England into centuries of turmoil as _____, some Catholic and some Protestant, would enforce their preferred religion and persecute their subjects if they did not follow suit.

Which choice completes the text so that it conforms to the conventions of Standard English?

A) England's following monarchs

B) English rulers that followed

C) British kings that later ruled

D) England's later–ruling kings

18

In many of Charles Dickens' writings, he explored themes of the social inequality he was witnessing during the Victorian Era. In his novel, *Oliver Twist*, he focused on the plight of orphans; in *Hard Times* he _____ the struggle of the working class; and in *Bleak House*, Dickens revealed the injustice of the courts that displayed favoritism to the upper classes. Ultimately, he used his skill as a writer to make a living and as a source of social commentary for Victorian readers.

Which choice completes the text so that it conforms to the conventions of Standard English?

A) highlights

B) was highlighting

C) highlighted

D) had highlighted

19

Theories have been put forth about what most influences our cultural _____ experience, or environment. Of the three options, the findings suggest that family background is the strongest determinant in molding an individual's cultural preferences.

Which choice completes the text so that it conforms to the conventions of Standard English?

A) tastes: genes,

B) tastes; genes,

C) tastes, genes,

D) tastes genes,

20

Signs of red paint were found on skulls from _____ Valley dating back to somewhere between 1000 and 1825 C.E. Of the twenty–five discovered skulls, the majority painted upon were male, though a few were the bones of females and children.

Which choice completes the text so that it conforms to the conventions of Standard English?

A) Perus Chincha

B) Perus's Chincha

C) Perus' Chincha

D) Peru's Chincha

21

Bladder cancer is becoming more treatable due in part to AI algorithms that can both diagnose the disease and predict the outcome. AI can be used to identify tumors, diagnose the stage, predict the likelihood of _____ determine survival chance.

Which choice completes the text so that it conforms to the conventions of Standard English?

A) recurrence and

B) recurrence; and

C) recurrence, and

D) recurrence: and

22

There is a common misconception that all cats detest _____ fishing cat, *Prionailurus viverrinus,* proves this assumption is false. This wild cat that lives in Southeastern Asia can not only swim long distances but also relies on fish for roughly 75 percent of its diet.

Which choice completes the text so that it conforms to the conventions of Standard English?

A) water; the

B) water, the

C) water the

D) water – the

23

The Victorian Era is a period named for its ruler, Queen Victoria of England. _____ she reigned from 1837–1901, the era corresponds roughly with the years of 1820–1914. The era is characterized by many features that were modeled after its namesake including conservatism, expansion, and invention.

Which choice completes the text with the most logical transition?

A) Additionally,

B) Although,

C) Furthermore,

D) For example,

24

India is one of the oldest still–existing civilizations in the world today dating back over 4,500 years. Over the years, it has contributed significant achievements in the field of medicine, mathematics, and architecture. _____ until recently, Western societies have not always looked upon India with approval.

Which choice completes the text with the most logical transition?

A) Indeed,

B) Regardless,

C) Moreover,

D) As a result,

25

While researching a topic, a student has taken the following notes:

- In 79 C.E., the stratovolcano Mt. Vesuvius erupted near the Roman city of Pompeii.

- Herculaneum and other cities by the volcano were also affected by the explosion.

- There were several earthquakes in the months preceding the eruption.

- Nearby residents were not concerned as earthquakes were a common occurrence and it was not known that Mt. Vesuvius was a volcano.

- On the day of the eruption, a large plume of ash was seen coming out of the volcano.

- Later that day, molten rock and ash flew into the nearby cities destroying buildings and making it hard to breathe.

- The pyroclastic flow and damage from the volcano killed 2,000 people in total.

The student wants to demonstrate the tragedy caused by the eruption of Mt. Vesuvius. Which choice most effectively uses the relevant information from the notes to accomplish this goal?

A) Mt. Vesuvius's pyroclastic flow destroyed buildings and suffocated residents in Pompeii in 79 A.D.

B) Pompeii residents were unaware that the earthquakes indicated a forthcoming explosion from Mt. Vesuvius.

C) The molten rocks, ash, and pyroclastic flow from Mt. Vesuvius's eruption killed at least 2,000 people in nearby cities.

D) Ancient Romans did not realize Mt. Vesuvius was an active volcano that would later kill many residents living in its shadow.

While researching a topic, a student has taken the following notes:

- Ancient Egypt created one of the earliest peace treaties ever recorded to end the conflict between their nation and the Hittites.

- Egyptian women had many rights including the ability to serve in government, participate in juries, and buy property.

- Workers went on strike when they felt as if they were not being fairly treated and were often rewarded for letting their grievances be known.

- The pharaohs were viewed as descendants of their Egyptian gods.

- Approximately 118 pyramids were built by the ancient Egyptians.

- Ancient Egypt was divided into three kingdoms from 3100 B.C.E.–332 C.E. — Old, Middle, and New.

The student wants to explain how ancient Egypt advocated for human rights. Which choice most effectively uses relevant information from the notes to accomplish this goal?

A) Ancient Egypt was a long–lasting civilization that dominated the landscape for roughly 3,000 years.

B) Some humans in Ancient Egypt were elevated to the status of a god, specifically their pharaohs.

C) Ancient Egyptians were concerned with the welfare of their citizens as shown by creating peace treaties.

D) Women in ancient Egypt were allowed several of the freedoms that men had and laborers went on strikes if they were not given fair rations.

27

While researching a topic, a student has taken the following notes:

- Microplastics are small pieces of plastic that are less than 5 mm in length.

- In the past 20 years, the presence of microplastics on the ocean seafloor has tripled.

- These microplastics do not degrade once they reach the ocean floor since they are no longer exposed to sunlight and oxygen.

- Microplastics can affect marine life by limiting food intake, inhibiting growth, and causing abnormal behavior.

- Microplastics contain harmful chemicals like phthalates and bisphenol.

The student wants to demonstrate the damage caused by microplastics on the ocean floor. Which choice most effectively uses relevant information from the notes to accomplish this goal?

A) The amount of microplastics found on the ocean floor has increased substantially over the last 20 years.

B) Once on the ocean floor, microplastics do not break down smaller than 5 mm as they are not exposed to oxygen.

C) Microplastics found on the ocean floor can be consumed by marine life and cause delayed growth and problematic behavior.

D) Microplastics found on the ocean floor contain toxic elements such as phthalates and bisphenol.

Reading Test

27 QUESTIONS | 32 MINUTES

DIRECTIONS

The questions in this section address a number of important reading and writing skills. Each question includes one or more passages, which may include a table or graph. Read each passage and question carefully, and then choose the best answer to the question based on the passage(s). All questions in this section are multiple-choice with four answer choices. Each question has a single best answer.

1

A mother's mitochondria, an organelle found in many of the body's cells, may be able to help her ailing children. A suggestion has been put forth to soak the blood cells of children with mitochondrial disease in the mother's healthy mitochondria. As early research shows _____, follow-up clinical trials will follow.

Which choice completes the text with the most logical and precise word or phrase?

A) aspiration

B) potential

C) ability

D) improbability

2

Videoconferencing through platforms like Zoom and Google Hangouts has become a necessary form of communication in light of a greater move toward remote work. Along with this trend, a _____ has developed which has become known as "videoconferencing fatigue," resulting from a lack of work–life balance and family conflicts while working from home.

Which choice completes the text with the most logical and precise word or phrase?

A) miracle

B) phenomenon

C) disaster

D) case

3

American painter Georgia O'Keeffe was _____ for her beautiful and bright depictions of flowers. Though these gained her fame and recognition, a biographical essay of her life written by Joan Didion, reflects the idea that O'Keeffe may have been frustrated by the constant demand from the public and her contemporaries to paint more flowers, when she was capable of painting a wider variety of objects and landscapes.

Which choice completes the text with the most logical and precise word or phrase?

A) despised

B) renowned

C) commended

D) infamous

4

Rococo art spread during the 1730s in Paris and was characterized by its pastel colors, depictions of frivolous scenes, ethereal atmosphere, and display of the aristocratic lifestyle. While these depictions were well–liked for a time, their popularity waned while the disparity among French classes created tension. Eventually, this style fell out of grace completely once the French Revolution began, and the lower classes revolted, resenting the difficult lifestyle they were forced to endure while the upper classes enjoyed a leisurely existence.

Which choice best states the main purpose of the text?

A) To prove that the French Revolution was a direct result of Rococo art falling out of style.

B) To demonstrate that Rococo art was only appreciated for a brief time due to rising tension in French society of the 1700s.

C) To argue that Rococo art would have become more popular had it not been for the French Revolution.

D) To explain that the aristocratic lifestyle of the upper classes displayed in Rococo art was unfair and needed to be overthrown.

5

An experimental gene–editing therapy that alters the DNA of donor cells has proven effective in treating leukemia. The first patient to be treated with this therapy, a 13–year–old girl who had acute lymphoblastic leukemia, is in remission after receiving the genetically modified T–cells. Though she still needs to be closely monitored, six months after receiving the treatment she still had no detectable cancer in her body.

Which choice best states the function of the underlined sentence in the text as a whole?

A) It elaborates on a claim that a new gene therapy that alters T–cells can cure various types of cancer.

B) It notes a possibility of the new gene therapy not having long–lasting curing results.

C) It provides further details about the success of the new gene therapy in treating a specific type of cancer.

D) It illustrates an example of the new gene therapy having long–lasting success in treating cancer.

6

Scholars have analyzed the period of the Italian Renaissance (approximately 1350–1550 C.E.) for a number of different factors including its cause. This era is particularly known for its increased interest in the arts, literature, and philosophy of ancient Greece and Rome, with many of its scholars becoming known as humanists. As a result, numerous experts believe that one of the most significant contributions to the growing love of individual learning during this time period can be traced back to the invention of the printing press by Johannes Gutenberg. After its creation, over the coming years, movable type allowed for the production of multiple copies of books that could be bought, sold, and distributed across Europe.

Which choice best states the main purpose of the text?

A) It argues that the Italian Renaissance is one of the most important time periods in world history.

B) It explains that most scholars believe that there are numerous reasons why the Italian Renaissance saw many people inspired to learn.

C) It discusses expert opinions on the origin of the Italian Renaissance with emphasis on the invention of the printing press.

D) It presents findings that the invention of the printing press was the sole reason why the era of the Italian Renaissance transpired.

Text 1

Australian bats have experienced both food shortage and habitat loss due to deforestation and climate change. This scarcity has led to bats relocating to urban and agricultural settings where they can infect intermediate hosts with the Hendra virus. From there, the virus can be spread to humans living closer to the bats, proving that climate change is a danger to not only wildlife but also humanity.

Text 2

The Hendra virus was first discovered in infected horses in Australia during the 1990s. Meanwhile, a horse trainer experienced flu–like symptoms and was diagnosed with the virus, later passing away from the illness. In the years following, more outbreaks occurred with at least seven people infected and four others dying from the disease. If humans experience further exposure to the disease it will likely result in more deaths.

Based on the texts, how would the author of Text 2 most likely respond to the theory discussed in Text 1?

A) It is inaccurate as it does not properly interpret the observations.

B) It could be true, but more proof of bat migration into habitats near people needs to be found.

C) It is most likely untrue since climate change may not be the reason for Australian bat migration.

D) It is most likely true as climate change further exposes humanity to the Hendra virus.

Text 1

After the American Revolution, the first wave of feminism gained popularity as proponents urged that women's suffrage must exist if the nation were to be equal. Many of these feminists also began to argue for abolition of slavery. Some have theorized the reason these two injustices were supported by many of the same advocates was because both were associated with freedom and equality.

Text 2

Many early feminists such as Susan B. Anthony and Lucretia Coffin Mott argued for a woman's right to vote and for an end to slavery. In her speech, *The Law of Progress* (1848), Mott argued that though slavery was increasing in America, people could still take heart that racial equality was beginning to spread in other countries as slaves were being freed. Mott spent much of her life supporting freedom for her own sex and for the enslaved peoples of America.

Based on these texts, how would Mott and her peers (Text 2) most likely view the theories presented in Text 1?

A) It is mostly accurate, as one can hardly advocate for the equality of a group of people without supporting another that experiences injustice.

B) It may seem believable; however, there are not enough instances of early feminists arguing for abolition in order to prove the theory.

C) It is not reasonable despite some of the concrete examples provided.

D) It is probably true, but only applies to specific early feminists and cannot be applied to the movement as a whole.

9

Archeologist Thomas Rune Knudsen led a team that discovered remnants of a Viking–era hall that likely dates back to the mid–'900s C.E. He theorizes the area the hall was found on belonged to a family whose name is engraved on a runestone nearby. He anticipates evidence of adjacent houses will be found, along with land that was farmed.

Which choice best states the main idea of the text?

A) Evidence of a Viking hall was found, while more nearby Viking–era discoveries are being searched for.

B) Remnants of a Viking–era house and farmed land were discovered by an archeologist and his team.

C) Archeologist Thomas Knudsen hopes to find evidence of a Viking hall dating back to the '900s C.E.

D) Thomas Rune Knudson believes that a Viking–era hall dating back to the '900s C.E. belonged to a family whose name was inscribed on a stone nearby.

10

The following text is from Margaret Mitchell's 1936 novel, *Gone with the Wind,*. Scarlett O' Hara is the daughter of a Southern family in Georgia before the start of the American Civil War.

"Scarlett O'Hara was not beautiful, but men seldom realized it when caught by her charm as the Tarleton twins were. In her face, were too sharply blended, the delicate features of her mother, a Coast aristocrat of French descent, and the heavy ones of her florid Irish father. But it was an arresting face, pointed of chin, square of jaw. Her eyes were pale green without a touch of hazel, starred with bristly black lashes and slightly tilted at the ends. Above them, her thick black brows slanted upward, cutting a startling oblique line in her magnolia–white skin—–that skin so prized by Southern women and so carefully guarded with bonnets, veils, and mittens against hot Georgia suns."

Which choice best reflects the main idea of the text?

A) The main character is not beautiful, but her features and grace still appeal to men.

B) The main character is beautiful and many men give her attention as a result.

C) The main character has obtained her good looks from her Irish father and French mother.

D) Her physical features are the aspect of her that most draws attention from men, like the Tarleton twins.

11

"The Road Not Taken" is a poem written by Robert Frost in 1915. The poem reflects on the theme that the decisions one makes can have a far–reaching impact on one's future.

Which quotation from the poem most effectively reflects the theme?

A) "Two roads diverged in a yellow wood,/ And sorry I could not travel both/ And be one traveler, long I stood/ And looked down one as far as I could/ To where it bent in the undergrowth."

B) "Then took the other, as just as fair,/ And having perhaps the better claim,/ Because it was grassy and wanted wear;/ Though as for that the passing there/ Had worn them really about the same."

C) "And both that morning equally lay/ In leaves no step had trodden black./ Oh, I kept the first for another day!/ Yet knowing how way leads on to way,/ I doubted if I should ever come back."

D) "I shall be telling this with a sigh/ Somewhere ages and ages hence:/ Two roads diverged in a wood, and I—/ I took the one less traveled by,/ And that has made all the difference."

12

Economic sociologists have compiled data over the years of 1989–2010 to determine the potential connections between parental status and wealth. Findings suggest that due to societal pressure for home ownership when married and raising a family, these adults were more likely to own a home. Since home ownership is a key factor in increasing wealth in the United States, evidence found that married parents had a greater amount of wealth when compared to other household types.

Median wealth a by household type, 2016 and 2019

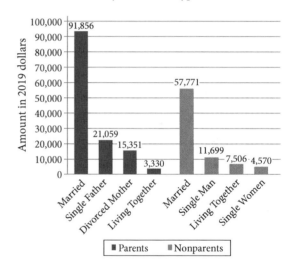

Which choice best describes data from the graph that support the researchers' conclusion?

A) Couples living together whether parents or nonparents had the lowest median wealth in the years 2016 and 2019.

B) Parents' average median wealth was higher in 2016 and 2019 than the average median wealth of nonparents.

C) Married parents had a median wealth of over $90,000 in the years 2016 and 2019.

D) Married nonparents had a median wealth of nearly $60,000 in the years 2016 and 2019.

13

Estimated Human Injuries and Deaths Caused by Captive Exotic Animals From 1990–2022

Animals	Injuries	Deaths
Big Cats	244	20
Reptiles *	57	28
All Other Exoctic Animals	361	43
Total	662	91

* Reptiles include snakes, iguanas, water dragons, and bearded dragons

Advocates of owning exotic pets believe that by keeping unusual animals such as snakes, alligators, and chimpanzees, they are providing a safe home for these wild creatures that would otherwise live in dangerous habitats. However, though they may be providing these animals with a safer home, most owners do not realize that they are putting their own health and safety at risk. For instance, monkeys can transmit the ebola virus, most reptiles carry salmonella, and many others carry diseases like rabies, herpes, and even the bubonic plague. However, there are safety concerns much more worrisome than disease since _____

Which choice most effectively uses data from the table to complete the example?

A) Owning reptiles like snakes have accounted for roughly 57 injuries over approximately 30 years.

B) Captive big cats have resulted in the death of approximately 20 people from 1990–2022.

C) Many types of exotic pets, other than big cats and reptiles, have injured 361 people in 32 years.

D) The total number of deaths that have occurred by captive exotic animals is 91 over the last 32 years.

14

Studies have found that students who do not get enough sleep are at a higher risk for a number of health problems including obesity and diabetes, among other diseases and issues. Furthermore, the CDC found that anywhere between 30–40% of students are not getting the recommended amount of sleep. Despite this, most schools start the school day before 8:30 a.m. These findings imply that _____

Which choice most logically completes the text?

A) The start of the average school day is not affecting a student's sleep schedule as there are many other factors to consider.

B) Obesity and diabetes in students can be directly linked to the school day starting too early.

C) A later start time would most likely help students get the additional sleep they are missing and lead to a healthier life as a result.

D) If schools started even earlier, it would encourage students to go to bed earlier and therefore, get more of the recommended amount of sleep.

15

Between 2011 and 2019, the U.S. dollar appreciated by approximately 23 percent and has continued this trend in the years following. Factors that _____ to this rise include global investing, the U.S. central bank policy, and investor demands leaning towards the U.S.

Which choice completes the text so that it conforms to the conventions of Standard English?

A) have contributed

B) contribute

C) contributes

D) will contribute

16

Roughly 70 percent of Nigerian inmates are still awaiting trial. Some theorize that creating a portal system with a stored database would speed up this process due to its easy access, available materials related to the trials, and ability _____ cases.

Which choice completes the text so that it conforms to the conventions of Standard English?

A) to allocating

B) allocating

C) to allocate

D) allocate

17

Previously, geologists thought the Bering Land Bridge emerged earlier in the last Ice Age. Recent studies place it much later, in the Ice Age known as the Last Glacial Maximum, _____ around 35,700 years ago.

Which choice completes the text so that it conforms to the conventions of Standard English?

A) appear

B) appeared

C) appearing

D) to appear

18

A new method for creating crystalline materials using two or more elements _____ by chemists. By using these elements, one of which cannot be metal, they can produce improved superconductors, batteries, magnets, and more.

Which choice completes the text so that it conforms to the conventions of Standard English?

A) developed

B) had developed

C) will develop

D) has been developed

19

Author Jean Craighead George's time in the Alaskan wilderness observing the language of wolves influenced her award–winning novel, *Julie of the Wolves*. Her first–hand experience with these animals taught her of their pack mentality and the non–verbal communication they use to establish order. This was also noted by her main _____ whose life was saved by these lessons while she was lost in the tundra.

Which choice completes the text so that it conforms to the conventions of Standard English?

A) character, Julie

B) character, Julie,

C) character Julie

D) character Julie,

20

The stories of Greek mythology date back to the Bronze Age. The Greek gods such as Zeus and Aphrodite, who most are familiar with today, did not originate in the well–known tales by _____ they were introduced in the 7th Century in Hesiod's *Theogony*.

Which choice completes the text so that it conforms to the conventions of Standard English?

A) Homer; instead,

B) Homer, instead,

C) Homer; instead

D) Homer instead,

21

During the Industrial Revolution, many factories moved from rural areas to large cities. While this meant more opportunity and a better life for _____ it made life much more difficult for others. For example, an abundantly populated city life required people to live in small, crowded areas with poor health standards. Additionally, children from impoverished families worked in dangerous environments for up to fifteen hours a day to help support their families.

Which choice completes the text so that it conforms to the conventions of Standard English?

A) some

B) some:

C) some,

D) some;

22

An issue with our immunity as we age has been discovered as playing a role in the development of Alzheimer's disease. _____ the cerebrospinal fluid coats the brain in nutrients and immune protection, but can become dysregulated as people get older.

Which choice completes the text with the most logical transition?

A) Still,

B) Specifically,

C) Thus,

D) Ultimately,

23

For many years, astronomers believed that gamma–ray bursts (GRB) either lasted no longer than 2 seconds or for even less time. _____ they were shocked when two NASA telescopes observed a GRB that lasted for 50 seconds.

Which choice completes the text with the most logical transition?

A) Understandably,

B) Surprisingly,

C) Interestingly,

D) Conclusively,

24

American lawyer and politician Elliot Abrams stated that first impressions are lasting and important. Sociologists have, _____ studied the effect of first impressions. Research has been conducted to determine whether or not one's clothing had an impact on treatment. The results determined that when individuals went into high–end retail stores dressed more formally, they were given assistance immediately, while they received delayed assistance or even no assistance at all when dressed in clothing that appeared old, inexpensive, or substandard.

Which choice completes the text with the most logical transition?

A) although,

B) also,

C) nevertheless,

D) in fact,

25

While researching a topic, a student has taken the following notes:

- New observations found that particular supermassive black holes project jets of high–energy particles into space.

- Shockwaves are produced along the jets and contort magnetic fields.

- This accelerates the speed of light as particles escape.

- Astronomers observing this believe this is the reason why some black holes shine so brightly.

- Further research needs to be done to determine the details of how the light particles flow.

The student wants to explain the insights these new observations have provided. Which choice most effectively uses relevant information from the notes to accomplish this goal?

A) New observations show that particles of light escape from jets launched from some black holes.

B) Jets shooting from supermassive black holes project light that increases the speed of light.

C) By observing jets launching from supermassive black holes, astronomers have realized a possibility as to why certain black holes shine so intensely.

D) Astronomers have witnessed shockwaves from black holes that explain why the light particles accelerate the speed of light.

While researching a topic, a student has taken the following notes:

- Demographic trends show that during the COVID–19 pandemic, minority groups were disproportionately impacted in the U.S.

- Measures taken like lockdowns and social distancing created social and economic challenges despite contributing to public safety.

- A study was conducted from April 2020 to September 2022 noting a loss of employment, food scarcity, housing insecurity, and unmet health services.

- Online surveys were taken from approximately 117 million U.S. households.

- Findings showed that non–Hispanic Black, non–Hispanic other minorities, and Hispanics were more likely to report struggles in these areas.

The student wants to make a generalization about the conclusions reached from a study conducted during the COVID–19 pandemic. Which choice most effectively uses relevant information from the notes to accomplish this goal?

A) Social distancing and lockdowns implemented in the U.S. during the COVID–19 pandemic contributed to public safety.

B) Demographic research found that from April 2020 to September 2022, minority groups were unequally affected economically and socially as a result of the COVID–19 pandemic measures.

C) Studies were conducted with roughly 117 million U.S. housing units during the COVID–19 pandemic.

D) Research during the COVID–19 pandemic noted loss of employment, food scarcity, housing insecurity, and limited health services at 117 million U.S. households.

While researching a topic, a student has taken the following notes:

- In 1983, Howard Gardner published an educational book teaching that people have eight intelligences.

- These intelligences are Linguistic, Logical/Mathematical, Spatial, Bodily–Kinesthetic, Musical, Interpersonal, Intrapersonal, and Naturalist.

- He theorized that students have one or more intelligences.

- Gardner believed that many students struggled in school not because of lack of intelligence, but because teachers were not engaging their intelligences.

- Gardner argued that in order to teach effectively, one must engage all of these intelligences in the classroom through various strategies.

The student wants to present this topic and its theory. Which choice most effectively uses relevant information from the notes to accomplish this goal?

A) Students struggle in school because they are not being taught well, therefore, teachers must do a better job in the classroom.

B) Howard Gardner taught that students have multiple intelligences and that teachers need to use strategies to incorporate them into the classroom.

C) Howard Garnder taught that people have multiple intelligences and that to have more success, they must engage them.

D) In 1982, Howard Gardner wrote a book about people having multiple intelligences and that no one is truly unintelligent.

No Test Material On This Page

No Test Material On This Page

Answer Key

Reading and Writing

	Module 1				Module 2		

Questions	Correct	Mark your correct answers	Questions	Correct	Mark your correct answers
1	C		1	B	
2	B		2	B	
3	C		3	B	
4	B		4	B	
5	A		5	C	
6	B		6	C	
7	A		7	D	
8	D		8	A	
9	B		9	A	
10	D		10	A	
11	A		11	D	
12	A		12	C	
13	C		13	D	
14	A		14	C	
15	B		15	A	
16	D		16	C	
17	A		17	C	
18	C		18	D	
19	A		19	B	
20	D		20	A	
21	C		21	C	
22	A		22	B	
23	D		23	A	
24	B		24	D	
25	C		25	C	
26	D		26	B	
27	C		27	B	

1. **Level:** Easy | **Domain:** CRAFT AND STRUCTURE
    Skill/Knowledge: Words in Context

    Key Explanation: Choice C is the best answer because in the context of the passage "swam" indicates that the character is "searching" through the suitcase to find his particular clothing.

    Distractor Explanations: Choice A is not the correct answer since "examined" indicates more of a close observation of something. **Choice C** and **Choice D** are not correct because they take the term "swam" literally as being associated with water which is not taking the context of the passage into account.

2. **Level:** Medium | **Domain:** CRAFT AND STRUCTURE
    Skill/Knowledge: Words in Context

    Key Explanation: Choice B is the best answer because "administered" indicated providing and conducting an activity. In this passage, what is being provided and conducted is surveys.

    Distractor Explanations: Choice A is not the correct answer since "managed" indicates supervising, but not conducting. **Choice C** and **Choice D** are wrong because they refer to merely giving someone something, and not necessarily conducting an activity the way the correct answer does.

3. **Level:** Medium | **Domain:** CRAFT AND STRUCTURE
    Skill/Knowledge: Words in Context

    Key Explanation: Choice C is the best answer because "adopted" refers to not only learning the culture, but also making it a part of their own culture.

    Distractor Explanations: Choice A is not the correct answer since "learned" means to understand something, but not necessarily to apply it. **Choice B** is wrong because it only refers to copying something but not making it a part of one's life, or in this case, one's culture. **Choice D** is wrong because it is the opposite of the context of the passage.

4. **Level:** Hard | **Domain:** CRAFT AND STRUCTURE
    Skill/Knowledge: Text Structure and Purpose

    Key Explanation: Choice B is the best answer because the passage is discussing a new model that has not been released yet, but shows results that are more accurate than current products.

    Distractor Explanations: Choice A and **Choice C** are not the correct answers because the passage is not trying to persuade anyone that smart watches are not reliable overall. **Choice D** is wrong because the passage does not indicate that this new model will be available anytime soon.

5. **Level:** Medium | **Domain:** CRAFT AND STRUCTURE
    Skill/Knowledge: Text Structure and Purpose

    Key Explanation: Choice A is the best answer because the previous sentence discussed a character who was unwanted. The underlined sentence then introduces a brand new character who is living a very different life; thus it introduces a character in contrast with the previous character.

    Distractor Explanations: Choice B is not the correct answer since the following sentences do not add any further description of the character, but focuses on the perspective of the people of England. **Choice C** is wrong because the setting is not established in this sentence. **Choice D** is wrong since it discusses a different character from the previous sentence.

6. **Level:** Medium | **Domain:** CRAFT AND STRUCTURE
Skill/Knowledge: Text Structure and Purpose

Key Explanation: Choice B is the best answer because the passage is about results found in mice that could potentially be "given to people in pill form." This indicates that the findings could help humans with their motivation to exercise.

Distractor Explanations: Choice A is not the correct answer since it is too limited and fails to take into account how humans could be supported with these findings. **Choice C** is wrong because the passage is doing more than just "explaining" the findings. **Choice D** is wrong because the passage never states or indicates that not exercising is "not controllable," merely that this might be one of the reasons.

7. **Level:** Hard | **Domain:** CRAFT AND STRUCTURE
Skill/Knowledge: Cross–Text Connections

Key Explanation: Choice A is the best answer Text states that some of Franklin's biggest issues were the way he communicated arrogantly and aggressively. Silence would be the best virtue to practice of the options, since it would allow him to listen more and avoid talking in a manner that would be off–putting to those he was communicating with as French ambassador.

Distractor Explanations: Choice B, Choice C, and **Choice D** are not the correct answers since order, resolution, and frugality as explained in Text 2 would not help him deal with initial issues

of communication in the same direct way that silence would.

8. **Level:** Easy | **Domain:** INFORMATION AND IDEAS
Skill/Knowledge: Central Ideas and Details

Key Explanation: Choice D is the best answer since the passage reflects the idea that the narrator is going to leave the neighborhood to pursue other options, but that she will come back to help her neighbors who could not make it out on their own.

Distractor Explanations: Choice A is not the correct answer because the narrator says she will return to the neighborhood. **Choice B** is wrong, Although the narrator mentions books and paper, it is not directly stated that she wants to become a writer. **Choice C** is wrong because though she mentions that she will leave, it does not include that she will come back. Therefore, it is too narrow of an answer and does not explain the main idea.

9. **Level:** Medium | **Domain:** INFORMATION AND IDEAS
Skill/Knowledge: Central Ideas and Details

Key Explanation: Choice B is the best answer since it explains that the language developed as a result of many factors that are mentioned in the passage.

Distractor Explanations: Choice A is not the correct answer since a missing comma would make this a run–on sentence. **Choice B** is wrong because a colon is used to emphasize or clarify the previous part of the sentence, introduce a list, or present quotations or definitions. **Choice D** is wrong because semicolons most often separate two complete sentences. Though they have other uses, they are not used in between a dependent and independent clause.

10. **Level:** Hard | **Domain:** INFORMATION AND IDEAS
Skill/Knowledge: Command of Evidence (Textual)

Key Explanation: Choice D is the best answer since the question asks what evidence proves that the story struggles to accept her racial identity in a specific setting. This answer choice shows that she struggles with her race in the South because she is aware that it makes her different.

Distractor Explanations: Choice A is not the correct answer since it shows that she is aware that her race is different, but not that she is struggling with her racial identity. **Choice B** is wrong because it does not express either concept brought up in the question. **Choice C** is wrong because although it does show her insecurity with an aspect of her racial identity, it leaves out the setting.

11. **Level:** Medium | **Domain:** INFORMATION AND IDEAS
Skill/Knowledge: Command of Evidence (Textual)

Key Explanation: Choice A is the best answer since the question asks to focus on the claim that there is a darker side to this time period. This answer choice most effectively illustrates the darker side of the 1960s and 1970s.

Distractor Explanations: Choice B is not the correct answer because it shows that people were anxious about the time period, but provides no specifics about the downside of the time. **Choice C** and **Choice D** are wrong because they do not

show the downside as effectively as the correct answer.

12. **Level:** Medium | **Domain:** INFORMATION AND IDEAS
Skill/Knowledge: Command of Evidence (Quantitative)

Key Explanation: Choice A is the best answer because the passage indicates that it can be hard to predict an eruption and the data shows that the seismic activity was not consistently high. Thus, it provides a reason that it can be difficult to determine when an eruption will occur even though seismic activity is monitored.

Distractor Explanations: Choice B and **Choice C** are not the correct answers since they correctly interpret the data, but do not reflect the geologist's conclusion that "forecasting is difficult." **Choice D** is wrong; it does not correctly interpret the data.

13. **Level:** Easy | **Domain:** INFORMATION AND IDEAS
Skill/Knowledge: Inferences

Key Explanation: Choice C is the best answer since it addresses the stereotypes that Shakespeare used for his female characters without inferring anything that is not based on the passage.

Distractor Explanations: Choice A and **Choice B** are not the correct answers since they draw conclusions outside the scope of the passage. **Choice D** is wrong because it makes an inference about all women during the time period, rather than focusing on his female characters like the passage calls the reader to do so.

14. **Level:** Medium | **Domain:** INFORMATION AND IDEAS
    Skill/Knowledge: Inferences

    Key Explanation: Choice A is the best answer because the passage indicates from the start that these experiments were performed to gain a better understanding of "people living with PTSD." This answer infers something based on the main idea of the text.

    Distractor Explanations: Choice B and **Choice D** are not the correct answers since they focus on trying to understand the effect of PTSD on mice and further study instead of people, as the passage indicates from the start. **Choice C** is wrong because although these realizations were true, they were not the reason for conducting the experiment, rather an observation made.

15. **Level:** Medium | **Domain:** INFORMATION AND IDEAS
    Skill/Knowledge: Inferences

    Key Explanation: Choice B is the best answer because the passage clearly says that the "children hated those marigolds…they said too much that we could not understand."

    Distractor Explanations: Choice A is not the correct answer since the passage does not say the marigolds are the only beautiful part of the neighborhood. **Choice C** is wrong because though the children acknowledge their beauty, it does not say they are "intimidated" by this feature. **Choice D** is wrong because though Miss Lottie clearly cares for the flowers, there is no indication that she cares more about them than anything else in her house.

16. **Level:** Medium | **Domain:** STANDARD ENGLISH CONVENTIONS
    Skill/Knowledge: Form, Structure, and Sense

    Key Explanation: Choice D is the best answer since "them" is the pronoun to replace "ideas," which means the pronoun must be plural like the word "ideas."

    Distractor Explanations: Choice A is wrong because while "it" is a pronoun, it is singular and does not match the plural word "ideas" that it replaces. **Choice B** is wrong because "that" is a singular demonstrative pronoun used to refer to something far away. **Choice C** is wrong because "this" is a singular demonstrative pronoun used to refer to something close by.

17. **Level:** Medium | **Domain:** STANDARD ENGLISH CONVENTIONS
    Skill/Knowledge: Form, Structure, and Sense

    Key Explanation: Choice A is the best answer because it is grammatically correct with the possessive "England's" for monarchs, but it is written in the most concise manner.

    Distractor Explanations: Choice B, Choice C, and **Choice** D are incorrect. While all are grammatically correct, they are overly wordy and none of them are as concise as the correct answer.

18. **Level:** Easy | **Domain:** STANDARD ENGLISH CONVENTIONS
    Skill/Knowledge: Form, Structure, and Sense

    Key Explanation: Choice C is the best answer because the verb is in past tense and fits in grammatically with the sentence.

Distractor Explanations: Choice A is incorrect because the verb is in present tense and the context is specific to what was written in the past. **Choice** B is wrong since this is in the past continuous which refers to ongoing past events. **Choice D** is wrong since it is in past perfect tense which is used to describe a past event that happened before another past event.

19. **Level:** Hard | **Domain:** STANDARD ENGLISH CONVENTIONS
    Skill/Knowledge: Boundaries

    Key Explanation: Choice A is the best answer since colon is used to emphasize or clarify the previous part of the sentence, introduce a list, or present quotations or definitions. After the word "tastes" the sentence lists three influences of cultural tastes "genes, experience, or environment."

    Distractor Explanations: Choice A is wrong because semicolons most often separate two complete sentences. Though they have other uses, they are not used in between a dependent and independent clause. **Choice C** is wrong because placing only a comma here is grammatically incorrect and creates a run-on sentence. **Choice D** is wrong because no punctuation after "tastes" makes the sentence a run-on.

20. **Level:** Medium | **Domain:** STANDARD ENGLISH CONVENTIONS
    Skill/Knowledge: Boundaries

    Key Explanation: Choice D is the best answer since when adding a possessive to a singular noun, the proper format is —'s.

    Distractor Explanations: Choice A is not the correct answer since it is missing the possessive.

Choice B is wrong because it turns Peru into a plural noun with an additional — s. **Choice C** is wrong because an apostrophe by itself is only added if the noun is plural, and making "Peru" plural is grammatically incorrect.

21. **Level:** Medium | **Domain:** STANDARD ENGLISH CONVENTIONS
    Skill/Knowledge: Boundaries

    Key Explanation: Choice C is the best answer since it separates a dependent clause from an independent clause. When a dependent clause precedes an independent clause, a comma is required.

    Distractor Explanations: Choice A is not the correct answer since a missing comma would make this a run-on sentence. **Choice B** is wrong because semicolons most often separate two complete sentences. Though they have other uses, they are not used in between a dependent and independent clause. **Choice D** is wrong because a colon is used to emphasize or clarify the previous part of the sentence, introduce a list, or present quotations or definitions.

22. **Level:** Medium | **Domain:** STANDARD ENGLISH CONVENTIONS
    Skill/Knowledge: Boundaries

    Key Explanation: Choice A is the best answer because a semicolon is the correct option for separating two independent clauses.

    Distractor Explanations: Choice B is wrong because a comma separating two independent clauses is insufficient. **Choice C** is incorrect because there is no punctuation. **Choice D** is wrong because dashes are used in sentences to mark the beginning and end of a series. There must be both a beginning dash and an ending one.

23. **Level:** Easy | **Domain:** EXPRESSION OF IDEAS
Skill/Knowledge: Transitions

Key Explanation: Choice D is the best answer because it provides specifics to the previous sentence.

Distractor Explanations: Choice A and **Choice C** are not correct because another point or concept is not being explored; "additionally" and "furthermore" would indicate this. **Choice B** is wrong because this sentence is not contrasting the previous sentence.

24. **Level:** Medium | **Domain:** EXPRESSION OF IDEAS
Skill/Knowledge: Transitions

Key Explanation: Choice B is the best answer because "regardless" essentially means "despite this." The sentences before details accomplishments of Indian society and that "despite this," Western societies have not taken it seriously until recently.

Distractor Explanations: Choice A is incorrect as "indeed" is used to agree with something. **Choice B** is wrong because "moreover" is used when wanting to add on to the concept brought up previously. **Choice D** is used to show direct cause and effect and that is not the relationship between these two sentences.

25. **Level:** Medium | **Domain:** EXPRESSION OF IDEAS
Skill/Knowledge: Rhetorical Synthesis

Key Explanation: Choice C is the best answer since it shows the most tragedy of the answer choices, with 2,000 people being killed by the destruction and violence of the volcano.

Distractor Explanations: Choice A and **Choice D** are not correct because they do detail destruction, but not on a large, specific scale like Choice C provides. **Choice B** is wrong because it does detail any destruction or damage.

26. **Level:** Hard | **Domain:** EXPRESSION OF IDEAS
Skill/Knowledge: Rhetorical Synthesis

Key Explanation: Choice D is the best answer because it details specific freedoms and rights that the people of ancient Egypt had.

Distractor Explanations: Choice A is not correct because it does not provide information on any human rights. **Choice B** is wrong because it shows the status of the pharaohs who were rulers, not the civilization providing its people with rights . **Choice C** is wrong because it does show concern for the people, but not as clearly and specifically as Choice D.

27. **Level:** Medium | **Domain:** EXPRESSION OF IDEAS
Skill/Knowledge: Rhetorical Synthesis

Key Explanation: Choice C is the best answer because it shows specifically how the microplastics can cause damage to sea life.

Distractor Explanations: Choice A and **Choice B** are not correct as they do not provide information about damage. **Choice D** is wrong because though it does show that there could be potential damage from the toxic elements, it does not provide any specific information on the damage that occurs as Choice C does.

1. **Level:** Medium | **Domain:** CRAFT AND STRUCTURE
   Skill/Knowledge: Words in Context

   Key Explanation: Choice B is the best answer because "potential" matches the tone of the passage that research is positive and lines up with the following part of the sentence. Follow–up research would make sense if early results showed "potential."

   Distractor Explanations: Choice A is not the correct answer because although it is positive, it indicates that one is hoping to achieve something; this does not match the context of the passage. **Choice C** is wrong because "ability" refers to the "skill to do something." **Choice D** is wrong because the tone of this word is negative and the passage is clearly positive due the results found

2. **Level:** Medium | **Domain:** CRAFT AND STRUCTURE
   Skill/Knowledge: Words in Context

   Key Explanation: Choice B is the best answer because "phenomenon" refers to an observable event that can be asked and theorized about. In this passage, observers are noticing the event of "videoconferencing fatigue" and drawing conclusions about it.

   Distractor Explanations: Choice A is not the correct answer since "miracle" implies something positive and the observations do not match this tone. **Choice C** is wrong. "disaster" is too strong to fit in with the tone of the passage that is mostly neutral and observational. **Choice D** is wrong because it is too general.

3. **Level:** Medium | **Domain:** CRAFT AND STRUCTURE
   Skill/Knowledge: Words in Context

   Key Explanation: Choice B is the best answer since "renowned" refers to being positively well–known as is indicated by the descriptions of her "fame and recognition" for her "beautiful and bright depictions of flowers."

   Distractor Explanations: Choice A is not the correct answer since there is no indication of her being unliked. **Choice C** is wrong because though it refers to being praised, it does take into account her "fame and recognition." **Choice D** is not accurate since "infamous" refers to being well–known for something negative.

4. **Level:** Hard | **Domain:** CRAFT AND STRUCTURE
   Skill/Knowledge: Text Structure and Purpose

   Key Explanation: Choice B is the best answer because it most accurately reflects the ideas presented in the passage that appreciation for Rococo art was ended by the values emphasized leading up to the Revolution, particularly because of its subject matter that contradicted ideas of the Revolution.

   Distractor Explanations: Choice A is not the correct answer as the passage does not indicate that the art style led to the Revolution, rather that it fell out of style because of it. **Choice C** is wrong because the passage does not say anything about this theory. **Choice D** is wrong because although some people living during the French Revolution may have felt this way, there is no indication that the writer of the passage believes this.

5.   **Level:** Medium | **Domain:** CRAFT AND STRUCTURE
    Skill/Knowledge: Text Structure and Purpose

    Key Explanation: Choice C is the best answer because the sentence gives more information about the current results of the gene therapy upon the patient who has lymphoblastic leukemia, or a "specific type of cancer."

    Distractor Explanations: Choice A and **Choice D** are not the correct answers since the passage focuses on the effect of this therapy upon one type of cancer. **Choice B** is wrong because this sentence does not indicate that the gene therapy will not have "long-lasting curing results."

6.   **Level:** Hard | **Domain:** CRAFT AND STRUCTURE
    Skill/Knowledge: Text Structure and Purpose

    Key Explanation: Choice C is the best answer since the passage focuses on the possible reason for the origin of the Renaissance. This answer reflects the opinion that the printing press is one of the most significant contributions to this time period, but not necessarily the only one.

    Distractor Explanations: Choice A is not the correct answer since there is no indication that this time period is the most important in history. **Choice B** is wrong because the passage does not refer to multiple reasons that the Renaissance occurred. **Choice D** is not accurate since the passage clearly states that the printing press was "one of the most significant contributions," but not the sole reason.

7.   **Level:** Hard | **Domain:** CRAFT AND STRUCTURE
    Skill/Knowledge: Cross–Text Connections

    Key Explanation: Choice D is the best answer because Text 2 understands that Hendra virus will spread if humans are further exposed to the disease through the spread of it.

    Distractor Explanations: Choice A is not correct because Text 2 is very factual and there is no indication of Text 1 improperly interpreting the results. **Choice B** is wrong because Text 1 does detail evidence of bat migration moving closer to human habitats. **Choice C** is wrong because Text 1 clearly details climate change affecting the migration of the bats.

8.   **Level:** Hard | **Domain:** CRAFT AND STRUCTURE
    Skill/Knowledge: Cross–Text Connections

    Key Explanation: Choice A is the best answer since Mott in Text 2 was both an abolitionist and supporter of women's suffrage. Text 1 focuses on the theory that both were supported historically by many of the same advocates.

    Distractor Explanations: Choice B is not the correct answer since Text 2 clearly details several early feminists who supported both issues. **Choice C** is wrong because there is no indication in Text 2 that it is an unreasonable theory. **Choice D** is not accurate since it limits the theory presented in Text 1, but Text 2 does not limit these ideas to only certain feminists, rather it provides examples of "many early feminists."

9.   **Level:** Easy | **Domain:** INFORMATION AND IDEAS
    Skill/Knowledge: Central Ideas & Details

    Key Explanation: Choice A is the best answer since the passage is about a historic hall that was discovered by archeologists and the expected discoveries that they believe will be found nearby.

Distractor Explanations: Choice B is not the correct because the discovery made was a hall, not a house. **Choice C** is wrong because a hall was discovered; the hope is to find a house and farmland. **Choice B** is wrong because though that information is in the text, it does not thoroughly incorporate the entire main idea of the passage and is too limited of an answer.

10. **Level:** Easy | **Domain:** INFORMATION AND IDEAS
    Skill/Knowledge: Central Ideas and Details

    Key Explanation: Choice A is the best answer. The passage focuses on Scarlett being appealing to men despite the fact that her physical features are not traditionally beautiful. However, her personality and ability to charm men draws them to her.

    Distractor Explanations: Choice B is not the correct answer since the passage clearly states that Scarlett is not beautiful. **Choice C** is incorrect because though she looks like a blend of her parents' features, it has not resulted in good looks but features that are "too sharply blended." **Choice C** is inaccurate since what actually draws men to her is her charm which distracts them from the fact that her physical features are not beautiful.

11. **Level:** Medium | **Domain:** INFORMATION AND IDEAS
    Skill/Knowledge: Command of Evidence (Textual)

    Key Explanation: Choice D is the best answer as the theme focuses on decisions that have long–lasting effects. In this answer, the narrator is reflecting, many years later, upon the choice

he made to walk down one road and that made a significant difference in his life.

Distractor Explanations: Choice A is not the correct answer since the narrator is not making a choice. **Choice B** is wrong as the narrator makes a choice but there is no indication of any consequence. **Choice C** is not accurate as the narrator implies that there will most likely be a consequence of not being able to come back, it is not a certain consequence that will last years as it is in **Choice D**.

12. **Level:** Medium | **Domain:** INFORMATION AND IDEAS
    Skill/Knowledge: Command of Evidence (Quantitative)

    Key Explanation: Choice C is the best answer since it correctly interprets the data and supports the conclusion that married parents have the greatest accumulation of wealth.

    Distractor Explanations: Choice A does not correctly interpret the data. **Choice B** is wrong because it correctly interprets the data but is too broad to specifically support the conclusion as effectively as the correct answer. **Choice D** is wrong since it correctly interprets the data, but does not support the conclusion.

13. **Level:** Medium | **Domain:** INFORMATION AND IDEAS
    Skill/Knowledge: Command of Evidence (Quantitative)

    Key Explanation: Choice D is the best answer since it correctly interprets the chart and finishes the example most logically as it shows the greatest number of deaths. This is more significant than disease.

Distractor Explanations: Choice A and **Choice C** are not correct since they highlight injuries, not something as serious as death. **Choice B** is wrong since it shows death, but only from big cats, not from all exotic pets.

14. **Level:** Medium | **Domain:** INFORMATION AND IDEAS
    Skill/Knowledge: Inferences

    Key Explanation: Choice C is the best answer since the passage details that students are suffering from not getting enough sleep. This is the only option that clearly provides a solution that would allow students to get more sleep, and thus suffer from fewer problems.

    Distractor Explanations: Choice A is not the correct answer since it is implied that such an early start time is affecting their sleep. **Choice B** is incorrect since it is too narrow of an answer and makes a direct statement not clearly suggested in the passage. **Choice D** is wrong because there is no indication that this would be a helpful solution.

15. **Level:** Easy | **Domain:** STANDARD ENGLISH CONVENTIONS
    Skill/Knowledge: Form, Structure, and Sense

    Key Explanation: Choice A is the best answer because the verb is in present perfect tense which is used for something that has started in the past and is continuing presently.

    Distractor Explanations: Choice B and **Choice C** are incorrect because both verbs are in present tense. **Choice D** is wrong because it is in the future tense.

16. **Level:** Easy | **Domain:** STANDARD ENGLISH CONVENTIONS
    Skill/Knowledge: Form, Structure, and Sense

    Key Explanation: Choice C is the best answer because the verb is in infinitive form and acts as a noun, properly fitting into the sentence.

    Distractor Explanations: Choice A is wrong because the grammar is incorrect as when paired with a "to," the verb must be in present tense. **Choice B** is wrong because "allocating" is a gerund which means it acts as a noun and does not fit in the sentence grammatically. **Choice D** is wrong because "allocate" is a present tense verb and does not fit in.

17. **Level:** Easy | **Domain:** STANDARD ENGLISH CONVENTIONS
    Skill/Knowledge: Form, Structure, and Sense

    Key Explanation: Choice C is the best answer because the verb is in gerund form and acts as a noun, properly fitting into the sentence.

    Distractor Explanations: Choice A is incorrect as the verb is in present tense. **Choice B** is wrong because the verb is in past tense. **Choice C** is wrong because "to appear" is an infinitive.

18. **Level:** Medium | **Domain:** STANDARD ENGLISH CONVENTIONS
    Skill/Knowledge: Form, Structure, and Sense

    Key Explanation: Choice D is the best answer because this form of the verb is in the present perfect continuous tense which is used for events that started in the past, but are continued in the present which matches this passage's context.

Distractor Explanations: Choice A is not correct since this tense would limit it only to the past. **Choice B** is wrong because this tense is used for an event in the past that has happened before another event. **Choice C** is wrong because it refers to the future and this passage implies the development has already begun.

19. **Level:** Easy | **Domain:** STANDARD ENGLISH CONVENTIONS
    Skill/Knowledge: Boundaries

    Key Explanation: Choice B is correct because when a specific name follows the noun it refers to, then commas need to surround the name. In this case, if it can be removed without changing the meaning of the sentence, then commas must be around it.

    Distractor Explanations: Choice A is incorrect because a comma after "Julie" is missing. **Choice C** is wrong because neither of the required commas are there. **Choice D** is wrong because the preceding comma is missing.

20. **Level:** Medium | **Domain:** STANDARD ENGLISH CONVENTIONS
    Skill/Knowledge: Boundaries

    Key Explanation: Choice A is the best answer because a semicolon is the correct option for separating two independent clauses. Furthermore, the comma is required as the word "instead" is used as an adverb to start out the second independent clause, which requires a comma to follow.

    Distractor Explanations: Choice B is incorrect as a comma is insufficient when separating two independent clauses. **Choice C** is wrong because a comma is missing after "instead." **Choice D**

is wrong because there is no punctuation after Homer.

21. **Level:** Medium | **Domain:** STANDARD ENGLISH CONVENTIONS
    Skill/Knowledge: Boundaries

    Key Explanation: Choice C is the best answer since it separates a dependent clause from an independent clause. When a dependent clause precedes an independent clause, a comma is required.

    Distractor Explanations: Choice A is not the correct answer since a missing comma would make this a run–on sentence. **Choice B** is wrong because a colon is used to emphasize or clarify the previous part of the sentence, introduce a list, or present quotations or definitions. **Choice D** is wrong because semicolons most often separate two complete sentences. Though they have other uses, they are not used in between a dependent and independent clause.

22. **Level:** Easy | **Domain:** EXPRESSION OF IDEAS
    Skill/Knowledge: Transitions

    Key Explanation: Choice B is the best answer because it gives a specific example of what the previous sentence makes a general statement about.

    Distractor Explanations: Choice A is not right because "still" is used to show an exception or contrast. **Choice C** is wrong because "thus" is used to indicate a result of the previous. **Choice D** is not right, as "ultimately" indicates a conclusive thought.

23. **Level:** Easy | **Domain:** EXPRESSION OF IDEAS
Skill/Knowledge: Transitions

Key Explanation: Choice A is the best answer because it indicates that it was reasonable for the astronauts to be shocked by their findings as it contrasts what they previously believed about an extreme amount.

Distractor Explanations: Choice B and **Choice C** are not right because it should not be "surprising" or "interesting" that they are shocked by the findings, as they are very different from what they previously thought. **Choice D** is wrong because "conclusively" is used to reach a clear conclusion based on previous information.

24. **Level:** Easy | **Domain:** EXPRESSION OF IDEAS
Skill/Knowledge: Transitions

Key Explanation: Choice D is the best answer since "in fact" places emphasis on a specific example of the previous sentence.

Distractor Explanations: Choice A and **Choice D** are not correct since they refer to contrast and this sentence does not contrast the previous sentence. **Choice B** is wrong because there is no indication in Text 2 that it is an unreasonable theory. **Choice B** is not correct because it also refers to something additional, but this sentence is not another example. It is an example of the previous sentence.

25. **Level:** Hard | **Domain:** EXPRESSION OF IDEAS
Skill/Knowledge: Rhetorical Synthesis

Key Explanation: Choice C is the best answer because the notes show the insights that astronomers have learned a reason why specific types of black holes shine so brightly. This answer choice provides the information learned from these observations the most clearly.

Distractor Explanations: Choice A is not correct because it merely states that there were insights, not what those insights were. **Choice B** is wrong since it details a part of the observation, but not what was learned from this information. **Choice D** is wrong since it explains that they have learned why the particles accelerate the speed of light, but does not make the connection to the conclusion that this contributes to a reason why certain black holes shine so brightly.

26. **Level:** Hard | **Domain:** EXPRESSION OF IDEAS
Skill/Knowledge: Rhetorical Synthesis

Key Explanation: Choice B is the best answer because the notes conclude that certain minority groups were unfairly affected by measures taken during the COVID pandemic. This answer provides the best generalization of the findings as it provides dates, information about minority groups, and the general effects they faced during the pandemic.

Distractor Explanations: Choice A is not correct because it does not detail a general conclusion reached as a result of the study. **Choice C** is wrong because it merely discusses the study that was conducted, but not the results. **Choice D** is wrong since it does not detail who specifically was affected by pandemic measures, which is an important aspect of the conclusion.

27. **Level:** Hard | **Domain:** EXPRESSION OF IDEAS
Skill/Knowledge: Rhetorical Synthesis

Key Explanation: Choice B is the best answer. It reflects Gardner's theory that students "have one or more intelligences" and that effective teaching requires engaging "all of these intelligences in the classroom."

Distractor Explanations: Choice A is not the correct answer since it is making a claim of poor teaching that is not reflected in the student's notes. **Choice C** is wrong since the notes do not talk about "people" have multiple intelligences but students and focus on classroom strategies, not general "success." **Choice D** is not accurate since it is too limited and does not include his theory that these multiple intelligences need to be taught in the class for students to see improvement.

NOTES

Made in the USA
Columbia, SC
08 August 2023

21418299R00165